THE END OF BRITISH POLITICS?

THE END OF BRITISH POLITICS?

Scots and English Political Behaviour in the Seventies

BY

WILLIAM L. MILLER

CLARENDON PRESS · OXFORD
1981

Oxford University Press, Walton Street, Oxford OX2 6DP

OXFORD LONDON GLASGOW
NEW YORK TORONTO MELBOURNE WELLINGTON
KUALA LUMPUR SINGAPORE HONG KONG TOKYO
DELHI BOMBAY CALCUTTA MADRAS KARACHI
NAIROBI DAR ES SALAAM CAPE TOWN

*Published in the United States
by Oxford University Press, New York*

British Library Cataloguing in Publication Data

Miller, William L
  The end of British politics
  1. Scotland – Politics and government – 20th
century
  I. Title
320.9411   JN1211   80–41309

ISBN 0–19–827422–X

*Printed in Great Britain
at the University Press, Oxford
by Eric Buckley
Printer to the University*

Typeset by Macmillan India Ltd., Bangalore

Preface

The 1979 referendum on the Scotland Act provides, at the least, a natural break in the progress of Scottish politics: a time to review the hectic decade of the seventies.

This book is not about Scottish nationalism, still less about the SNP. It is a book about Scottish political behaviour in the seventies viewed from the perspective of British politics. So there is a lot about Scottish nationalism in it, and a lot about the SNP; but also a lot about Labour and the Conservatives in Scotland. And a lot about England.

In the first chapter I trace the development of Scottish political issues, especially in the years from 1945 to 1974. I try not to tell some secret tale of what 'really' went on. Quite the reverse. I try to convey some sense of how Scots politics looked to the man in the street. If the politicians and the press spent their time and space on rhetoric or trivia, then so do I. But in the main the special Scottish issues that gained increasing attention were far from trivial.

In the second chapter I begin a detailed analysis of Scots and English public opinion in the mid-seventies by using the British and Scottish Election Surveys of 1974 to find out whether Scots and English voters were different on anything except voting and, if so, how different. In addition I consider whether Scots–English differences were truly national or whether Scotland simply marked the far end of a centre–periphery spectrum.

Chapter 3 examines public demand for Scottish devolution both across time and across different sections of the public. Here I am using the word 'demand' almost in the economics sense: the demand for devolution should not conjure up visions of street parades. Chapter 4 examines the perceived supply of policy, including devolution policy. What did people in Scotland and England think the parties were offering? Considering party records on devolution policy it comes as something of a surprise that so few voters claimed not to know.

Chapters 5 to 8 look at voting patterns in Scotland and England, starting with social alignments. These had most effect on Labour versus Conservative voting and showed a high level of cross-national similarity. Chapter 6 deals with a variety of influences whose effect was mainly on the level of third-party success: balanced or contradictory attitudes towards the old parties or the old issues; the pull of special Scots issues; and the interaction between balance and Scots issues. These two chapters compare the Con–Lab–SNP split in Scotland with the Con–Lab–Lib split in England. Was the SNP vote simply a Scots version of a protest vote or did it indicate real support for the constitutional policies of the SNP?

Chapter 7 gives a brief review of Scottish electoral geography. I interpret 'electoral geography' as the political consequences of territorial constituencies, and spatial or environmental effects. So I discuss the properties of the British first-past-the-post electoral system when applied to the territorial distribution of Scots votes. Why did the British system produce such pathological results in Scotland? Second, I review geographic and other spatial varia-tions in political attitudes and show how the SNP was able to concentrate its vote so much more effectively than the English Liberals despite remarkably uniform attitudes towards devol-ution and independence throughout Scotland. Finally, a study of constituency class alignments in Scotland and England allows me to calculate the 'normal' difference between Scots and English support for Conservative or Labour and so identify the good times and the bad times for Scots Labour or Conservative.

Chapter 8 brings together, summarizes, and synthesizes much of the earlier analysis of voting by constructing causal models of three-party voting for Scotland and England. It compares the power of class and devolution attitudes with other influences on voting when all are operating simultaneously in a multivariate model.

Some elections, alas, have causes but not consequences. Not so 1974. The two elections of 1974 put Scottish devolution so firmly onto the British agenda that it took a referendum to push it off again – whether temporarily or not we have yet to see. So in Chapter 9 I complete the story of the 1974 elections by tracing their consequences up to the devolution referendum of March 1979 and the consequent collapse of Mr Callaghan's Govern-ment.

A short Chapter 10 presents a few thoughts on the future of Scottish politics and in particular on the 'issue of '74': devolution.

W. L. MILLER
Glasgow, December 1979

Contents

Chapter 1

The Course of Scottish Politics
to 1974

The number '1707' is a political slogan with as much power in Scotland as '1690' in Ireland. It is the date of the union of the parliaments of Scotland and England: the Treaty of Union.

The visitor to Scotland is most unlikely to find '1707' chalked or painted on the walls of derelict buildings. Indeed he would be much more likely to come across '1690'. The Scottish slogan '1707' appears in another context: at the start of almost every description of Scottish government and every debate about it.

Often the discussion begins with some tale of what 'really' went on in 1707. Were the Scottish signatories bribed or not? Was there popular support for the treaty at the time? Was it in Scotland's best interests or not? Did the Scots negotiators want federalism or even understand what federalism meant? What was the nature of the union bargain? I will spare my readers the agony of going through ancient history yet again. It is irrelevant to current Scottish politics. But the myth of the Union is not.

The significance of the 1707 myth is that in recent times there has been widespread acceptance, both in London and Scotland, that Scotland exists as a nation in more or less voluntary union with England. The perpetual Treaty of Union, despite all its references to provisions 'remaining in all time coming', is thus almost as renegotiable as the perpetual Treaty of Rome which forms the basis for the EEC. Both ultimately depend upon each succeeding generation making the calculation that the treaty serves their interest sufficiently well for it not to be worth the trouble of renegotiation.

Not everyone accepts that view. At least one Conservative MP in the late seventies told a public conference in the North of England that the Scots could have their independence only 'if they were willing to fight for it' and I have found at least one minister on the other side who had an alarming tendency to mix comments about devolution with references to the American Civil War. None the less, there is a widespread and officially accepted view that Scottish government should be in the hands of Scots living in Scotland subject only to the restrictions necessary to give Scotland positive benefits from participation in a wider state. Guided by this spirit, Scots and English politicians continue to take positive action to prevent a full integration of Scotland and England.

INSTITUTIONAL CONVERGENCE

The Union was to be a marriage of convenience that would give the Scots economic prosperity and the English military security. The parliaments, the military and economic systems would be united but the social systems would be guaranteed a separate existence by the Union institutions—the law, the courts, religion, education, local government. After the Union these institutions preserved a distinct Scottish national consciousness and also a very real measure of home rule.

Of the Union institutions, the Scots Kirk was the most significant. Its doctrine and discipline were regarded as a principal 'output' of government, to use modern jargon. Doctrine and discipline were matters of life and death, the cause of wars and rebellions. At a more mundane level the Kirk controlled morals, education, social welfare and, outside the burghs, it supplied most government activity.

Scottish industry, trade and commerce may not look like post-Union institutions but they too preserved a large measure of home rule in the days before nationalization. There was a world of difference between the economic unity of equal access to markets and today's unity of centrally run nationalized industries.

But for the last century or so, the institutions which at first guaranteed Scottish home rule have been in decline. They have contributed to convergence and integration rather than independence. They no longer provide a sound basis for the separation of Scotland from England.

In the middle of the last century, the Kirk split into two almost equal parts and lost its control of education and social welfare.

Though reunited and enjoying much greater active membership than the Established Church in England it has lost most of its control over morals and its total freedom on matters of doctrine seems to our twentieth-century minds to be almost irrelevant to government. Church and State have been divorced. The Kirk's Church and Nation Committee still tells the government what to do but, on purely secular affairs, it is doubtful whether the Committee or the Kirk's General Assembly carries any authority within the Kirk, let alone outside it. After years of urging successive governments to set up a Scottish Assembly the Kirk decided on the eve of the 1979 referendum to forbid its ministers even to remind their congregations of the Kirk's own previous statements on devolution.

The last traces of post-Union local government institutions were abolished in 1974. They had lost their independence of central government, and their prestige, long before that. Turn-out rates in local elections were low and voting trends in local government elections reflected attitudes to the central government of the day. Whichever party was in office at Westminster could expect to do badly in Scottish local government elections just as in English local elections or in the Gallup poll. In status local government had been reduced to a by-product of an opinion poll on the central government of the day. Only councillors and officials could regard it as truly local.

Scots education has become very similar to education in England, partly because the English have come into line with Scots on such matters as encouraging working-class children to go to university. But whoever came into line with whom, education no longer distinguishes Scots and English as once it did.

Scottish courts continue a separate existence but the law they administer is increasingly the same as in England. Scottish law still exists to guarantee a career for Scottish lawyers but has been overlaid by vast quantities of British law. And in the Scottish sector of the North Sea English commercial law takes precedence over Scottish.

Nationalization, mergers, and take-overs by English and multinational firms, plus trade union amalgamations mean that little of either side of Scottish industry still remains distinctively Scottish. On the trade union side, higher wages in England at least until the mid-seventies meant that Scots trade unionists had a special interest in 'national', i.e. British, wage bargaining. And the logic of British wage bargaining implied British unions. At the close of the nineteenth century there were about 200 independent Scottish trade unions but they gradually merged with English unions. The process was almost complete by the early seventies. In 1971 the last big Scots union – the Scottish Commercial Motormen – voted overwhelmingly to join the TGWU. Paradoxically perhaps, their general secretary, Alex Kitson, who had negotiated the merger not only went on to high office in the TGWU but pushed the cause of political devolution for Scotland. Scottish teachers' unions are still independent but their independence is derivative, the product of a separate educational bureaucracy. Few other Scots workers remain outside the British unions.

On the entrepreneurial side, Scots companies with headquarters in Scotland have become a minority within Scotland itself. In manufacturing industry only two Scots workers in five now work for Scottish companies.

Though individual firms and unions typically operate on a Britain-wide basis, their Scottish elements come together in the Scottish CBI and the STUC. The STUC is separate from the British TUC and has a well-developed sense of Scottish national consciousness but it has tended to be more nationalist in political than industrial affairs.

More generally, the twentieth century has been a period of rapid expansion for central government and that means for London government. It has taken over much of the activity and the prestige of the Kirk, the burghs, the universities, industry, and commerce as well as fostering its own entirely new types of activity. Inevitably that has meant a reduction in local rule, and so in home rule.

INSTITUTIONAL SEPARATION

Scotland is separated from England by more than institutions. It is still a long way from the concentration of Scotland's population in its central belt to the nearest concentration of English population and further still to the political and economic centre of England. Even with an air-shuttle service to London, it is still more convenient and certainly a great deal less expensive to visit people or locations elsewhere in Scotland than to journey to London not least because Scotland's population is so concentrated within a small part of Scotland. For most of the period since the War the Scottish Council has been complaining about Scotland's poor communications with, among other countries, England. The contrast between Scotland and Wales is striking. Geography splits Wales up and binds the pieces to England but it keeps Scotland apart and united.

The peoples are almost as separate as the lands. Because Scotland has suffered from continuous emigration, not immigration, most Scots residents are Scots by birth. And because the English population is so large relative to Scotland's, emigration from Scotland to England has little effect upon the population mix in England. Again there is a striking contrast between Scotland's separate population and the English–Welsh mixture in Wales, especially North Wales.

So land and people might continue to divide Scotland and England even if institutions ceased to do so. But as the Union institutions have decayed or withdrawn from government, other separatist institutions have taken their place.

Scottish news media serve to divide Scots politics from English politics. Not that the media have a separatist political stance on issues but they very self-consciously cater for a different audience from the London media. They may not create special Scottish political reactions but some certainly try and most are likely to amplify Scottish deviations, if nothing more, by their intensive news coverage of Scottish affairs.

By the seventies only two daily papers had a mass readership in Scotland: the *Express* and the *Record*. Both were owned furth of Scotland but edited in Scotland and, until 1974, both were printed in Glasgow. When the *Express* switched printing to Manchester it lost a circulation war with the *Record*, and lost very badly.

The *Record* aimed entirely at a Scots audience. It had practically nothing in common with its London sister-paper, the *Mirror*. The *Scottish Daily Express* had more in common with London's *Daily Express* but two-thirds of its content was Scottish and on occasion it could take a violently different political line from its London counterpart. After the defeat of the 1977 Scotland and Wales Bill the *Daily Express* applauded Parliament's wisdom while the *Scottish Daily Express* thundered 'Scotland will never forgive the Devo Traitors'. In fairness, I should add that by the time of the devolution referendum in 1979 no newspaper could have taken a more anti-devolution position than the *Scottish Express*. Its letters column, for example, offered small prizes not for the best letter for or against devolution but for the best letter on what to do with the Scottish Assembly building after the hoped-for defeat of the Assembly in the referendum.

In the mid-seventies, the *Mail*, the *Mirror*, and the *Sun* which reached 14 per cent, 42 per cent, and 30 per cent (respectively) of Londoners were read by only 4 per cent, 3 per cent, and 6 per cent of Scots. English middle-class newspapers – the *Telegraph*, *Guardian*, *Times*, and *Financial Times* – were scarcely read at all in Scotland: each had only about 1 per cent of Scots for readers. Instead, four Scottish newspapers each combined the function of a serious middle-class paper with that of a lively single-city paper: the *Herald* in Glasgow, the *Scotsman* in Edinburgh, the *Courier* in Dundee, and the *Press and Journal* in Aberdeen. Of these, the *Scotsman* was closest to being a purely national paper, followed by the *Herald*; while the Dundee and Aberdeen papers tilted more towards city and local papers. After the War all these papers were Conservative but with the passage of time and a series of take-overs only the *Express* remained openly and violently Conservative in the seventies: the *Herald* inclined towards the Conservatives, the *Record* towards Labour, and the *Scotsman* towards the Liberals or the SNP. By the time of the 1979 referendum, the *Scotsman* and *Record* were enthusiastically pro-devolution the *Herald* less enthusiastically but still on balance pro-devolution, and the *Express* anti-devolution to the extent of being little more than a campaign broadsheet.

But their editorial viewpoints matter less than their concentration on Scottish affairs which has helped to make Scots self consciously aware of Scotland as a unit; aware of Scotland's problems, particularly economic problems; and aware too of Scots political responses. The press can amplify political trends through publicity and self-awareness even though it has not created and perhaps does not approve those trends. An SNP by-election victory or a package of devolution proposals was an important news story badly covered by the London media. In the drive for status and circulation Scots media could hardly avoid giving such stories extensive coverage. They were always in competition both with each other and collectively with the London media. Anything that enhanced the status of Scots politics enhanced the status of the Scots media relative to the London media.

Unlike the press, most radio and television programmes were made outside Scotland but then much of their content was pure entertainment, irrelevant to politics. The Scots proportion of news and current affairs broadcasting was far higher than the Scots proportion of entertainment broadcasting.

In the early seventies both BBC television and ITV broadcast about half an hour of Scots news every weekday plus one or two regular weekly current affairs programmes and special coverage of the STUC conference, the General Assembly of the Kirk, Scottish local government elections and Scots party conferences, which traditionally occur in the spring and so avoid being overshadowed by the British party conferences.

BBC radio was more like the press. In the early seventies it broadcast four times as much Scots material as television. Its daily output included a two-hour breakfast-time news magazine with another half-hour in the early evening.

The political parties used the media to reinforce the notion of a separate Scots politics by 'opting out' from their London-originated party political broadcasts, screening special programmes featuring Scots politicians and themes. Since the War it has become a regular practice for Labour and Conservative to issue separate Scottish election manifestos and, of course, the Scottish Liberals and SNP are purely Scots parties. Even neglecting the Liberals and SNP, Labour and Conservative manifestos and television programmes have on occasion been so different in Scotland as to give a real policy content as well as a personality content to separate coverage of Scots politics.

An insignificant number of people actually attend Parliament in Westminster. Much therefore of its function as a forum of the nation is discharged by media reports or media contributions by Members of Parliament. To some extent the separate Scottish media perform the function of a non-existent Scots parliament. Collectively they provide something of a forum for the Scottish nation. They have been criticized for a lack of sufficiently tenacious investigative reporting but they still provide a national focus and an outer boundary for a Scottish debate.

The second set of separatist institutions has grown up within central government itself. On the administrative side, the Scottish Office, and on the parliamentary side, the special Scots legislative and investigatory committees. When Whitelaw offered the Northern Irish a range of options on devolution he reportedly described the Scots system as 'integration', but the Scots system has evolved precisely because there has been so little support for integration either in Scotland or London. Successive governments have maintained and even increased the separation of Scots affairs from English rather than gone for integration which would imply treating Scotland like Yorkshire.

The office of Secretary for Scotland was abolished after the 1745 rebellion but re-established in 1885. The Secretary picked up powers from the Scottish Lord Advocate and from the Home Office, Treasury, Local Government Board, and Privy Council. His office was in the same city as the India Office, that is in London, and the first Secretary was the Duke of Richmond. He began with a handful of staff and no powers over the various Boards which ran much of Scottish affairs. Still the headquarters of the independent Scottish Education Department, for example, remained in London until 1922 so at least the Scottish Office was in the right city for liaison.

Gradually the Scottish Office and its Secretary acquired more responsibilities, more status, even more pay. From 1892 the Secretary has been a Cabinet member though always a junior and peripheral one, excluded from any 'inner Cabinet'. He became a Secretary of State but until 1927 was paid less than other Secretaries of State. He also became more Scottish over the years and it would now be quite exceptional for an Englishman to be appointed.

Scottish Unionists pressed for the re-establishment of the Scottish Office and the Conservatives have repeatedly extended its powers. Yet the whole logic of the Scottish Office has made it a basis for separation, even for nationalism. Just as central government in Westminster and Whitehall is inevitably Unionist in the sense that when it takes powers from sectors of society it transfers control from Scotland to Britain, so the Scottish Office is inevitably separatist for when it takes powers from other sectors of the government machine it transfers powers back from Britain to Scotland. Certainly, the Scottish Office can be described *by definition* as a part of unified central government but to the extent that real discretion is given to the Scottish Office it goes to

Scotland. That is usually given as the justification for any transfers to the Scottish Office. The secret intention may well be to keep the Scottish Secretary on so short a leash that London will not lose any effective control. But the justification itself, whether true or false, stimulates nationalism first by raising expectations and second by creating a separate Scottish government machine ripe for political control.

In 1939 the Conservatives reformed Scots government along new coherent and separatist lines. From then on the Secretary was to be identified with all government in Scotland whether formally under his control or not. A new Scottish Office was set up in Edinburgh instead of London with four administrative departments – Home, Health, Education, and Agriculture – responsible not to parliament but to the Secretary of State. His old London headquarters staff which had only totalled about a hundred in 1937 moved to Edinburgh to join the headquarters units of the four new departments leaving only a very small, subordinate, liaison staff at Dover House in London. The term 'Scottish Office' changed from a description of a small back-up team for a minister to meaning Scottish central government. The Office became a place as much as a function; 'of Scotland' rather than 'about Scotland'. These 1939 reforms marked the end of an era in which the Secretary had acquired powers by absorbing other, independent Scots bodies and the beginning of a period in which the Scottish Office continued to expand by taking powers from British ministries: the end of its role as a national unifier within Scotland and the start of its role as separatist within Britain.

Today, if the visitor to Edinburgh has no more than an hour and a half to spare but steps out briskly, he can begin by inspecting the Scottish crown jewels in the Castle, walk down past the parliament of 1707 to the Royal Palace, turn up past the building Labour prepared for the Scottish Assembly, pass the huge office blocks that house the civil servants of the Scottish Office, and end up at the minor palace which is the official residence of the Secretary of State. The city has all the appearance of a long-established capital except that the Assembly building is unoccupied.

From 1939 onwards there was a piecemeal transfer of functions from British ministries to the Scottish Office: the main additions being electricity, roads, some transport, agriculture, health, social work, Highland development and aspects of economic planning, oil, and industrial development. The departments were reorganized and increased to five – Agriculture and Fisheries, Development, Home and Health, Education, and eventually even Economic Planning. The Secretary headed a political team that grew to two ministers of state, and three under-secretaries backed up by ten thousand civil servants. Scottish national consciousness made it more difficult to remove than to add powers and the only major loss has been national insurance.

Though Scottish civil servants are theoretically part of the British Civil Service and applicants for senior posts are interviewed in London, the overwhelming majority are Scots. Scottish Office civil servants are considerably more Scottish even than civil servants in the Scottish parts of UK ministries. Very few move between Edinburgh and London during their careers, though in an unprecedented move just before the 1974 election three of the top six civil servants at the Scottish Office, including the permanent under-secretary were replaced by Englishmen.

According to the Kilbrandon Commission survey in 1970 only half the Scots electorate admitted any knowledge of the Scottish Office. Many of the remainder felt it had no freedom of action. And recent surveys have shown that the Scottish Secretary may remain a fairly unknown face to the Scots electorate.

None the less it is impossible to overlook the fact that under successive governments a Scottish governmental machine has been constructed complete with prime minister, subordinate ministers, its own civil service, and unlimited responsibilities if not unlimited powers. At the very least it makes devolution or independence a more credible option for Scotland than for Yorkshire and it continually reinforces the significance of a line on the map dividing Scotland from England.

As a means of preventing political devolution the build-up of the Scottish Office has proved a Danegeld. It stimulates rather than satisfies the appetite for self-government. It has made Scots government at once more Scottish and less subject to parliamentary control. A political top-tier to this administrative machine appears ever more credible and more necessary. Yet the irony is that it owes so much of its growth to the actions of Unionists.

A Scottish Grand Committee of the House of Commons had a brief existence in 1894–5 before reappearing in 1907 as a standing committee to take the committee stage of bills. In 1948 the Labour Government widened its functions to include debates on the principles of legislation and on Scottish estimates. Frequently, it has been suggested that the SGC meet in Scotland. Tom Johnston tried it during the War but abandoned the idea when few MPs turned up. Willie Ross tried again in the late sixties but also ran into practical difficulties.

There is a joke that the SGC is neither Scottish, nor grand, nor a committee: not Scottish because up to fifteen non-Scots can be added to the Scots MPs to adjust the party balance; not a committee because it debates points of principle; and not grand because it has little parliamentary authority or public visibility. Unfortunately, while everyone would agree that it is not very grand, it is both Scottish and a committee and these attributes contradict each other.

The SGC really is a committee of the Commons and no more. Controversial bills are kept on the floor of the House. The outcome of the 1974–9 parliament would have been very different if the Scotland Act had been taken by the SGC instead of by the Commons as a whole. It only sees the technical, non-controversial part of Scottish legislation and even then only half the bills given to it for detailed consideration are given to it for a vote of principle. And at the final stage everything goes back to the full House for approval. So the SGC is clearly a sub-committee.

But paradoxically it is also Scottish. Even the addition of a full fifteen English Conservatives still leaves Labour with an absolute majority on the SGC at times like 1970 or 1979 when Labour has a two-to-one majority of Scottish seats. Moreover, the English MPs are not welcomed when they attend nor listened to when they dare to speak. The problem can be solved simply by avoiding votes on the SGC: after all, what is the point of taking decisions one way on the SGC only to find that they are reversed in full House? The whole system therefore depends first upon keeping controversial, that is party-controversial, matters away from the SGC, and second upon deference by Scots MPs to the Westminster majority.

There are other ways of choosing Scottish committees than the 'topping up' procedure used for the SGC. If the British system were truly integrated there would, first of all, be far less work for Scots committees to do. And when committees were required to deal with special Scots affairs they would be chosen – like the members of the Kilbrandon Commission – from a cross-section of those with an interest in the particular topic. Scots would quite properly be in a minority on committees dealing with Scots affairs. This method is not used explicitly though it is implicit whenever Scottish legislation is kept on the floor of the full House.

Instead, for the Scottish standing committees set up in 1957 and 1962 to take the committee stages of Scots bills, and for the Select Committees which investigated Scots economic planning in 1969 and land use in 1971, the problem of party balance was solved by making them so small that there were enough Scots Conservatives around to provide the Westminster government with a majority. As a further safety device the·rules allowed sufficient padding with English MPs to turn these committees into the integrated form described above but this facility was not used.

Of course, Scots Conservatives have to work especially hard to run Scots committees when the Conservatives have a Westminster majority but perhaps as few as twenty-two Scots MPs. Pure exhaustion contributed to the decision to discontinue the Select Committee after its report on land use.

These Scots committees are a peculiar anachronism in a supposedly unitary state. They could be reconciled with an integrationist philosophy if they were 'about Scotland' rather than 'of Scotland' but they are not. So they contribute to a sense of national consciousness by their names, their composition, their whole style. And by accident or design the Scots committees, together with the Scottish Office, help to separate Scots MPs from their colleagues at Westminster.

By convention Scots MPs are now considered unsuitable for junior office in ministries whose functions in Scotland are performed by the Scottish Office – the Home Office for example. No convention specifically excludes them from committees concerned with British affairs but the work of the Scots committees puts so much pressure on their time that they cannot participate in non-Scottish affairs as much as English MPs. Though Scots MPs attend far more committee sittings than other

MPs they attend British committees less than others, and English committees hardly at all.

A significant change seems to have taken place in the early fifties. Before that Scots MPs' membership of British committees was only slightly less (proportionately) than non-Scots but afterwards the Scots joined British committees at only half the rate of their non-Scots colleagues. And even in their participation in British committees there is a distinctive pattern. Scots turn up frequently on trade, industry, transport, agriculture and fisheries committees, all of which have special significance for Scotland, but neglect commonwealth, colonial, defence, and foreign affairs committees.

Proposals to make the SGC more 'grand' by sending it up to sit in Edinburgh under the cameras of Scots television would only accelerate these moves toward separation. English MPs drafted onto the Scots committees might have to be removed, and would certainly be very reluctant to travel north. Scots MPs would find it even more difficult to participate in non-Scots affairs at Westminster. And Scots MPs deference to the Westminster majority would be strained to the limit outside the confines of Westminster and under the glare of Scottish television. Sending Scots MPs back to Scotland, to join the Scottish administration, has overtones of the Dail withdrawing to Dublin: far more separatist than plans for devolution or federalism which depend upon keeping Scots MPs at Westminster and freeing them from the excessive burden of purely Scots affairs so that they could participate more fully in British affairs.

The third group of separatist institutions are to be found among the parties and pressure groups: not all the parties and not all the pressure groups because some have been so committed to squeezing resources out of London that their very nationalism has made them Unionists. Like a pick-pocket thief they need to stay close to their victim. The analogy is perhaps a little unfair but it dramatizes the position of those who see the UK as a context for pushing Scottish interests. It explains the ambiguity and the rapid turn-abouts by many individuals and organizations in their attitudes to devolution or independence as they recalculate where Scots interests lie.

However, the Scottish National Party and its offshoots have been unambiguous separatists. At times they have even agonized over whether to press London for special benefits for Scotland in case that compromised their separatist logic.

Home rule organizations of one kind or another have existed in Scotland since Victorian times. In the earlier years they attempted to secure all-party agreement but had more success in persuading Liberals to give at least lip-service to the cause. The Commons debated Scots home rule on numerous occasions and voted on it at least eight times between 1889 and 1920. With the exception of the 1889 vote a substantial majority of Scots MPs always voted in favour of home rule. On the second reading of the 1913 bill, for example, they divided forty-five in favour to eight against. The bill itself passed its second reading but was quietly forgotten during the War.

In 1928 and 1932 two political parties were formed to make self-government a party issue. They united in 1934 to form the Scottish National Party. Today's SNP is formally that same party founded in 1934 but its membership has changed so much that the link with the party of 1934 is slight.

The inter-war SNP fought a number of by-elections and won votes ranging up to 16 per cent: not a derisory performance but still a very modest achievement. It lost more deposits than it saved. There were two candidates at the 1929 general election, five in 1931, and eight in 1935, but nine of the fifteen lost their deposits. The party was divided on how far to go towards full independence and also on how separate the SNP should be from other parties. Something of the old pressure-group attitude lingered in the way the SNP allowed dual membership so that even its most senior officers could simultaneously belong to other parties.

During the war the SNP's best propagandist, John Mac-Cormick, led his followers out of the party in a return to pressure-group politics. The rump of the SNP were firmly committed to party politics and were mainly, though not exclusively, hard-line nationalists who wanted a totally independent party fighting for a totally independent Scotland.

A wartime electoral truce between the major parties provided the opening for all sorts of small parties and fringe candidates. As the sole, or sole significant opponent of the sitting party, the SNP scored large votes for the first time in its history, votes that were not to be repeated for more than twenty years. In 1940 they took

37 per cent in Argyll against the Conservatives and in 1944 41 per cent against Labour in Kirkcaldy. Then in the closing stages of the War Dr Robert MacIntyre took Motherwell from Labour with a vote of 51 per cent. Motherwell stands on the gently rising hills to the north of the Clyde, facing Hamilton on the south bank where the SNP won their next victory twenty-two years later. MacIntyre campaigned for an independent Scotland, for a road bridge over the Firth of Forth, and for international status for Prestwick airport: a blend of separatism and immediate demands which formed the pattern for later campaigns. His specific demands were Scottish rather than purely local however, since neither Prestwick nor the proposed Forth Bridge were anywhere near Motherwell. Before the 1945 general election the Government gave Prestwick international status. The bridge came much later.

These by-elections in Argyll, Kirkcaldy, and Motherwell showed that Scots had no deeply rooted objection to voting SNP: it was not a completely unacceptable option. But the by-elections gave no evidence that Scots would vote for the SNP when a full range of party options were available nor in a general election when the control of government was at stake. Motherwell has to be seen against a background of similar war-time by-election successes by fringe parties in England and Wales. Common Wealth scored 42 per cent at Rusholme and won Skipton with 45 per cent and Chelmsford with 58 per cent. The ILP won 46 per cent in Newport and 49 per cent in Bilston, and the Welsh Nationalists took 16 per cent at Neath and 25 per cent in Caernarvon. Various independents also did well.

At the 1945 general election Dr MacIntyre lost his seat even though Common Wealth retained Chelmsford and, within Scotland, seven of the MPs elected stood outside the three major parties. The SNP vote was down to 17 per cent in Kirkcaldy and 27 per cent in Motherwell.

SCOTTISH POLITICS SINCE 1945

Since 1945 we might distinguish five phases of Scottish politics.

Phase One lasted until the 1955 election. The issue in Scotland as in England was 'controls', resistance and reaction to the introduction of what Conservatives called 'socialist planning'. For Scotland the Conservatives pointed out 'nationalization meant denationalization': socialist control meant London control. Conservatives saw Scottish desires for more independence as a weapon to use in their attack on the London socialist government. In 1979 Mrs Thatcher returned to the same theme when she said the kind of devolution she wanted was devolution back to the people themselves. The argument may have been less than persuasive in 1979 but it gave the Conservatives the initiative on Scottish affairs for the first decade after the War.

Phase Two ran from the late fifties until the mid-sixties. The key issue was Scotland's apparent exclusion from the prosperity of the South. Key statistics were first, the rate of Scots unemployment relative to English unemployment – the so-called 'unemployment relative'; second, the rate of migration from Scotland to England; and third, the gap between Scots and English wage rates or earnings. Often we summarize this syndrome by talking about unemployment but the basic worry was employment not unemployment. You may remember Chaplin's film *The Great Dictator* in which he proposed to shoot a factory full of striking workers because he did not want any 'unhappy workers'. Similarly migration out of Scotland kept the unemployment rate down by removing the unemployed but Scots politicians regarded that cure as every bit as bad as the disease. Scotland should not be emptied of its population just to solve the people's problems on an individual basis. Willie Ross, for example, strongly attacked the situation in the borders region of Scotland in the late sixties where there was very little unemployment but a declining population.

The problem was relative. Scots unemployment was not high and over-all Britain was prosperous. The need was to switch resources from the so-called 'congested areas' of the South to Scotland, to keep Scots employed in Scotland, to increase the number of Scots jobs rather than lower the number of Scots unemployed.

Planning and controls no longer appeared to be necessarily against Scots interests. Why go for more independence when the need was for more Scottish control of what went on in England? The initiative on Scottish affairs passed to Labour as the party of planning, and Labour used a distinctly nationalist rhetoric to attack the Conservative Government.

During Phase Three, from 1964 to 1970, Labour had the

opportunity to show how planning and controls could shift resources and, above all, jobs from the congested South to the North. The unemployment relative did fall. But the experiment was not a total success because the whole British economy ran into difficulties. So the unemployment relative moved in the right direction because the English lost their jobs instead of Scots gaining them.

Both Labour and the Conservatives were now in danger of losing the initiative on Scottish affairs. The SNP scored its first run of consistently maintained success against a full panel of opposition. It won a parliamentary by-election and dozens of local government elections. But in 1967 and 1968 the Labour Government was no more popular in England. As the general election approached Labour recovered support on both sides of the border and the SNP challenge faded.

Phase Four, from 1970 to 1974, was characterized by the interaction of two circumstances, each without precedent. The Conservatives won a Westminster majority at the 1970 election and Scotland got a Conservative Secretary of State as a consequence. But Labour had a clear lead in Scots votes and a two-to-one majority of Scots MPs. With the exception of the single year 1922–3 we have to go back to 1895 to find the last occasion when the Secretary lacked the support of both Scots votes and Scots MPs. Even in 1959–64 the Conservatives had more Scots votes though fewer seats than Labour. The only real precedent for an externally imposed Secretary was the period 1885–95 when Unionist Secretaries faced a Liberal electorate in Scotland. But with over half working-class men and all the women excluded, the late nineteenth-century electorate could not claim to represent Scots as a whole. Moreover, the office was a minor one at that time and had been set up by the Unionists themselves.

In short, there was no real precedent for the imposed Secretaryship of Gordon Campbell. Circumstances made it extremely difficult for him to pose as a protector of Scotland when his very existence testified to the power of external influences. By an unfortunate coincidence three current issues pointed the need for protection from external exploitation.

Scots may not have much respect for their fellow Scotsmen but they have some pride in the land coupled with the rather guilty feeling that they have permitted far too much spoliation in the past. In this respect the seas around Scotland became a natural extension of the land itself. It was not just the authors of the popular musical 'The Cheviot, the Stag and the Black Black Oil' who could see a connection between Highland clearances and North Sea oil.

Three land issues caught popular imagination in the early seventies. They were, first, external control of the oil wealth whose existence only became public knowledge after the 1970 election; second, oil blight on the Scots mainland, as beautiful coastal sites were destroyed to make oil-rig construction yards. Some of these yards never won an order. It was pure destruction without construction. Third was the EEC issue. EEC entry raised a whole complex of issues but in Scotland there were special fears that the EEC wanted to grab Scotland's oil and Scotland's fish.

Finally, Phase Five centred on the constitutional issue of devolution – the creation of a Scots parliament or assembly. This phase began with the general election of February 1974 and ended with the referendum in March 1979. Despite the rumble of debate and the report of the Kilbrandon Commission, it was the sudden and largely unexpected election of seven SNP MPs in February 1974 which put devolution on the agenda for action. The October election confirmed devolution as a major issue. The end came equally suddenly with the unexpectedly narrow 'Yes' vote in the 1979 referendum. In a longer time perspective we may come to see the referendum as no more than a temporary set-back for the devolutionists, or as the start of a trend towards integration. But for the first few months after it the referendum seemed to mark the start of a period of benign neglect: everything that could be said about Scotland either by Scots or non-Scots had been said in the run-up to the referendum; now was the time to talk about something else.

Inevitably, this five-phase view of recent Scots politics must be something of a caricature. Unemployment remained a worry in Phases Four and Five; indeed it got steadily worse. Devolution was discussed in the late sixties as well as in the late seventies. Oil revenues still appeared in political speeches during the devolution phase. None the less, I think the five phases do convey an impression of the dominant Scots issues since the War and sometimes the switch between issues was remarkable for its abruptness – as with the sudden awareness of North Sea oil after, but not before, the 1970 election.

Phase One (1945–55): Controls

The central issue at the 1945 general election was whether or not to continue wartime economic controls into peacetime and use them to move towards a planned socialist economy. The campaign was livened up by Churchill's claim that Attlee would need a Gestapo to enforce socialism in Britain, and by a row between Attlee and Laski over who should control a Labour government if Labour won the election. Churchill made a triumphal tour up through England to a climax at rallies in Glasgow and Edinburgh. The terms 'National' or 'Nationalist' were applied in Scotland as elsewhere to supporters of Mr Churchill's National Government.

Dr MacIntyre's success at Motherwell earlier in the year encouraged Labour and Liberal candidates to voice support for a Scottish parliament and MacIntyre's father, the Revd J. E. MacIntyre, persuaded the General Assembly of the Kirk to vote for an SBC (Scottish Broadcasting Corporation) rather than a post-war re-establishment of BBC regional radio services. But it was all a fairly ritual exercise with little hope or expectation or probably even concern for success. Churchill's Government produced a pre-election sweetener by conceding MacIntyre's demand for international status for Prestwick, adding that an independent Scots airline would be given a monopoly of the Scandinavian trade. Tom Johnston, Labour's legendary Secretary of State for Scotland in the wartime coalition, used his radio party political broadcast to argue the case for controls, not devolution.

The SNP put up the same number of candidates as in 1935, scoring much the same vote but losing one more deposit, making six lost deposits for eight candidates. MacIntyre lost the seat he had just won at the by-election. For the rest of Phase One, the SNP was eclipsed by Scots pressure groups led by the former SNP leader, John MacCormick.

After taking his followers out of the SNP in 1942, MacCormick joined the Liberals and urged his supporters to infiltrate all the other parties. MacCormick stood as a Liberal candidate in 1945.

In 1947 MacCormick's 'Convention' organized a Scottish

National Assembly inviting representatives from every pres-
bytery, local authority, chamber of commerce and trade union.
The STUC organized a similar Assembly in the early
seventies. About 600 delegates attended the 1947 meeting and it
became an annual event. At the third Assembly 1,200 delegates
met in the Kirk's General Assembly hall and began signing the
'Covenant' which pledged them 'in all loyalty to the Crown and
within the framework of the UK, to do everything in our power
to secure for Scotland a Parliament with adequate legislative
authority in Scottish affairs'.

The Covenant ran away from its sponsors. Everyone, it
seemed, wanted to add their name. In the end over two million
signatures were claimed. Though many were later ridiculed or
disputed the Covenant certainly revealed widespread emotional
commitment to the idea of a more independent Scotland.
However, MacCormick and the Covenant have grown in the
imagination of some nationalists as the years have passed. To put
his achievement in perspective we should note that the present
Conservative Secretary of State, George Younger, organized a
'Save the Argylls' petition in the late sixties and claimed well over
a million signatures.

Perhaps there is more than a passing similarity between
MacCormick's and Younger's petitions. Both revealed an emotional commitment. Both seemed to involve no real cost to the
signatory. And both were used by Scottish Unionists to embar-
rass a Labour government beset by economic and industrial
problems.

Labour's Scottish conference passed vaguely pro-home rule
motions in 1941, 1945, and 1947 but the issue was never given a
high priority. Words like 'examine the possibilities' of home rule
were used; and the British Labour Party did not adopt a home
rule policy. MacCormick probably did as much harm as good,
especially when he stood at the 1948 Paisley by-election.

He fought a glittering campaign. The press reported 6,000
turned away from his final rally, unable to get in to the packed
town hall. MacCormick had come to an agreement with the local
Unionists and stood as the sole anti-Government candidate. He
had the same advantage as MacIntyre in Hamilton during the
War and, for a year past, Labour had suffered swings of up to 10
per cent at other by-elections. MacCormick stood as a National-

ist though more in the Churchillian than the SNP sense. On the platform at his final rally he was backed by Scots and English Conservative MPs, by John Bannerman from the Scottish Liberal Executive, and by William Power, President of Scottish Convention. 'Never before', he said, 'has a by-election been fought in which the issue is so straightforward and essentially so simple: it is one between freedom and totalitarianism. If the Government is allowed to pursue its present course our retrogression towards State tyranny is inevitable.'

There was a perfectly valid argument that Labour's nationalization of industry, the national health service, and other British national plans represented a centralizing tendency inimical to Scottish independence. Free marketeers and free Scots did have a common enemy in London socialism. But MacCormick's Paisley campaign – which even included an attack on PAYE – chained Scots national demands to a crude right-wing attack on Labour government. Small wonder, then, that the 1948 White Paper on Scottish Affairs, which appeared during the Paisley campaign, ignored Convention's demands and merely reformed the Scottish committee system at Westminster.

Despite the enthusiasm shown at his meetings, and the absence of any alternative anti-Labour candidate, MacCormick lost the Paisley by-election and Labour even increased its vote slightly.

A week before the 1950 general election Winston Churchill made a remarkable speech in the Usher Hall, Edinburgh. He had two themes. Outside Scotland his speech was reported as a statement on foreign affairs: only the atom bomb preserved peace. But his second theme was as coherently argued, and more extremist, than his first:

The principle of centralisation of government in Whitehall and Westminster is emphasised in a manner not hitherto experienced or contemplated in the (1707) Act of Union . . . I frankly admit that it raises new issues between our two nations . . . *I would never adopt the view that Scotland should be forced into the serfdom of socialism as a result of a vote in the House of Commons.*

Having rejected the notion that parliamentary sovereignty extended north of the border Churchill said there was still time for Scots and English to act together against socialism.

[But] the socialist menace has advanced so far as to entitle Scotland to *further guarantees of national security and internal independence* . . . we shall advise the creation of a new office of Minister of State for Scotland . . . of Cabinet rank . . . Such an appointment would enable a senior minister of the Cabinet to be constantly in Scotland. . . . We shall appoint a Royal Commission to review the whole situation between Scotland and England and we shall take good care that this does not become an instrument of delay upon practical action.

Scotland was apparently to get two representatives in the Cabinet and their function was to 'guarantee internal independence'.

The Conservative's UK manifesto repeated Churchill's promises in scarcely less inflammatory language and added the promise of another under-secretary, separate Scots boards for coal, electricity, gas, and the railways 'in no way subordinate to the English boards'; the status of heads of UK ministries in Scotland would be enhanced; more power would be devolved to Scots local government; and the Conservatives would end the practice of tacking Scots clauses onto English legislation.

The *Daily Record* persuaded Secretary of State Arthur Woodburn and Walter Elliot for the Conservatives, to answer the question 'who speaks for Scotland?' Woodburn, clearly on the defensive, listed the parliamentary committee reforms and claimed that Scotland benefited from controls imposed on English firms. Elliot, who had been behind the Scottish Office's move from London to Edinburgh in 1939, was confident and aggressive. 'Not a word now of devolution,' he chided Labour, 'let alone a Scottish parliament – twenty years of promises and propaganda gone with the wind.' Hugh Gaitskell now ran Scots gas and half her electricity: the Secretary of State for Scotland 'has to ring up London to get permission to have another bar turned on in his office radiator'. Elliot then attacked three Labour MPs for being born outside Scotland and ended: 'let free Scots enterprise be developed in Scotland by Scotsmen.' This was the voice of Unionism in 1950.

Conservatives offered devolution within the central government machine: ministerial devolution and administrative devolution. They offered devolution from central government to the citizen or local authority. But they never offered the sort of devolution proposed by the 1974–9 Labour Government. They never offered a devolution of accountability. The Scots electorate, as a body, was offered nothing at all. Yet the problem for the future was that the Conservatives offered almost everything else. After the early fifties they had come close to the end of the road they had chosen. Administrative devolution had been pushed almost to the limit. And so much administrative devolution, explicitly justified as a 'guarantee of national security and internal independence' was itself an argument for Scots political control of this devolved administration.

When they returned to office in 1951 the Conservatives set up the promised Royal Commission, known as the Balfour Commission. The report was published in July 1954. There was a sharp contrast between Balfour's diagnosis and its prescription. The report began with a reference to the 1707 Treaty of Union as a 'voluntary union of two proud peoples' and warned of a resurgence of that 'old fear that Scotland is being downgraded from a nation to a province of England'. But it launched into a detailed attack on all current radical proposals for reform. The Covenant, it said, had been signed in a wave of emotion with no real debate about its implications, and many of the signatures were invalid. It listed the Scots organizations which had proposed home rule, and those which had rejected home rule; then derided the numerical strength of the home rulers.

On practical grounds it opposed Scottish meetings of Scots committees of the Westminster parliament, dismissed the idea of a Highland Development Authority and rejected any transfer of trade and industry functions to the Secretary of State.

In Balfour's view the 'Scot's pride in Scotland is no mere creation of the last few decades. It is his heritage from centuries of history and tradition'; there had been no recent growth in nationalism only a growth in frustration caused (a) by the massive growth of central, hence London, government; (b) by insensitive handling of Scots affairs by English politicians; (c) by ignorance in Scotland of the degree of devolution that already existed and (d) by the economic gap between Scotland and England. To see whether Scotland was getting fair treatment, Balfour compared housing and unemployment statistics for Scotland with those for England and Wales. Per capita Scotland had benefited from 16 per cent more new houses than England since the War but unemployment ran at twice the rate in England. Still, both unemployment rates were very low –

roughly $1\frac{1}{2}$ per cent in England and 3 per cent in Scotland and 'if there had been any effective measure of separation between England and Scotland there can be no doubt that most of the factories which have in fact been established in Scotland by English concerns would have been located within the regions of England and Wales'.

Balfour diagnosed frustration and prescribed more under-standing, more sensitivity by the London government. Two decades later politicians were to diagnose inflation and prescribe a popular willingness to forgo wage increases. A change of behaviour rather than a change of institutions. But without a change of institutions where was the constant incentive to change behaviour? At Christmastime 1965 Willie Ross, then Secretary of State, was moved to a written protest by the House of Commons Christmas card showing Simon de Montfort's English parlia-ment in 1278 with the King of Scotland 'doing homage at Westminster' – a caption that was both inaccurate and insulting. The incident itself is not important except as an indication that no Royal Commission report could produce 'sensitivity' without some routine method for encouraging or enforcing it.

Meanwhile, the Covenant Association had run out of ideas and support, while the SNP won only 7 per cent of the vote in the 1952 Dundee by-election – their only by-election contest be-tween 1948 and 1961. Indeed the party fought far fewer elections in the fifties than the thirties – a dozen contests spread over four general elections with lost deposits in eight of the twelve. Home rule came to be associated with the theft of the Stone of Destiny from Westminster Abbey or attacks on post-boxes carrying the EIIR symbol.

Until 1968 the *Glasgow Herald* published on index similar to the London *Times* index. Figure 1.1 shows the number of lines in the *Herald* index devoted to the heading 'home rule' for each year between 1940 and 1968. It provides a simple objective measure of the amount of public attention given to the issue: very little until 1946; then, in response to MacCormick's assemblies, a swift rise to a peak in 1950, followed by a sharp drop in 1951 and 1952 and a progressive decline until 1960. Interest revived slightly between 1960 and 1966 and exploded in 1967 and 1968.

'Who speaks for Scotland?' was not the main issue at the 1950 general election but it was a significant secondary theme.

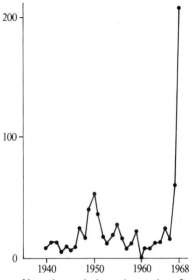

Note: the graph shows the number of
lines devoted to home rule in the
Glasgow Herald index for each year up
to 1968, after which it ceased publication.

Fig. 1.1. Public interest in home rule, 1940–68

Reports from around Scotland showed that controls were justified or attacked not only in socialist versus free market terms but in Scottish terms. Controls were a means for shifting industry from England to Scotland as well as restraining capitalist excesses; or controls took power from Scotland as well as from individual citizens. Glasgow University's study of the election reported that home rule was raised in questions at election meetings in Glasgow though often coupled with an expressed fear that a devolved Scotland would be permanently Conservative.

In 1955, despite fading public interest and SNP electoral failures, the Conservatives' UK manifesto gave three times as much space to Scotland as in 1950. The language was more restrained, perhaps because in 1955 it was a government rather than an opposition manifesto. For the same reason it was backward looking instead of forward looking: a list of promises honoured instead of reforms proposed. Its 'general theme [was] that within the Union the responsibility for managing Scottish affairs shall be in the hands of Scotsmen', but it had no 'general' proposals. There were specifics like a road bridge over the Forth and a tunnel under the Clyde, plus a repetition of promises made elsewhere in the manifesto about England – more schools and hospitals, for example. But Balfour had concluded that things were generally satisfactory; so there were no general reforms to propose.

From the Scottish Office reforms in the late thirties to Balfour in the mid-fifties the Conservatives bolstered up Scots national consciousness, used Scots nationalism as a weapon against socialism, and built up the Scottish Office. And over the same period their electoral performance in Scotland was significantly better than they could normally expect.

Before the First World War the Unionist's lead over the Liberals was about 15 per cent less in Scotland than in England (or the Liberal lead was 15 per cent more in Scotland). And from the early twenties to the present, the Conservative lead over Labour has averaged about 8 per cent less in Scotland than in England. In a later chapter I will show that we should expect it to be about 8 per cent less simply because the class mix in Scotland is different from that in England. So for both social and historical reasons the Conservatives had reason to expect that the norm was a lead 8 per cent less in Scotland than in England. Neglecting third parties that meant, for example, a Conservative vote 4 per cent less in Scotland and a Labour vote 4 per cent higher in Scotland.

But in 1945 and 1955 the Conservatives did as well against Labour in Scotland as in England. (Better if ILP votes are not grouped with Labour.) And in 1950 and 1951 the Conservatives had a greater margin over Labour in Scotland than in England. This was a very considerable achievement gained against the weight of class interests and historic traditions. It would be quite wrong to regard 1945–55 as the electoral norm and then look for special explanations of election results from 1959 onwards.

In this first phase of post-war politics the Scots Conservatives succeeded in using special Scots political factors to outweigh their natural class disadvantage in Scotland.

Phase Two (1955–64): the Failure of Freedom

Towards the end of the fifties the Conservative attack on controls ran out of steam. Throughout Britain people had grown used to the massive post-war extension of state intervention. Scots in particular began to see more national advantages than disadvantages in controls and planning.

The key to this change of attitude lies in the unemployment ratio that worried the Balfour Commission. As unemployment rates edged upwards in the late fifties and early sixties the unemployment ratio remained high: indeed it increased rather than decreased, and was coupled with increasing migration losses (see Figs. 1.2 and 1.3). The ratio of Scots to English GDP per capita also fell throughout the fifties and early sixties (see Fig. 1.4).

The unemployment ratio had varied around 1.25 in the twenties and thirties. Unemployment rates had been high but Scottish rates had been only one and a quarter times over-all GB rates. During the War the ratio shot up to around 2.00 but that reflected a 1 per cent unemployment rate in Scotland against half

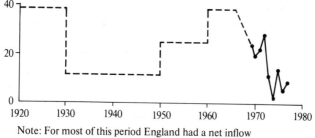

Note: For most of this period England had a net inflow

Fig. 1.2. Net annual migration loss to Scotland (thousands)
   Sources: *Modern Scotland* (Kellas) and *Scottish Economic Bulletin*

Note: Scots rate as fraction of GB rate to 1946 and as fraction of UK rate from 1949 onwards

Fig. 1.3. Unemployment ratio
   Sources: *Modern Scotland* (Kellas) and *Scottish Economic Bulletin*

Note: Scots GDP per capita as fraction of UK. GDP of North Sea excluded from both

Fig. 1.4 GDP per capita ratio
      Sources: *Scotland's Future* (McCrone) and *Scottish Economic Bulletin*

a per cent in GB. But when unemployment rose again after the War the ratio stayed obstinately close to 2.00. And the ratio showed no tendency to decline when annual unemployment rates rose again at the end of the fifties to fluctuate around 4 per cent in Scotland and 2 per cent in England. Politicians had accepted 2 to 3 per cent unemployment as a definition of 'full employment'. That meant a qualitative difference between Scotland and England: a difference between full employment and unemployment.

Central economic planning became more popular in Scotland and its new popularity had two important political effects. It silenced the campaign to picture socialism as inevitably anti-Scottish and gave Labour the chance to regain the initiative in Scotland. But at the same time it encouraged Labour to ditch its half-forgotten commitment to parliamentary devolution.

At the beginning of 1957 Labour's Scottish executive drew up a statement regretting that there were now 'compelling economic grounds' for rejecting its earlier policy of home rule. Yet when the statement was put to conference in Perth, conference revolted. John Mackintosh's motion to send the statement back for further consideration was carried by 108 votes to 71. The following year a special autumn conference was called to debate the revised devolution statement which now called for a Speaker's Conference and demanded the 'maximum possible self-government for Scotland consistent with the right to remain in the UK parliament and continue full Scottish representation there'. It got a large majority but some supported it because it failed to present an unambiguous demand for a Scots parliament while others supported it because it failed to reject a Scots parliament. As the party veered later towards favourable or unfavourable attitudes to devolution it could always quote the 1958 vote as proof of consistency.

But the 1958 vote has to be seen against the background of the 1957 vote. At a time when the SNP posed no electoral threat whatsoever, was indeed scarcely visible in Scots politics, and at a time when economic conditions stressed the value of centralized control, the Scots Labour Party proved remarkably reluctant to ditch political devolution completely.

The Conservatives all but forgot Scotland in the 1959 election. It was the first television-dominated election and they had a superb performer in Harold Macmillan . But the medium was ill-suited, in its early days, to sending different messages to different parts of the country. Even in his signed articles in the Scots press, Macmillan showed too much of that insensitivity which Balfour had deplored. 'I do not remember any period in my lifetime when the economy has been so sound and the prosperity of our people at home so widely spread' – reduced by his opponents to 'you've never had it so good' – sounded differently in Scotland and South-East England. It was too complacent, and all the stress on prosperity somehow made regional variations that much less easy to bear.

But it would be wrong to suggest that Scots were so irritated by Macmillan's message that they swung against the Conservatives in 1959. Scotland did swing to Labour while England moved further towards the Conservatives but that only represented a drift back towards the norm. The Conservatives still won more Scots votes than Labour, despite having one candidate less. And the gap between Conservative performance in Scotland and England still remained rather less than the norm. The Conservatives lost most of the special Scottish advantage they had enjoyed since 1945 but they lost no more than that.

During the next parliament economic difficulties increased. Unemployment never fell back to the pre-1958 level and went on to a new peak in 1963 when the rate in Scotland averaged almost 5 per cent for the year as a whole.

Scotland's semi-official substitute for a Board of Trade – the Scottish Council (Development and Industry) – commissioned a team under J. N. Toothill, general manager of Ferranti, to report on 'what makes Scotland's economy tick and what would make it tick better?' Toothill responded in July 1961 with a 200-page report and eighty-one detailed recommendations. This report stimulated government interest in regional planning but also encouraged the notion that Scots could plan their own economy as well as manage their own education system.

Since the 1930s regional policy in Britain had been a relief operation for areas of high unemployment: an uneconomic and vaguely disreputable charity to be abandoned as soon as unemployment in an area declined to an acceptable level. In the fifties the acceptable level was fixed at $4\frac{1}{2}$ per cent. Toothill, however, saw regional policy as part of a modernization process and switched the emphasis from maintaining employment to encouraging growth. Encouraging growth implied investment in transport and communications both within Scotland and between Scotland and the rest of the world; it implied helping Scots industries to expand as well as attracting incomers. But the distinctive feature of Toothill was its strong advocacy of a 'growth point' strategy.

Designated 'growth points' were to get enough infrastructure investment to make them as attractive and convenient to industry as the South-East of England. They were to get government aid until they had solved their own economic problems – just like old-fashioned unemployment blackspots. But then they were to get further injections of government help until they had sucked in the surrounding unemployment and solved the economic problems of other areas. So boundaries were not to be defined by local economic conditions: aid to one area was to be justified by the problems of other areas. It implied a broad perspective, Scotland-wide rather than local. Toothill also suggested a new department of economic planning within the Scottish Office.

Toothill was published when even the Conservatives had come to see the need for planning. Macmillan established a National Incomes Commission and a National Economic Development Council and in the 'night of the long knives', a year after Toothill, he emphasized the new Conservative direction by sacking a third of his Cabinet and many ministers outside the Cabinet. Early in 1963 the NEDC published *Growth of the UK Economy to 1966*, a 150-page economic programme based on a 4 per cent per annum growth rate. Later in the year the Government published simultaneous White Papers on Scotland and the North-East of England. 'Central Scotland: a Programme for Development and Growth' was openly modelled on Toothill and claimed to 'represent a more positive approach to regional economic development than any government in this country has yet attempted'. Popularly known as the 'Central Scotland Plan' the White Paper was published on a Tuesday but Labour increased its majority at the Dundee by-election on Thursday of the same week.

The Central Scotland Plan was welcomed by the Scottish Council but it had several economic and political faults. It lacked a time-table, showed little understanding of the causes of growth, and applied to only a part of Scotland. The initiative on all industrial matters, including even the provision of information about the advantages Scotland offered for incoming firms, was retained by Edward Heath, the Minister for Industry, Trade, and Regional Development. The Scottish Secretary would play a minor, supporting role.

Early in 1964 the Central Scotland Plan seemed to be negated by a South East England Plan which envisaged an enormous growth of population in the South East and set out plans to house and otherwise provide for this population increase including the establishment of three new cities. It did seem very odd that a government should produce within six months of each other one plan to stop emigration from Scotland and the North plus another plan to accommodate the expected immigration into the South.

In Scotland, the South East England Plan got almost as much publicity as the Central Scotland Plan and all the publicity was bad. Six weeks after the South-east Plan was published Labour took Rutherglen from the Conservatives with a swing of 8 per cent between the 1959 general election and the by-election.

Even without the contrast between its Central Scotland and South-east England Plans it would have been difficult for the party which had campaigned so recently and so strongly against controls to become the natural party of planning, whether regional planning or national planning.

Conservatives could, and frequently did, list the prestige projects approved during their period in office – the Dounreay reactor, Ravenscraig strip mill, Linwood motors, Bathgate trucks, Fort William's pulp mill, the Clyde tunnel and the Forth and Tay road bridges. But as for general regional policies they could only point back to the 1960 Local Employment Act which assisted factory building in areas of high unemployment. The incentives and planning they adopted in 1963–4 seemed, perhaps unfairly, to owe their inspiration jointly to the non-governmental Toothill Report and the approaching election.

For the first half of the Parliament Labour was in no position to profit from the Conservatives' problems . Labour had suffered three general election defeats and four increasingly adverse swings in a row: its gloom was epitomized by the title of Abrams and Rose's *Must Labour Lose?* To add to its divisions on the EEC and the Bomb it plunged into a fratricidal quarrel over Clause 4, the section of its constitution which committed the party to socialism. Conference defeated the party leader, Hugh Gaitskell, and he vowed never to accept the verdict of Conference. Throughout Britain third parties enjoyed a surge of support.

Liberals throughout Britain had been reduced to 2½ per cent of the vote at the 1951 and 1955 general elections. In 1959, they doubled the number of Liberal candidates to 216 but still won only 6 per cent of the vote and six seats in parliament. In Scotland they had only 4 per cent of the vote and one MP, Jo Grimond. The SNP had less than 1 per cent.

In the early fifties Liberals contested only one by-election in every seven and in the late fifties only one in three, but in the 1959–64 parliament they contested fifty out of sixty-two. Where they did contest by-elections before 1959, the Liberals, unlike the SNP, sometimes achieved substantial votes especially in rural or resort areas. They won 36 per cent or more in Ross and Cromarty (1954), Hereford (1956), Carmarthen and North Dorset (1957), Rochdale and Torrington (1958). Other sizeable Liberal votes in Scotland were 28 per cent in Argyll, 24 per cent in Aberdeen East (1958), and 26 per cent in Galloway (1959). Every one of these Scottish by-election votes was obtained where the Liberals had had no candidate at the preceding general election and every one of these seats was subsequently won by the Liberals or SNP. Perhaps with a more vigorous party the Liberals could have won even more votes at by-elections in the fifties but it was not until after 1959 that the party put itself to the test.

At first there was nothing special about Scots by-elections in the 1959–64 parliament. In 1960 there was only one – Edinburgh North. Turn-out dropped by more than the average for English by-elections that year and the Liberal vote was smaller than in England. Next year, at Paisley and East Fife, turn-out dropped less than in English by-elections and the Scots Liberals did better than English Liberals. John Bannerman pushed the Liberal vote up to 41 per cent in Paisley – within 4 per cent of victory. But in the autumn the Liberals made a tactical blunder when they failed to contest Bridgeton. Their decision fitted into a general pattern. Throughout the parliament the by-elections they avoided were in safe Labour areas – Bridgeton, Blyth, Pontefract, Rotherham, Manchester Openshaw, and Liverpool Scotland. They had their sights on prosperous suburbia. In England this merely deprived already deprived areas of an opportunity to cast a protest vote. In Scotland it let the SNP collect the protest.

It was the SNP's first by-election contest since 1952. While turn-out dropped by only 11 per cent in Paisley it dropped a full 27 per cent in Bridgeton and the SNP won less than 19 per cent of the vote compared with the Liberals' 41 per cent in Paisley. Since Bridgeton's electorate was also small the SNP won just 3,549 votes there compared with 17,542 for the Liberals in Paisley. But Ian Macdonald, the SNP candidate, was so delighted by his modest achievement that he sold his farm and offered himself to the SNP as full-time national organizer for a nominal salary. The SNP was so used to a negligible electoral performance that 19 per cent in Bridgeton was a cause for rejoicing. At that time the party had only a little over a thousand members, most affiliated directly to headquarters. Macdonald set about constructing a branch-based party structure with branches or cells of twenty members. It maximized the number of junior office holders, maximized participation generally, and helped a rapid growth in membership.

In 1962 the English Liberals did far better than either Scots Liberals or the SNP, averaging 26 per cent of the vote in fourteen by-elections and winning Orpington with 53 per cent. Billy Wolfe stood for the SNP at West Lothian. He got 23 per cent, less than the average English Liberal but better than previous SNP by-election votes; and he had the satisfaction of beating both Liberal and Conservative candidates. Tam Dalyell held the seat for Labour.

Late in 1962 the Scots Liberals pushed the SNP back to fourth place at Woodside where Labour took the seat from the Conservatives. English Liberal support faded in 1963 and so did votes for Scots Liberals and the SNP. Scots Liberals took 20 per cent in Kinross, 11 per cent in Dumfries, and failed to contest Dundee West. The SNP contested all three but each time got less than 10 per cent of the vote. Neither party had a candidate for Rutherglen in 1964.

Over all, the SNP had gained votes only when the English Liberals were being even more successful at harvesting a protest vote. Bridgeton and West Lothian were enough to breathe some life into a moribund party and attract ex-supporters of the defunct Scottish Convention but they were not evidence of any significant shift in attitudes or allegiance by the electorate at large.

Just before the 1964 general election Billy Wolfe persuaded the SNP to offer the Liberals an electoral pact if they would give top priority to their declared policy of a federal Britain. The move foundered as the SNP set impossibly rigid conditions and the Liberals denounced separation. For the next decade, however, a succession of Liberal and SNP politicians pursued the chimera of a united home rule front. They produced a bewildering variety of detailed proposals. Some were trying to give priority to an issue that transcended party politics: others were manoevring to expose the other party, to show the Liberals' frivolity or the SNP's extremism.

Scottish Labour MPs, led by the future Secretary of State, Willie Ross, ran a strongly nationalist campaign throughout the 1959–64 parliament but it centred on their promise to use central UK planning and controls to restrict development in what they called the 'congested areas' of the South. By a fortunate accident of electoral arithmetic Labour won seven more Scots seats than the Conservatives in 1959, despite taking fewer votes. That gave Labour MPs half a justification for their own view that they and not the Conservative Secretary 'spoke for Scotland'. Labour's by-election gains at Woodside in 1962 and Rutherglen in 1964 confirmed this view. Sometimes it was difficult to disentangle the nationalist from the partisan aspects of Scots Labour's attack on the 1959–64 Government.

UK Labour's principal policy document at this time was *Signposts for the Sixties*. It compared the UK with more prosperous European countries, America, and Japan, and enthused over the need for socialist planning. It cost sixpence. If you lived in Scotland you could pay another ninepence to get the much shorter *Signposts for Scotland*. This compared Scotland with England and enthused over regional planning. I will give some lengthy quotations from *Signposts for Scotland*, firstly because they epitomize the nature of the Scottish Labour campaign in the early sixties, and secondly because they provide the benchmark for judging the performance of the 1964–70 Labour Government.

On unemployment and emigration, *Signposts for Scotland* noted that:

from 1951–61 the number of males in employment in Scotland has decreased by 16,000 while increasing by 839,000 in Great Britain . . . the truth is that the prosperity so often claimed for Britain has been more or less confined to the range of new and expanding industries that have settled overwhelmingly in the area running from Birmingham to London. The economic experts call this *the coffin* because of the shape it makes if drawn on a map. It is a suitably sombre title, for the *hopes of Scottish prosperity have been buried in this area during the years of Toryism.* [To combat this] the policy of restricting development in the *congested areas* will be rigorously applied.

As for Dr Beeching's rail cuts,

the vast increase in motor traffic in the *congested areas* is no argument for depriving the crofter and holiday maker of railway services and an adequate road system to link the Highlands and Islands with other parts of the country. . . . It is unjust that, while millions of pounds are spent on motorways and trunk roads in the south to which the public has free access, tolls should still be imposed on the essential [Forth, Tay, and Erskine] bridges and ferries in Scotland. . . . Already the little South-East corner of England has three times the population of Scotland. To go on draining Scotland of some of our most vigorous people and to go on overcrowding the South is absurd.

The old argument that socialist controls implied centralization was dismissed with the claim that

a rigid national plan for the whole of Britain is neither desirable nor necessary. All that will be required at the centre is a small planning staff with powers which will enable it to coordinate the regional plans . . . In Scotland the main responsibility will rest with the Scottish Office.

At the end, *Signposts for Scotland* outlined Scots Labour ideology. The basis was the socialist principle – to each according to his needs, from each according to his ability . . . We believe that the vast majority of the people of this country – in the prosperous Midlands and South as well as in Scotland and other less fortunate areas – regard a fair sharing of improved living standards as a far more worthy and desirable objective [than] personal gain.

Ten lines further down it pointed out 'Scotland will stand to gain more from this fairer sharing of both benefits and burdens just because of our present relatively greater needs.'

Then it ended by making the case for the Union.

Separation would give Scotland the worst of both worlds. It would throw us back on our own resources at a time when the process of decline in our traditional industries is far advanced and before our economy has had the opportunity to benefit fully from new scientific developments. [But there was room for] further measures of devolution in Scotland and a major increase in the powers and scope of the Scottish Office.

No doubt relatively few people bought and read *Signposts for Scotland*. I quote it because it exemplifies the style and content of the arguments Labour used in the press, on television, in weekend speeches, and wherever it could get a hearing.

It stressed Scottish interests as a prime criterion for judging policy. By opening on unemployment coupled with emigration, on jobs in Scotland rather than Scots without a job, it elevated the interest of the land above even the interests of the people. It sharpened the contrast between Scotland and the South, publicizing the statistics of the prosperity gap while using belittling or abusive language to describe the South: 'congested areas', a 'coffin', a place where 'hopes of Scottish prosperity have been buried'. Restrictions and controls were to be applied to these 'congested areas'. Centralized planning, as opposed to internal Scottish planning, would be the minimum necessary to squeeze the South effectively. An independent Scotland was not *at present* economically desirable because Scotland could *not yet* rely on its own resources.

Add North Sea oil or subtract an effective squeeze on the 'congested areas' and you have a pamphlet that an SNP activist would be happy to distribute. Between 1959 and 1964 Labour made much of the case for a reviving SNP. Like the Conservatives up to 1955 Labour was now able and willing to play the Scottish card.

Phase Three (1964–70): the Failure of Planning

Scotland gave Labour its UK majority in 1964 and made it possible for Harold Wilson to call the 1966 election in circumstances favourable enough for Labour to win a large majority in England as well. But Scotland was able to tip the balance in 1964 only because votes in England were so evenly divided – 44.1 per cent for the Conservatives against 43.5 per cent for Labour. The gap between Scots and English voting was little more than might be expected on class grounds alone. It marked the final elimination of the Conservatives' special Scots advantage but not much more. Indeed the only post-war election when Labour did very much better in Scotland than the social mix implied was 1979, though 1970 and October 1974 were also good elections for Labour in Scotland.

In a sense, then, the period 1964–70 was a time of relative Labour success in Scotland: relative to the Conservatives and relative to Labour's loss of support in England. And Labour's relative political success matched its relative economic success: the Scots–English unemployment ratio fell as unemployment increased in both countries.

Several background factors, none of them particularly Scots, were specially significant for political developments within Scotland at this time. Shortly after Labour's huge victory at the 1966 election the seamen began a long strike which lasted until the end of June. At the beginning of July George Brown published his Prices and Incomes Bill. A fortnight later the Government introduced the 'July measures': a pay and prices freeze and an economic squeeze. It was the end of Brown's Ministry of Economic Affairs and of his National Plan with its assumptions about growth. Brown switched to the Foreign Office. From July 1966 onwards Scots politics – like English politics – operated in an atmosphere of economic gloom and of disillusionment with planning.

Less than a week before the formal announcement of the July measures but in the midst of an obvious economic crisis Gwynfor Evans won the Carmarthen by-election for the Welsh Nationalists. Evans had lost his deposit in Carmarthen in 1964, and took only 16 per cent of the vote at the end of March 1966 but he won 39 per cent in July. He lost the seat again in 1970. It was a timely reminder to Scots that they had other options than Liberal or Conservative if they wished to desert Labour.

A third background factor was the decision to reform local government into larger units. The Conservatives formally adopted the idea of a Scottish Assembly but explicitly gave it lower priority than reform of local government and, in particular, insisted that their Assembly proposals must remain in suspense until the new local authorities had been established. Labour went further and claimed that local government reform was devolution, or as much devolution as they now wanted. Simultaneously the move towards larger local government units increased separatist tendencies in the Orkney and Shetland Islands which were then used as a further block on devolution for Scotland.

Finally, renewed violence in Northern Ireland and on an horrific scale, damaged the reputation of devolved parliaments. Whatever the faults or merits of the Stormont system over the last half-century, it now became all too easy to equate devolution with Stormont, Stormont with the Irish, and the Irish with intolerance and violence. In the seventies, several leading English politicians used the Irish analogy to justify devolution: block Scottish aspirations and you might encourage revolutionary violence, they claimed. But within Scotland the Irish analogy was more often used to suggest that a devolved Scotland would be permanently Labour, a one-party state that might somehow oppress Scots Conservatives or sink into uncontrolled corruption.

From the start in 1964, the Scottish Office under Willie Ross made much of the running on economic planning. A Scottish Economic Planning Board was set up in the Scottish Office and a Scottish Economic Planning Council outside it. This was one of eight such Councils spanning Britain but, typically, it was the first to meet. At the same time a bill was published to create a Highlands and Islands Development Board with wide powers of compulsion. George Brown's National Plan was issued in September 1965 and Ross's Scottish National Plan followed in January 1966. It aimed to halve Scots emigration by 1970 and thereafter to increase the number of jobs in Scotland and the size of the Scots population.

Though now criticized for diluting the growth points strategy,

Labour won broad approval in 1966 when it made the whole of Scotland (except Edinburgh) a development area. The following year areas affected by pit closures were designated as 'special' development areas with even higher incentives. In 1967 Labour introduced what James Callaghan described as the 'blockbuster' of REP (Regional Employment Premium) – a payroll subsidy for the whole of Scots industry. At first REP was worth about £40 million per annum to Scotland but it was doubled in 1974 before being abolished in 1977.

In addition the Government approved another reactor at Dounreay, a major expansion at Linwood motors, and an aluminium smelter at Invergordon. Restrictions were placed on developments in the South through a system of Industrial Development Certificates. Within a month of coming to power Labour restricted office developments in London and soon extended the restrictions to Birmingham.

But the whole of Labour's regional economic strategy had to be applied in conditions of general British economic stagnation symbolized by the 1966 July measures. Seventy Labour MPs commemorated the first anniversary in July 1967 with a motion criticizing their own government for having 'no credible policy for bringing the economy out of stagnation'. Restrictions on development in the South might have helped Scotland even more if there had been more pressure for development in the South.

The STUC was particularly critical. Labour's Scottish National Plan was described as no more than a 'preliminary guide', Regional Economic Premium as a 'sop', and the Scottish Economic Planning Council as 'impotent'. Both the Council and the Highland Board disappointed the wilder hopes of Labour supporters. In its first five years the Highland Board was reckoned to have created only 5,000 jobs and was never given the political backing necessary for it to use its compulsory powers or its powers to set up its own industries in a radical way. The Planning Council turned out to be an advisory body, not always consulted on major decisions.

Unemployment in Scotland declined from 1964 to 1966 but thereafter it was always marginally higher than it had been in 1964 though the ratio of Scots to English unemployment fell sharply. Emigration continued and an SEPB report showed that in the fifties and sixties Scotland's loss was unique – greater than the losses of all three northern English regions put together. Even the net loss concealed the dangerous fact that Scotland was exporting her young, economically active population and importing retired Englishmen. But Labour could claim that it reduced the Scots emigration rate by half. Scots were still paid less than the English but the earnings gap was reduced by two-thirds under Labour – from about $7\frac{1}{2}$ per cent to $2\frac{1}{2}$ per cent behind. And GDP per capita in Scotland climbed back to over 90 per cent of the UK level – roughly where it had been in the early fifties. Relatively speaking Scotland did rather well between 1964 and 1970. Only the absolutes were disappointing.

Something should be said about North Sea oil if only to stress its absence from Scots politics before 1970. According to the *Scottish Economic Bulletin* table of 'significant discoveries' in 'UK northern waters', there was none before 1969 and only one in each of 1969 and 1970. By a remarkable coincidence North Sea oil discoveries occurred after the 1970 general election almost as if the election turned on some undersea tap. Throughout 1964–70 the Scots press carried pictures of rigs drilling in the Channel and the southern part of the North Sea. But it was a story of English natural gas, not Scottish oil.

Back in opposition, the Conservatives were once again ready to play on Scots national sentiments in their attack on labour. They could hardly compete in terms of regional aid since they were developing an intense dislike for 'lame duck' industries or regions. Keith Joseph, among others, promised that a Conservative government would end REP and Labour's system of regional incentives though some of the savings would come back to the regions. Instead the Conservatives linked themselves to non-economic Scots national demands, emotional and constitutional. Let me describe three examples of such emotional nationalist issues, each of which inspired a long-running Conservative campaign: NALGO, the Argylls, and BST.

The NALGO affair was a direct consequence of the July measures. Scots local government staff negotiated their pay rises slightly later than in England. So the Scots NALGO award was frozen but the English award was paid. Early in 1967 the Scots Conservatives took up the issue and pushed it to a vote of censure in the Commons just a week before the Pollok by-election. It put

Conservatives in the position of demanding an immediate pay rise for local government workers and Labour in the position of refusing to Scots what they had granted to the English. The Conservatives took Pollok from Labour but the SNP came a close third. Scots Conservatives continued their NALGO campaign right through until after the 1967 local government elections when Labour again suffered large losses but the SNP again got much of the benefit.

As part of their military cuts the Government proposed to abolish Scottish Command and drastically cut the number of Scots regiments. They were in the process of withdrawal from East of Suez. But withdrawal was a messy business. Whatever the rights and wrongs of Aden politics the Argylls were pictured as heroes, particularly when, in July 1967, they played reveille from the rooftops of the Crater district of Aden, a former 'no-go' area. Yet the Argylls were to be disbanded. In 1968 Colonel Mitchell of the Argylls resigned and launched a 'Save the Argylls' campaign. Scots Conservatives, notably the present Secretary of State, George Younger, took a leading part in this campaign and Mitchell became the Conservative candidate for West Aberdeen. He took the seat from the Liberals in 1970. The Argylls campaign centred on a public petition for which over a million signatures were claimed. As soon as the Heath Government took office the Argylls were reprieved but reduced to a company. After protests the Argylls got a full reprieve.

Then there was BST – British Standard Time. Callaghan introduced year-round British Summer Time in the autumn of 1968 as a gesture towards harmony with Europe. Five hundred miles to the north of London BST meant children going to school in complete darkness. Stornoway immediately opted out of BST and introduced Western Isles Time. Though the early evidence suggested an over-all drop in road accidents in Scotland Scots Conservatives called loudly for an end to this 'disastrous experiment'. It was presented as a perfect example of London parochialism. Heath's government abolished it soon after taking office.

NALGO, the Argylls, BST may seem small matters and certainly none of them could form the basis for a very long-term campaign. But collectively they could be part of a continuing attack on what the Balfour Commission identified as a major cause of Scots discontents: London's insensitivity to Scotland's nation status.

For a party which had won over half the Scottish vote as recently as 1955, the elections of 1964 and 1966 were a bitter blow. Conservative politicians could hardly take the detached academic view that the sixties were the norm and the fifties the aberration. They blamed their failure on what one conference delegate described as 'sychophantic complacency' and a failure to identify with Scotland. Emotional issues were one way towards restoring that identification, but in Pollok their own victory had been marred by a shockingly good vote for the SNP candidte. Shortly after Pollok they set up a committee under Sir William McEwan Younger to study the possibility of going beyond purely administrative devolution. This was the logical outcome of their policies since 1885 even if it was the logic of the slippery slope.

As the committee met, the SNP won the Hamilton by-election. Labour reacted by taking a tough no-concessions line against political devolution and went on to suffer badly in the 1968 local government elections. It seemed that a pro-devolution policy might help the Conservatives compete against the SNP for the anti-Labour protest vote. And Labour's hard-line response would ensure that devolution was a Conservative policy that would help in the general election fight against Labour.

Heath made his 'Declaration of Perth' at the Scots conference in May 1968. The Conservatives' initial proposals were based on those of the McEwan Younger committee: a partly nominated Assembly without financial powers that could consider and even initiate legislation but would send everything back to the Westminister parliament for final consideration. Thus Scotland would get an Assembly but Westminster would retain detailed control of Scots legislation. The idea won few friends either inside or outside the party. Strict Unionists were opposed to any Assembly while devolutionists wanted a body which could take decisions that would only be reversed in exceptional circumstances by exceptional methods. To them, McEwan Younger proposed a sub-committee, not an Assembly.

After Perth, Heath set up a Scottish Constitutional Committee chaired by the former Prime Minister, Lord Home, backed by a dozen very distinguished members. It reported in March 1970 with a plan for a 125-man, elected Convention which would meet

for about forty days per year. It would take over much of the
work of the Scottish Grand and Standing Committees. Legislation would be referred to it by the Commons and could be
referred back by the Secretary of State. Quite clearly a
committee of Parliament but with members chosen in a peculiar
way. The two Scots academics on the Constitutional Committee
submitted a memorandum of dissent, claiming there was no
'political living space' for the proposed body.

In addition the Constitutional Committee rejected the Stormont system but proposed a Scots Ministry of Development
modelled on the Northern Ireland Ministry of Commerce.

The balance of Scots Conservative MPs were thought to be
against the plan but in May 1970 Lord Home won conference's
support by 385 to 106 after a speech which stressed the long-term
and tentative nature of his proposals and the UK manifesto for
the general election in June pledged that the Home report 'will
form a basis for the proposals we will place before Parliament'.
Gordon Campbell pointed out that local government reform
would have to come first but he could 'guarantee' a White Paper,
while legislation to set up a Scottish Convention was at least a
possibility during the life of the next parliament.

However, Convention pledges, such as they were, formed a
minor part of the Conservatives' 1970 campaign in marked
contrast to Labour's Assembly proposals in October 1974.

Pressure for more far-reaching political devolution came from
the Liberals and the SNP. In the run-up to the 1964 election the
SNP were not allowed any official party election broadcasts.
They responded with pirate Radio Free Scotland broadcasts
directed by Gordon Wilson and the *Scotsman* printed the script of
their official party political broadcast which never was. After the
election they brought a court action for electoral malpractice. It
failed, but the other parties agreed to SNP and Welsh Nationalist
broadcasts in future. An official broadcast in September 1965
helped an SNP membership drive. Another just before the 1966
election stressed job losses in the pits and the car industry and was
clearly aimed at the heavily populated central belt.

At this time the Liberals fought more constituencies, and took
more votes than the SNP, and the Liberals were particularly
strong on the Scots periphery. In 1964 Liberals held four Scots
seats, all on the northern periphery – Orkney and Shetland,

Caithness and Sutherland, Ross and Cromarty, and Inverness – in fact, everything north of Inverness. David Steel picked up Roxburgh, Selkirk and Peebles at the 1965 by-election and in 1966 the Liberals added Aberdeen West which stretched across to meet the Inverness constituency, though the solid Liberal bloc was broken by a Labour gain in Caithness. Later in 1966 the Liberals won control of Greenock burgh council.

Scots Liberals favoured home rule within a federal Britain. Russell Johnston put forward a home rule bill late in 1966 but it made no progress. At the start of 1967 Jo Grimond resigned as leader of the British Liberals. His ten years as leader had been associated with the unsuccessful attempt to represent inter-mediate economic man of the suburbs instead of the traditional Liberal areas on the rural peripheries. But after his resignation in 1967 he spent most of his time and efforts on home rule, an issue that he claimed 'transcended party politics'. Jo's concern for home rule eventually led Willie Wolfe to observe that 'Grimond is obviously very close to the SNP but I doubt if he is very close to the Scottish Liberal Party'. Ludovic Kennedy, who had come close to winning Rochdale for the Liberals in 1958 and 1959 and was now a well-known broadcaster, also urged the importance of home rule and eventually quit the Liberals just before the Hamilton by-election because they would accept his policies but not his priorities. At various times, Steel, Johnston, and Thorpe also advocated some kind of home rule front or home rule pact with the SNP. In the end all this debate probably helped the cause of home rule while damaging the Liberal Party in Scotland. Roxburgh and Greenock were the party's last sig-nificant successes in Scotland. For the 1970 election they put up less than half as many candidates as the SNP and won less than half as many votes. Two of their five MPs were defeated, while the SNP won a seat in the Western Isles and established itself as a major force throughout the rural periphery.

In the autumn of 1968 Edinburgh played host to the British Liberal conference. While Grimond, Kennedy, and others gave ever more priority to home rule the English Liberals appeared to drop their commitment to have home rule all round by switching to a policy of twelve regional Assemblies throughout England instead of an all-England Assembly. Implicitly that demoted Scotland from a nation to a region.

Partly in response to this English change of heart Steel and other Scots Liberals devised a plan for what they called 'phased federalism'. As a first step there would be an elected Scottish Assembly without a corresponding English body. The Scots Assembly would have no tax powers, but would be financed by a block grant. There would be a Scots Executive and the Executive and Assembly would have powers roughly akin to the range covered by the Scottish Office. Scots MPs would not vote on purely English affairs. In many ways this 1970 Scots Liberal plan was hauntingly similar to the Labour schemes which were defeated in 1977 and 1979.

The first nationalist electoral breakthrough occurred outside Scotland when Gwynfor Evans won Carmarthen in July 1966. Evans appeared in Pollok the following spring to back up the SNP candidate. The Conservatives won Pollok from Labour but George Leslie's performance as SNP candidate made a much greater public impact. The votes were: Conservatives 37 per cent, Labour 31 per cent, SNP 28 per cent and Liberals 2 per cent. It was a disaster for the Liberals and an inspiration to the SNP.

Two months later the SNP scored their first widespread gains in local government elections, winning dozens of council wards and taking almost a fifth of the vote in the 'political' burghs. (Under the old local government system, much of Scotland especially in the counties was 'non-political': independent fought independent.)

As a natural result of Pollok and the local election results the SNP received so much media coverage that the Liberals protested. A great change from the days of Radio Free Scotland! By-election successes for minor parties tend to generate a wave of support throughout the land in the following months. The effect is similar to the 'honeymoon' period following the election of a new government. Post-by-election surges were particularly evident in England after Orpington and after each of the series of Liberal victories in the 1970–4 parliament. But these surges of support gradually dissipate unless reinforced by another spectacular event. Since Scotland has only seventy-one MPs the frequency of opportunities for SNP by-election successes is much less than for English Liberals. By chance there were none between 1974 and 1977 when by-elections might have seriously destabilized Scots politics to the SNP's advantage.

But in 1967 they were lucky. Labour handed them an unnecessary opportunity when Tom Fraser resigned his Hamilton seat to head the North of Scotland Hydro Board. Certainly Hamilton was a 'safe' Labour seat where Fraser had won 71 per cent of the vote at the general election. However, the SNP has seldom squeezed into the lead in a three-cornered fight against two evenly matched opponents. Safe Labour or Conservative seats were simply places where one of the two so-called major parties was too weak to be a credible challenge to the sitting party and often dangerously weaker in strength of organization and commitment than votes: in short, a plum, ripe for picking. At West Lothian in 1962 the Conservative vote dropped from 40 per cent to 11 per cent. Now in Hamilton it dropped from 29 per cent to 12 per cent and that on the same day as it rose substantially in the Leicester and Manchester by-elections. Labour's vote fell everywhere – 14 per cent in Manchester, 23 per cent in Leicester, and 30 per cent in Hamilton. For only the second time in its history the SNP had an MP – Winnie Ewing.

Labour was criticized for its choice of candidate. Mining was dead in Hamilton. According to the census about $4\frac{1}{2}$ per cent of Hamilton men worked in mining or quarrying in 1966, declining to $1\frac{1}{2}$ per cent by 1971. But the NUM still controlled the local Labour machine and imposed Alex Wilson, a miner from another part of Scotland, as candidate in the by-election. This criticism is probably unfair to Alex Wilson. He did, after all, win the seat back at the next attempt, and the 1967 SNP surge began in Pollok where Labour's candidate was a senior lecturer in economics, Dick Douglas, who later went on to lose East Stirling to the SNP.

After Hamilton the SNP's next opportunity was the 1968 local government elections (Table 1.1). They set out to contest almost every ward in the political burghs and won roughly a third of the vote. They took control of Cumbernauld. All the by-elections of 1966–70 and most of the political burghs were located in the central industrial belt and this urban SNP bias appeared to complement the strength of the Liberals on the periphery. A survey in Dundee suggested that former Labour voters were three times as likely as Conservatives to switch to the SNP. But this pattern began to fall apart from 1968 onwards.

Even before the peak success of spring 1968 stories were

Table 1.1 Votes in politically contested
burgh elections (1966–71)

	Right		Lab		SNP		Lib
1966	46	–	50	–	4	–	–
1967	40	–	42	–	18	–	–
1968	33	34	33	30	34	30	2
1969	37	39	37	32	26	23	3
1970	35	36	50	44	14	13	4
1971	–	35	–	52	–	8	3

Notes: Source for 1966–70 is Iain McLean, in *Political
Studies* (1970); source for 1968–71 is the Conservative Party
figures published in the *Scotsman* (6 May 1971). The two
sources disagree slightly because MacLean's figures are for
politically contested wards, and the Conservative figures
are for 'political' burghs. Both series agree on trends.
Liberal votes are excluded from McLean's series.

circulating in the press about SNP councillors' ill-preparedness.
In Glenrothes, where the SNP had won control in 1967, their
councillors resigned and handed power back to Labour. In
Glasgow several SNP men found themselves on the dole or
looking for new jobs after their election since their previous jobs
allowed insufficient time for council work. The Liberals were
demoralized and in 1970 they failed to contest several seats in
rural areas where they had polled well before, though their vote
dropped sharply even where they did fight. The SNP was badly
and progressively beaten in the 1969 and 1970 local elections and
the Gorbals and South Ayrshire by-elections. At the same time
the party decided to take a hard line as the only unequivocally
anti-EEC party.

Meeting in Oban a few days after their 1969 local government
defeat, the SNP had a major debate about policy: not what
policy, but whether to have any policy other than independence.
It was argued that the place for policy debates was the future
Edinburgh parliament not the Oban SNP conference. Wolfe and
Ewing argued the need for policy. Gordon Wilson and older
members like Dr McIntyre argued against. The results were
mixed: an unemployment policy was approved by 203 to 159 but
a welfare policy rejected by 322 to 312. At the same conference
Wolfe beat the holder, Arthur Donaldson, for the post of
chairman by 544 to 238 and this was, in part, a victory for policy.

In the run-up to 1970 and even more in the first years of the 1970–4 parliament the SNP pushed its anti-EEC policy even more strongly than home rule and gave a specific content to its general slogan of the sixties: 'Put Scotland First'.

So for a combination of reasons SNP support in the 1970 election was concentrated on the periphery instead of in the central belt where all its mid-term gains had been made. No burgh constituency gave the SNP as much as a 15 per cent vote in 1970, but in ten county seats the SNP won between 21 and 43 per cent. Seven of these were on the periphery: Aberdeen East, Angus South, Argyll, Banff, Galloway, Moray and Nairn, and the Western Isles. Such places had been natural Liberal territory in the past. But in 1970 the SNP forced a break with the past and set a new pattern for the future. Outside the periphery the only places with similarly large SNP votes were Hamilton and West Lothian where by-election effects persisted.

During the late sixties three processes were at work manufacturing trouble for the future though none caused immediate problems. First was Labour's reaction to SNP successes in 1967 and 1968; second, the Orkney and Shetland reaction to local government mergers; third, oil exploration in the North Sea. There is little to be said about oil except to re-emphasize that neither public nor politicians expected it to be enormously successful or profitable. It was not yet a political issue, but still the rigs were drilling.

Already by the autumn of 1969, Shetland County Council had sent its treasurer, Ian Clark, to visit Denmark and the Faroes to investigate home rule on the Faroese model. Well before the implications of oil began to filter through, Shetland was looking to home rule to preserve its existing independence which was under threat from radical local government proposals. Wheatley wanted the Islands to be a lower level of local government, with major services operated from Inverness, capital of a gigantic Highlands and Islands region. Now the distance from Inverness to the Shetlands is roughly the same as from London to the Scottish border, and the transport system is far more primitive. In 1969 the Islands had been forced into joint water, fire, and police authorities with the mainland, and the experiment was unimpressive. 'What will they do now if a brawl develops in Lerwick?' asked one Shetlander, 'Ship up a horse trained in crowd control from Wick?' What did happen was that they were charged 67 per cent more for the same police officers and equipment under a joint authority as under their own. So when oil and devolution did become political issues, the Shetlanders were already in the midst of a quarrel with Scotland which was not only based on romantic ideas about the distant past but on the economics of the present.

Early in 1968 the Labour Party in Scotland reached its conclusion on how to react to the SNP: attack separatism and defend the status quo. Ronald King-Murray tried to put the case for devolution but conference was far less sympathetic than it had been in 1958 when the SNP posed no threat. 'How can a separate government sitting in Edinburgh put the squeeze on firms in the South East and Midlands and drive them up to Scotland?' Ross asked the STUC and on the eve of the 1968 local elections Ross used a television party political broadcast to attack separatism.

But Ross's boradcast was followed by the SNP's greatest electoral success so far. Within the month Heath had made his Declaration of Perth and the General Assembly of the Kirk had called for a Royal Commission of Scots to consider schemes for home rule.

South of the border the party was less sure how to react. Ross's policy was not working in the very short term. King-Murray tried and failed to win support for devolution at the British Labour conference in the autumn but Harold Wilson hinted at a Royal Commission. Shortly after the conference Judith Hart, a long-time supporter of devolution, was given a special Cabinet post to oversee devolution strategy and a Royal Commission was announced in the Queen's Speech.

However, a Royal Commission can be used to gather facts or delay action: to test whether there is sustained demand for change or a temporary outburst of emotion. The Balfour Commission, promised during the Covenant agitation, had provided an excuse for four or five years of inaction and then ended up with no recommendation for major institutional changes. As the SNP declined, Hart was dropped from the Cabinet and the Queen's Speech promise of a Royal Commission to consider 'what' changes were needed turned into a remit to consider 'whether' change was needed. Only three of the fifteen members were Scots and under Crowther's chairmanship the

Commission's public hearings in Edinburgh were markedly unsympathetic to the devolutionists. Continuing its inflexible response, the Labour Party in Scotland advised the Royal Commission against devolution. By 1970 Labour's UK manifesto could pre-empt the Royal Commission's findings with a section on Scotland which began: 'The Labour Party in Scotland has welcomed any changes leading to more effective Government which do not destroy the integration of the UK or weaken Scotland's influence at Westminster. *They too reject separatism and also any separate legislative assembly.*' The Royal Commission itself was mentioned in the paragraph about regional economic planning councils in England.

A Royal Commission looked like an alternative to action in 1970. It looked much the same when it reported in the autumn of 1973; and the same again in 1979. But taken in combination with the elections of 1974, what was by itself a sleeping draught became a powerful stimulant. At the very least, there could be no excuse for another Royal Commission in response to the February election result.

Spurred by an estimated Scottish budget in the *Scotsman*, the Labour Government also produced official Treasury estimates of the Scottish budget in 1968 and 1969. The SNP responded with its version and various academics joined in with their own budgets. At the time these admittedly rough-and-ready estimates purported to show that Scotland would be £x worse off as a separate state. They contributed to the view that independence would not be impossible but would be costly. But once in the business of adding up profits and losses and deciding for or against independence on the basis of a financial balance sheet, it was difficult for Unionists a few years later to cope with the enormous wealth of North Sea oil revenues except by arguing that England, or the Shetlands, or some combination of the two would keep the oil out of Scottish hands.

Phase 4 (1970–4): External Control

From 1970 to 1974 the Conservatives under Edward Heath were occupied, even obsessed, with the drive to get Britain into Europe. Entry into Europe threatened Scotland with the prospect of becoming a periphery within a periphery and led to the resignation of Scotland's best-known Conservative, Teddy

Taylor. But even before entry the EEC question emphasized the nation's peripherality within Britain. The Conservatives never did manage to produce their promised White Paper on devolution. Entry into Europe plus the reform of local government left no room for active attention to further constitutional changes like devolution. At the same time Labour's opposition was muted. The party was demoralized by splits and front-bench resignations over EEC entry and either unwilling or unable to repeat its 1959–64 campaign. As the party of government up to 1970 it could hardly attack Scots conditions as strongly as before, and it had no wish to stir up nationalist feelings to the benefit of the SNP.

Labour had the material for a virulent nationalist or de-volutionist campaign had it not been so intent on defending the Union against the separatism of the SNP. There were an unusual number of Scots in the Cabinet – five in all – but that was little enough compensation for the fact that Gordon Campbell was almost the first Secretary of State since 1895 (and without exception the first since the office acquired extensive control of Scottish affairs) to be imposed from outside against both the popular vote and the seats won in Scotland. At the general election Labour beat the Scots Conservatives by a margin of 6½ per cent of votes and a two-to-one majority of seats. But the Secretary of State had to be a Conservative since the Conservatives formed the Westminster government. It made nonsense of George Younger's claim during the 1967 debates on Scots government that the Scottish Office 'is controlled *absolutely* by Scottish Ministers who are Scottish MPs backed by the 71 Scottish MPs'. The Scottish Office was to be run by totally unrepresentative and rejected Scots who owed their position 'absolutely' to the pattern of votes in England. Campbell was 'backed' by only twenty-two other Scots MPs.

No matter how a governor is chosen he may be competent and well intentioned but an externally imposed Secretary of State inevitably becomes something of a foreigner in his own land: able to speak for the Westminster government and able to report back on the Scots but unable to 'speak for Scotland', unable to pose convincingly as a natural protector of Scots interests. And in the face of issues like oil or EEC negotiations a natural protector was required. How could an externally imposed Secretary convince

Scots that their fishermen's interests would not be traded away in
the EEC negotiations or that he could prevent the oil situation
feared by Willie Ross: 'the maximum interference with life and
landscape and the minimum return in the form of new jobs.'

But while Gordon Campbell's predicament convinced some
Scots of the need for devolution it probably frightened off some of
the hesitant devolutionists in the Conservative Party. They saw
the troubles Campbell faced when Scots local authorities refused
to implement the Housing Act and wondered how much worse
the confrontation would have been if Campbell had been
opposed by a Scottish parliament.

Unemployment continued to grow, reaching a new post-war
peak in 1972 when it averaged $6\frac{1}{2}$ per cent for the whole year ($8\frac{1}{2}$
per cent among males). The unemployment ratio also rose until
1972, though not to the levels of the fifties and early sixties.
Emigration climbed back to a minor peak in 1972.

But after 1972 unemployment dropped sharply; so did relative
unemployment and net emigration. Scotland's relative GDP per
capita also rose throughout the parliament with only a temporary halt in 1972, so that by 1974 Scots GDP per capita was up
to 95 per cent of the UK level. By the end of the parliament it was
much the same story as under Labour: the economic gap between
Scotland and England had narrowed yet only because the
English economy had performed so badly.

But until the U-turns of 1972, Scotland suffered both absolutely and relatively. The Government began by confirming
that REP would be phased out by 1974. In 1971 it abolished
investment grants. Regional preferential assistance to Scots

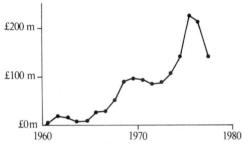

Fig. 1.5 Expenditure on regional preferential assistance to Scots industry (at current
     prices)
     Source: *Scottish Economic Bulletin*

industry had grown from virtually nothing in 1964 to £100 million per annum by 1970 (Fig. 1.5). The new Government reversed the trend and cut the aid even in monetary terms, still more once inflation was taken into account. The STUC accused it of 'dismantling' regional policy.

Then Rolls Royce went bankrupt, quickly followed by Upper Clyde Shipbuilders and the UCS 'work-in'. In the autumn of 1971 the Government set up Govan Shipbuilders under Hugh Stenhouse, the Scots Conservative Party's treasurer. They nationalized Rolls Royce and in the spring of 1972 they re-introduced investment grants, now called regional development grants, and preferential aid to Scots industry resumed its upward trend.

Without any sort of Scots backing, Campbell was in a false position and all the parties criticized him for his apparent weakness. At Hunterston he approved the ore terminal but failed to get the major prize of a new £1,000 million integrated steelworks. It went to Redcar on Teesside where BSC thought it could be run a little more cheaply. Lord Clydesmuir for the Scottish Council described the Redcar decision as 'the product of an over-centralized industrial system in which Scotland has no real voice'. In the EEC negotiations Britain first seemed willing to accept a 6-mile exclusive zone round Scots coasts but finally settled for 12 miles until 1982. Lord Boothby, former Conservative MP for one of the affected constituencies, described even that as a 'sell out'.

Though the Scottish Office acquired a new Scottish Economic Planning Department and began publication of Scottish *national* economic statistics (e.g. Scots GDP) in its *Scottish Economic Bulletin*, Ross attacked Campbell for allowing the Office to be bypassed and downgraded. Responding to a Scottish Council initiative Heath set up a ministry of regional development – officially called the Ministry of Industrial Development – but it was located within the giant Department of Trade and Industry. There was a Scottish Industrial Development Board and SID office in Glasgow but under the DTI. Oil also came under the DTI. Eventually in the spring of 1973 Lord Polwarth, former president of the Scottish Council, now a Minister of State in the Scottish Office, was given responsibilities for oil and the right of direct access to the Prime Minister. That right of access no doubt gave him more status in talking to the DTI but it also appeared to downgrade the position of the Scottish Secretary.

While non-Conservatives accused Campbell of failing to stick up for Scotland within the Government, Conservatives accused him of failing to defend Conservative interests within Scotland. They claimed he had agreed to a reform of local government boundaries that would help Labour, that he had agreed to a new airport runway in Edinburgh which destroyed the amenity of middle-class suburbs, that he had failed to block comprehensive education in Edinburgh and Glasgow, and had let the party conference slide into disarray over devolution.

His authority was certainly challenged by Labour-run councils which refused to implement the 1971 Housing Act. This Act proposed a regular annual rise in council house rents until a level of 'true rents' was reached. At one stage in 1972, twenty-five local councils representing half the Scots electorate were breaking the Act. Campbell's response was steady but undramatic pressure: he delayed payment of housing subsidies, held official inquiries, and took councils to the Court of Session. Those councils that refused to obey a court order to implement the Act were fined by the Court but they were treated more gently than the councillors of Clay Cross in England. Clydebank was the first to oppose the Act and the last to give in. The communist, Jimmy Reid, one of the leaders of the UCS work-in, was a Clydebank councillor and UCS money helped to pay the council's fine. In one sense it was a notable success for Campbell's quiet style though it drew attention to the fundamental difference between local government and political devolution and between the Scottish Office and political devolution, distinctions which Labour and Conservative politicians had so recently sought to dismiss.

From the start the Conservatives had clearly stated that Lord Home's proposals would have to wait until local government had been reorganized. That meant they could not be implemented before the late seventies. But at their Perth conference in 1973 they voted four to one against the Home plan. As Iain Sproat told the conference a Scots Assembly would be far worse than Clydebank in a confrontation with a Conservative Secretary of State. Heath stuck to the principle of devolution, however, and Campbell promised a Green Paper before the end of the parliament.

What saved the Conservatives from complete disaster was the condition of the opposition parties. Labour was split far worse than the Conservatives on EEC entry though, in the process of keeping the party together, Labour stole some of the SNP's thunder by advocating a referendum or special election to test the acceptability of the final terms of entry. Taverne's resignation and his Lincoln by-election campaign sparked off a series of third-party successes in England. And when the crisis election finally came unemployment statistics show that Scotland suffered far less than England from the effects of the three-day week which must also have helped the Scots Conservatives.

Labour added to its own troubles within Scotland. As the SNP declined Labour won massive victories in local elections but as a delegate to the 1973 conference complained Labour was 'in danger of becoming the party of the plant-hire boys, of the window-frame boys and the building contractors' friend'. Against executive advice conference passed an anti-corruption resolution. The party in Dundee was specially hit by splits and scandals.

The NUM had imposed an east-coast miner as candidate for the Hamilton by-election but for the Dundee by-election Labour selected George Machin, a Sheffield city councillor, because the AUEW promised lavish financial assistance. At much the same time Labour held an inquiry into the selection of Ed McGarry, a TGWU shop steward from Coventry, as candidate for Dunbarton East. Labour narrowly held Dundee at the by-election but both Machin and McGarry lost at the general elections of 1974: Machin to the SNP twice, McGarry to the Conservatives and then the SNP. Harry Selby, the Labour candidate for the Govan by-election, was a most uninspiring choice but he was at least a local man and regained Govan from Margo Macdonald after only three months.

Officially, Labour maintained its position of total opposition to devolution. Peter Allison, the Scottish Secretary of the Labour Party, claimed that there were fundamental differences on home rule between Labour and other parties: all the others wanted devolution, federalism, or independence while Labour was the only party of the status quo. As late as October 1973 the Scottish executive published the pamphlet *Scotland and the UK*, reaffirming, in changed circumstances, their unchanged view that the party had been correct to advise the Royal Commission against devolution. They rejected any 'assembly other than a committee of the UK parliament' as 'a mere talking shop' and attacked Liberal proposals for a dozen or so regional assemblies because that would imply an 'erosion of our special position arising from the fact that Scotland is a nation within the UK and not simply a region'. This pamphlet was expressly intended for submission to the 1974 Scots conference for formal approval. At the same time another pamphlet called for a Scottish National Enterprises Board in addition to a UK NEB and also put in a claim for the headquarters of the UK NEB to be located in a development area such as Scotland. The SNEB would be a 'subsidiary' of the UK NEB.

But behind the façade the unity of the late sixties was crumbling as Labour recovered from the shock of 1967–8, had to thole an externally imposed Secretary of State, and considered the implications of oil and EEC entry. Of the seventeen resolutions on Scottish government submitted for Labour's 1974 conference four were anti-devolution and two supported only a reform of the Scottish Grand Committee but eleven were in favour of Kilbrandon-style legislative devolution. Jim Sillars, noted for his pamphlet *'Don't Butcher Scotland's Future'* and his crushing defeat of the SNP in the 1970 South Ayrshire by-election, joined with King-Murray, Hart, and other Scots Labour MPs to study the implications of EEC membership for government structure within Scotland. He ended up an extreme devolutionist. At root, Labour's attitude to devolution in the late sixties owed as much to an hysterical reaction to party defeats as to consideration of the issue itself and was bound to weaken or change under a Conservative government. Even when devolution was an official Conservative policy and the status quo was official Labour policy there is evidence that Labour supporters were more inclined towards devolution: Labour's private opinion poll just before the February election, for example, showed that over half Labour supporters but only a quarter of Conservatives, wanted devolution. This large difference may have been due to a sampling error since later surveys found smaller party differences but always Labour supporters were more pro-devolution, irrespective of official party lines.

Looking back, too many commentators have quickly summarized 1970–4 as the years when Scottish oil became an issue and the SNP leapt to major party status. The reality was different. Despite some encouraging signs the over-all performance of the SNP was depressingly bad right up to the 1974 election. And as for oil, the SNP was reluctant to take up the issue and only joined in a campaign which others had started.

After the heady days of 1967 and 1968 the general election of 1970 came as a considerable disappointment to the SNP. Two-thirds of their candidates lost their deposits and over-all the SNP vote came to only 11½ per cent or just under 12½ per cent per candidate. SNP votes continued to decline in local elections partly, but only partly, because the SNP turned its attention away from local contests: dozens of sitting SNP councillors elected in the late sixties were dismissed when they appeared for re-election in the early seventies. In an economy drive the party closed its Glasgow office after thirty years as SNP HQ. In defeat, there was a danger of splits and a drift towards non-electoral politics. Late in 1971 the Revd Wotherspoon and a few others formed a breakaway Labour Party of Scotland in Glasgow. It disbanded in the spring of 1973. A rival Labour Party of Scotland was set up in Dundee and contested local elections and the Dundee by-election without much success. Since it had done so badly in the general election the SNP got no increase in party political time on television but had to be content with a quarter of the time given to the Liberals. A Radio Free Scotland broadcaster was arrested in the act of transmission and fined £30.

Wolfe condemned unconstitutional behaviour at the 1971 conference but those who advocated 'action' got more applause from a restless and impatient audience. The Wallace Sword was stolen from Stirling Castle. Wendy Wood, the veteran of pillar-box campaigns in the fifties, pushed onto the SNP platform at their annual Bannockburn rally to appeal for volunteers to picket Lancaster Court where a Scot was on trial for politically motivated bank robbery. She also went on a hunger strike to prompt the Conservatives into taking some action on their own pledge of a Convention but called it off a week later when Sillars claimed that Campbell would issue a Green Paper on devolution. By Irish standards a hunger strike to obtain a Green Paper was unbelievably moderate. Still, some of her admirers bombed a power pylon in Dumfries in sympathy with her strike and there were a variety of other violent but scantily reported incidents. A group of activists from the marxist Workers' Party of Scotland got eighty four years' gaol for a bank robbery but until cases came to court the Scots media seemed almost frightened to report them. No one knew quite how thin the ice might be.

There were four parliamentary by-elections: Stirling and Falkirk in 1971, Dundee East in March 1973, and Edinburgh North and Govan on the same day in November 1973. The SNP took 35 per cent in Stirling and Falkirk but the party had contested this seat at most elections since the war and in the 1971 local elections it had won 45 per cent in Stirling and 35 per cent in the parts of Falkirk it contested, despite a dismal showing throughout the rest of Scotland. So the by-election result was ambiguous. In Dundee the party took 30 per cent and, apart from an English Labour candidate, a badly split local Labour party, and the smell of local government corruption, there was no special local explanation. However, on the same day as Dundee, Dick Taverne won Lincoln with a 59 per cent vote for his own Democratic Labour Party and a Liberal took 39 per cent at Chester-le-Street where the Liberals had never fielded a candidate since the War. In Govan Margo MacDonald took the seat from Labour with a 42 per cent vote on a low turn-out of only 52 per cent. But on the same day a Liberal intervened in Hove and got 37 per cent, a Liberal won Berwick-upon-Tweed from the Conservatives, and the SNP's chairman standing in Edinburgh North only just scraped into third place with a vote of 19 per cent.

Clearly these by-elections suggest that the SNP had replaced the Liberals as Scotland's third party but they did not provide sound evidence to contradict the indications from local elections that the SNP was a weak third party. Govan, Dundee, and Stirling looked better SNP performances on a first inspection than on a second, and Edinburgh just could not be ignored. Three Scotland-wide opinion polls taken in the last three weeks of February 1974 put SNP voting intentions at 15 per cent, 17 per cent, and 18 per cent respectively. A local poll in Dundee shortly before the by-election there also put the SNP at 15 per cent. It would be wrong to use the by-elections as an excuse for projecting backwards the SNP's general election success.

And it would be equally wrong to suggest that the SNP concentrated entirely on oil. They attacked Scots – English

mergers in the co-operative societies, and in student unions;
attacked the number of English academics at Scots universities,
the appointment of an Englishman to the top job in the Scottish
Office, and the number of foreign-owned holiday homes; opposed the closure of rail lines, cuts in the Scots steel industry, and
the new steel plant at Redcar, the level of unemployment, polaris
missile bases on the Clyde, and tolls on Scots road bridges. They
backed Iceland in the 'fish war' against Britain and demanded a
50-mile exclusive zone round the Scottish coast while the
Government at one stage seemed ready to settle for 6 miles.

But until the end of 1971 the SNP concentrated mainly on
EEC entry, intensifying the compaign they had started shortly
before the 1970 election. One SNP member representing each of
the seventy-one constituencies invaded the old Scots Parliament
House to sign an anti-EEC declaration. Wolfe and Stewart flew
to Brussels with the message that Scotland would not be bound by
agreements that did not enjoy the full consent of the Scots people.
And the party organized a series of quota polls in over a dozen
constituencies to reveal local attitudes to EEC entry. They found
75 per cent against in Moray and Nairn – Gordon Campbell's
seat up on the north-east fishing coast – and 81 per cent against in
East Aberdeen. These polls were a modern equivalent of the old
local plebiscites on home rule. They were good publicity for the
SNP, good for keeping the activists active, good for creating the
feeling of being on the winning side at a time of electoral defeat.

The Stirling by-election occurred in mid-September 1971. At
the start Dr MacIntyre put forward EEC entry as the main issue,
with Scots unemployment second, but during the campaign he
found stirrings of public interest in the North Sea oil discoveries.
At this time public expectations about oil wealth were hazy but
certainly modest: perhaps it might be worth £100 million a year
or thereabouts. Nevertheless MacIntyre wrote a letter to Heath
claiming that 'Scottish oil will once and for all dispose of the old
wrong-headed notion that Scotland does not have the resources
for prosperity'. This argument was essentially about independence rather than oil unlike the sort of detailed oil issues raised
later which concerned development funds or extraction rates,
etc. At the end of the year David Simpson issued an SNP oil
briefing claiming that oil would be worth £350 million a year: it
was still a small bonus which even a convinced Unionist could

regard as a convenient source of aid to Scots industry. Ex-Secretaries of State like Willie Ross and Michael Noble called for *direct* oil benefits for Scotland. The Liberals wanted 50 per cent of the oil revenues for Scotland.

So when the SNP met for their 1972 conference at Rothesay in May, they were suffering from what Chris Baur of the *Scotsman* called an 'identity crisis': on oil and unemployment everyone seemed to be a nationalist. Paradoxically the SNP seemed to be drowning in a rising tide of nationalism. Gordon Wilson persuaded the SNP to mount an oil campaign but conference only voted 93 to 76 in favour of his motion. Opponents feared that the SNP could turn into just another pressure group holding out the 'begging bowl' for a bit more of the oil money, and Wolfe described oil as a set-back to the home rule movement.

The party began a three-month oil campaign in September and in the following spring the Dundee East by-election with Gordon Wilson as candidate provided a test of its success. The SNP were pleased with the result and some of their doubts were dispelled. Despite the slogans, 'Scotland's oil – to London with love?' and the elegantly simple 'It's Scotland's oil', Scots in all parties already felt Scotland had some special title to the oil revenue and were agitating for a sizeable share. The real purpose of the oil campaign was to convince Scots that oil made independence both economically possible and politically necessary. It succeeded more on the first point than the second and it also identified the SNP more than other parties with oil demands. Consequently, as I shall show later, oil proved to be one of the constraint breakers which allowed those who already wanted independence to vote SNP.

Oil turned out to be a usefully multi-faceted issue: the SNP demanded oil supply offices in Aberdeen, a Scottish Institute of Energy Studies, 100 per cent of the oil revenues, and a Scottish Oil Development Board; they attacked the Government for not standing up to the EEC, for not taxing the oil companies heavily enough, for not directing the oil companies to buy supplies – especially complete oil rigs – in Scotland, for permitting oil blight on Scotland's coasts in a mad rush to solve the UK's balance-of-payments difficulties, for charging Scots more than the English for English natural gas without making petrol and oil cheaper in Scotland, and for concealing the true magnitude of the oil wealth. In Dundee they ran an opinion poll on oil as they had done on the EEC in fishing constituencies. Yet though the party was well pleased by the result, Gordon Wilson's by-election performance was not as good as the Liberals' in Chester-le-Street or Democratic Labour's in Lincoln on the same day.

To some extent all the parties were upstaged by non-party politics during the 1970–4 parliament. First, there was a growing tendency to legitimate the tools of direct democracy. There was a referendum on Northern Ireland and the UK. Norway, Denmark, and Ireland held referendums on their entry into the EEC and the French even had a referendum on Britain's entry. Though they did it for party advantage the SNP helped by running their series of constituency polls on EEC entry. When Scotland voted three to two in favour of the EEC in the 1975 referendum the SNP could hardly complain or reject the result. But the SNP were not alone in sponsoring local polls. The Conservatives ran an EEC poll in Edinburgh. Campaigners for a united Fife region ran polls in the rural east and north of Fife which might have been expected to reject association with the heavily industrialized south but instead backed the idea of a united 'kingdom' of Fife. After many refusals the Government eventually gave way on Fife and destroyed the whole Wheatley concept of local government regions based on river estuaries. And there were local polls in the Shetlands on whether to accept on-shore oil developments. All this prepared the ground not only for the referendums of 1975 and 1979 but also for the idea of using opinion polls on devolution to help determine and publicly justify party and government policy.

Second, the UCS work-in and its communist leader, Jimmy Reid, stole much of the attention and glamour that might have gone to the established parties. The work-in followed by further government aid to Clydeside shipbuilding symbolized the Government's U-turn on industrial policy and the huge crowds that marched to Glasgow Green to support the work-in paid scant attention to the union leaders or Labour and SNP politicians who tried to address them: they came to hear Jimmy Reid. UCS was also linked to the local councils' defence of low council rents through Reid's membership of Clydebank council while the parliamentary Labour Party was scared of the constitutional implications of defying the Secretary of State. And

UCS shop stewards seem to have made the first public call for an STUC-backed Scottish Convention on unemployment. The SNP attacked the STUC for not responding to the UCS call and three months later the STUC announced plans for a Scottish Assembly on unemployment, claiming the idea as their own.

These STUC Scottish Assemblies – there was one in February 1972 and another in January 1973 with a Standing Commission in between – put the STUC rather than the political parties at the centre of Scots politics and Labour members criticized their union colleagues for this initiative. As with UCS these Assemblies took over the role which might have been performed by the SNP and more especially by Labour. The 1972 Assembly, for example, overshadowed the October 1971 Labour Party emergency conference on unemployment. Though they were called to discuss Scots unemployment rather than home rule the Assemblies were in many ways similar to MacCormick's Scottish Conventions of the late forties. At the first Assembly 1,500 representatives from a wide range of organizations including unions, employers' organizations, and all political parties met in the Usher Hall, Edinburgh. Teddy Taylor wanted greater decentralization of government offices to Scotland, David Steel advocated a Scottish Development Corporation financed by oil revenues, and John Mackintosh wanted a Scots Minister for Economic Development in the Cabinet alongside the Secretary of State. There was a fairly united demand for urgent action of any and every sort to cut Scots unemployment.

But the first Assembly met at the peak of unemployment. When the second met in 1973 unemployment was falling fast and the Government had already adopted several of the major proposals made at the 1972 Assembly. Fewer delegates turned up and the SNP sent four times as many as Labour and eight times as many as the Conservatives. Discussion switched more towards oil development than unemployment and the chairman accused the SNP of attempting to turn the Assembly into an SNP propaganda exercise.

Figure 1.6 shows the pace of oil discoveries in UK northern waters. From virtually none before the 1970 election the discovery rate accelerated continuously until 1975. Estimates of oil wealth steadily increased, so that SNP claims always proved more accurate than Gordon Campbell's. In the autumn of 1971

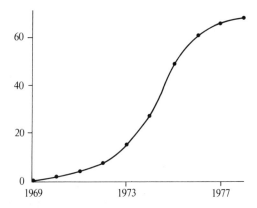

Fig. 1.6 Cumulative total of significant oil discoveries
Source: *Scottish Economic Bulletin*

the Scottish Council called for a special oil fund with a fixed percentage of the oil revenues to finance its ambitious Oceanspan and Hunterston proposals. Jeremy Thorpe and Russell Johnston for the Liberals north and south of the border called for a Scottish Oil Development Corporation financed by 50 per cent of the oil revenues. At that point MacIntyre for the SNP sent a letter to Heath virtually reiterating the Scottish Council suggestion. Heath replied that this was not possible because the oil revenues would come to less than the public expenditure bias towards Scotland. No one in Scotland had suggested trading oil revenues against existing public expenditure: existing public expenditure had clearly failed to solve Scotland's industrial problems and needed a supplement, not a substitute. However, it soon appeared that even the factual basis for Heath's response would be destroyed as oil discoveries continued.

In his chairman's address to the 1972 Labour conference John Pollok won rapturous applause for a list of nationalist demands which included a Scottish Development Agency based on oil revenues and a requirement that the oil companies should be forced to use rigs built in Scotland from Scots steel. Ross agreed with the proposal for an SDA 'manned and operated here in Scotland' and responsible to the Scottish Secretary but he rejected the idea of a special oil fund despite his earlier insistence on 'direct benefits' from the oil revenues.

All this happened before the SNP conference which accepted

Gordon Wilson's plan for an oil campaign. And though both Conservative and Labour leaders had ruled out special oil funds in 1971–72 both parties proved more flexible later. For the October election in 1974 (not February though) the Conservative manifesto promised a Scottish Oil Development Fund which would use oil revenues to finance additional services in the areas affected by oil development as well as abolishing road bridge tolls, providing new sports facilities including a new Hampden Park, and renovating out-of-date housing and obsolete industry. All this 'in addition to expenditure to which Scotland as an integral member of the UK is entitled'. On the Labour side, the manifesto in February and October only pledged that the oil revenues would be 'used to the maximum practicable extent to improve the economies of Scotland and other areas in need of development', but the party's official television broadcast just prior to the October election described the SDA quite unequivocally as being 'primed by North Sea oil'.

Late in 1972 and more especially in 1973 further oil issues grew up around the pace of exploitation. Ross and Cromarty Council suspended all planning applications for rig yards and the National Trust for Scotland attacked plans to site rig construction yards in natural beauty spots. Labour promised to nationalize oil to ensure that the oil companies did not make excessive profits. The Public Accounts Committee agreed with Labour and the SNP that the Government's tax policies failed to produce reasonable levels of oil revenue. And even Sir William McEwan Younger, the chairman of the Scots Conservatives, attacked his own government for failing to insist that the oil companies use British equipment. It all smacked of London haste and London incompetence quite apart from the question of whether Scotland should get any special benefit.

Another Middle East war began in October 1973 and the Arabs began to use the 'oil weapon' against the West. Petrol ration books were issued through post offices – my own was handed over the counter by a clerk with a lapel badge telling me 'It's Scotland's Oil'. The ration books were never used but the price of oil doubled and quadrupled, ensuring the economic viability of North Sea oil and the significance of the oil revenues while at the same time putting further balance-of-payments pressure on the Government to exploit oil fast.

Lord Crowther, the original chairman of the Royal Commission on the Constitution, died suddenly in February 1972 and was replaced by the Scots judge, Lord Kilbrandon. As early as 1966 Kilbrandon had gone on record as saying that Scots membership of the EEC would only be acceptable if balanced by devolution. Kilbrandon reported shortly before the Govan by-election, towards the end of 1973. The Commission were agreed on the need for change but disagreed on the form of devolution they recommended. Some wanted a version of the Lord Home plan, others a version of the English Liberals' regional assemblies while the majority favoured a Stormont-type system which they felt implied the end of Scotland's automatic right to a Cabinet seat, and a reduction in the number of Scots MPs from seventy-one to fifty-seven. The report got a tepid reception at Westminster and failed as the *Scotsman* put it to 'set the political heather on fire' in Scotland. The proposed loss of influence over British affairs at Westminster seemed too high a price to pay for devolved control of purely Scots affairs. There was a fairly general feeling that nothing much would happen: Kilbrandon would gather dust on the shelves of university libraries. Teddy Taylor – a pro-devolutionist at the time – called for a full parliamentary debate but his election agent joined the SNP. Labour MPs Sillars, Ewing, Robertson, and Eadie published a pamphlet welcoming the report and a majority of the resolutions for the 1974 Labour conference supported devolution. Most made specific references to Kilbrandon but several specifically insisted that there be no reduction in Scots representation at Westminster. Labour de-volutionists also objected to Kilbrandon's recommendation of proportional representation. And Peter Allison thought the anti-devolution policy of the Scottish executive would be upheld by conference.

Before Kilbrandon could be fully debated, the Government present its promised White or Green Paper, or Labour meet for its 1974 conference the miners' crisis led to a snap election. Though the Conservatives lost four rural seats, including Gordon Campbell's, to the SNP, their performance in February 1974 was rather better than they might have feared. Despite the odium of having imposed a Scottish Secretary for almost the first time in the century they lost only 5 per cent of the Scots vote compared to 8 per cent of the English; while Labour lost 8 per cent in Scotland but only 6 per cent in England.

There were three Scotland-wide opinion polls during the

February election campaign. They showed SNP support rising steadily from 15 per cent just as Liberal support grew in England in the last weeks before polling day. They also showed the Conservatives starting with a 5 per cent lead over Labour which turned into a 3½ per cent Labour lead on the day.

On the pollsters' question 'What do you yourself feel are the most important problems the government should do something about?' only 1 per cent of Scots quoted North Sea oil and 1 per cent self-government. Prices came top, followed by industrial relations and the miners' strike, housing and the EEC – much the same in Scotland as in England: a paradox that I shall investigate in the next chapter.

Yet 22 per cent voted for the SNP and seven SNP candidates were elected. True, English Liberal candidates scored a higher average vote than SNP candidates but relatively few Liberals were elected. Labour was in a particularly exposed position, holding forty of the seventy-one Scots seats but with an over-all vote of under 37 per cent. It was officially opposed to any form of devolution yet its own private polls showed that Labour voters were much more favourably inclined to devolution or independence than Conservatives and more Labour than Conservative supporters were willing to consider voting SNP.

Phase 5 (1974–9): Devolution

A week after the election Labour's Scottish executive endorsed a statement on devolution which had been drafted by a sub-committee that included Pollok, Dewar, Millan, and Ross. It was cautiously pro-devolution:

'there is a real need to ensure that decisions affecting Scotland are taken in Scotland wherever possible . . . we believe this might best be done by the setting up of an elected Scottish Assembly . . . [but] there can be no question of reducing the number of Scottish MPs or of abolishing the office of Secretary of State.'

At Ayr a fortnight later conference accepted this statement while rejecting all other pro- or anti-devolution resolutions. Had the statement appeared after years of commitment to devolution it would have represented a defeat for devolution since it was so cautious and conditional in its support. But after the line the party had taken from 1968 to 1973 it clearly implied a major shift

towards accepting devolution. Significantly this executive statement was issued several days before the Queen's Speech debate
on 12 March and Harold Wilson's promise of a White Paper and
a bill on devolution.

As Labour moved towards devolution the Conservatives found
the issue turning against them. They still had the 1970 Home
plan but it had been rejected by their 1973 Scottish conference.
Their Scots manifesto in February ended with a page on
devolution which referred back to 1970 but not to 1973. The
party's aim was 'to achieve the most effective and acceptable
form of further devolution' and its 'commitment to present
proposals still stands'. At conference in May 1974 they debated a
non-elected assembly made up of local councils' representatives
and included this idea in their October manifesto. A directly
elected assembly 'could evolve in the future'.

These 1974 Conservative devolution proposals would have
been seen as a pro-devolution move if they had been put forward
by Labour, but since they were a step back from the Home plan
they appeared anti-devolution when they came from the
Conservatives. Indeed, since they involved one retreat from an
elected to a non-elected Assembly, there was no reason to suppose
that they would not be followed by other, still less-devolutionary
schemes or even by benign neglect.

Meanwhile events forced Labour to take an unambiguous
stand on devolution if it was to get any electoral benefit out of the
issue at all. The Ayr conference was followed in April by the
STUC which also voted in favour of an elected Assembly and the
Government published its promised Green Paper on devolution
options. Then came the bombshell: at the end of June a sparsely
attended meeting of the Scottish executive voted six to five
against devolution and issued a statement to the press. The full
executive consisted of twenty-nine members.

The British NEC responded with a statement in favour of
devolution and a call for a special devolution conference of the
Scots party to decide the issue. A secret MORI poll carried out in
Scotland for the British leadership was leaked to the press along
with the conclusion that Labour could lose thirteen seats to the
SNP if it failed to accept devolution. Subsequent academic
research suggests that MORI's conclusions were about right.

The special conference met in the Co-operative Halls, Dalintober Street on the week-end of 17 August 1974 and was later known simply as the 'Dalintober Street' conference. Well attended, by 183 TU delegates, ninety-four from the constituencies, forty-two MPs and candidates plus a variety of others, it was asked to vote on five propositions. Dalintober unanimously resolved (1) against separation, and (2) for a fundamental and irreversible shift in the balance of power and wealth in favour of working people and their families.

Resolutions (3) and (4) were both prepared by the executive – one anti-devolution the other pro-devolution. Conference was obviously under some pressure to support the British leadership and the NEC and also to fend off SNP attacks. But many of the tales about Dalintober are without foundation. Tam Dalyell claims in his book on devolution (p. 110) that he later supported (briefly) Labour's 1974 devolution policy because he 'really imagined I was endorsing the super local authority which we understood had been agreed on 17th August. So did most of my colleagues'. . . . Given the text of the resolutions such stories sound like an attempt to rewrite history. The texts were:

Prop 3: That this conference opposes the setting up of a Scottish Assembly as being irrelevant to the needs and aspirations of the people of Scotland.

Conference believes that the social and economic problems of the Scottish people can only be solved by the implementation of socialist policies and that the setting up of a Scottish Assembly does not contribute towards our socialist objectives.

We reaffirm our belief in the need for unity of action by the working people of the UK.

This was defeated by a large majority.

Conference then passed by a large majority:

Prop 4: That this conference recognising the desire of the Scottish people for a greater say in the running of their own affairs calls for the setting up of a directly elected Assembly with legislative powers within the context of the political and economic unity of the UK.

No one in politics could possibly ignore the significance of the words 'with legislative powers'. Even super local authorities do not legislate.

Dalintober then unanimously accepted a fifth proposition which opposed any reduction in the numbers of Scots MPs, abolition of the Secretary of State, and proportional representation for Assembly elections – three changes which Kilbrandon had listed as the price of devolution.

Exactly one month later the Government issued the first of what proved to be a long series of White Papers on devolution. Another private MORI poll showed the SNP vote 'could crumble' now that Labour had so firmly adopted an Assembly policy. In the short-run the MORI forecast proved to be only half true: the SNP did not crumble until the Scotland Act was finally passed. But at least Labour lost no votes and gained one seat at the October election while the Conservatives lost a quarter of their vote and a quarter of their seats. *Scotsman*/ORC polls—polls carried out by ORC (Opinion Research Centre, London) paid for and published by the *Scotsman*—in May and September confirmed MORI's finding that devolution was a popular policy even if it was seldom mentioned as a priority for government attention.

Labour used this new policy in an aggressive campaign for the autumn election. Dalintober gave the party much more than a policy position: it conveyed a sense of firmness, finality, and authority. The policy had not only been announced, it had been debated. The Scottish executive had recommended the anti-devolution proposition (3) and only drafted propositions (4) and (5) in case conference would not accept its view. Ludovic Kennedy complained in the sixties that his resolution to the Liberal conference on priority for devolution had been unanimously accepted and unanimously ignored. Dalintober involved too agonizing a decision to be lightly accepted and then ignored. Moreover, Dalintober conveyed a sense of movement. It might not be easy to go back on devolution after Dalintober but the momentum towards devolution could carry the party towards stronger plans than those it first accepted.

Labour in Scotland 'opted out' of the British Labour election broadcasts and one such 'opt-out' suggested the party was still moving towards an even more devolutionary position. Though two of the four participants, Jim Sillars and John Mackintosh, later gained the reputation of rebels, their appearance was approved by the Scots Labour leadership and a Transport House official was present at the recording session which occurred ten hours before the broadcast. He approved the content and congratulated the participants. The other two participants were George Foulkes – later to defeat Sillars in South Ayrshire, and Helen Liddell – later to become Scottish secretary of the party. In short, it was a very 'official' broadcast, not an accidental misrepresentation of the Labour case. Yet the word 'parliament' was used repeatedly instead of 'assembly' – and the distinction between the words was stressed. This 'parliament' in Edinburgh would have 'powers of taxation and revenue' (Mackintosh), 'control of the Scottish Development Agency' (Liddell) which would be 'primed by North Sea oil so that the benefits of oil go to the ordinary working people of Scotland' (Liddell), and the 'parliament' would also get certain 'trade and industry' powers (Sillars).

These were large promises. Dalintober, the White Paper, and the television election broadcast committed Labour very firmly to a much greater degree of political devolution than the Conservatives had ever proposed. They made devolution the centre-piece of Labour's autumn campaign.

Both Labour and the Conservatives made a range of non-constitutional promises in addition. On the Conservative side these were more significant than their steadily shrinking plans for devolution. A Scottish Development Fund, said the manifesto, would 'ensure that every part of Scotland derives the fullest benefit from oil'. 'Projects financed by the fund will be in addition to expenditure to which Scotland as an integral member of the UK is entitled.' The Fund would pay for infrastructure needs caused by oil developments, would 'make good any damage to the Scottish countryside resulting from oil development' but would go beyond these oil-created needs to finance a 'major programme of renovation and replacement of out-of-date housing and obsolete industry', 'abolish the tolls on the Forth, Tay and Erskine Bridges', and 'provide better amenities and new facilities for sport and recreation' including a new national stadium to replace Hampden Park.

Labour's manifesto claimed to have done 'more for Scotland in the past few months than the Conservative Government did in four years'. Specifically, it claimed 'we have doubled Regional Employment Premium thus bringing another £40 million to Scotland every year', 'given Edinburgh and Leith development status bringing another £8 million per year', 'moved the offshore

Supplies Office to Glasgow', 'tightened the limits for industrial development certificates to 5,000 square feet in South East England and 10,000 square feet in the rest of England outside intermediate areas', given special help for housing and roads in oil-affected areas 'but the money has not been made available at the expense of road development elsewhere', 'called a halt to rail closures in Scotland' and given a total of £20 million to the Scots pig, cattle, and horticultural industries. If re-elected Labour would establish a British National Oil Corporation and a Centre for Oil Drilling Technology – both 'in Scotland', move '7,000 civil service jobs from London to Scotland', spend £12 million on Glasgow's underground railway, in addition to setting up a Scottish Development Agency and a Scottish Assembly and retaining seventy-one Scots MPs at Westminster.

These are long lists of special 'goodies for Scotland'. Our Scottish Election Survey found that after the election 76 per cent of Scots thought the SNP and its election victories had been 'good for Scotland' and only 14 per cent thought it had not. Almost 70 per cent of Labour and Conservative voters thought the SNP had been 'good for Scotland'. In a sense that was a measure of the SNP's failure to harvest all their potential supporters. Labour and Conservative voters approved the pressure SNP voters were exerting on Westminster. Whether those SNP voters merely wished to exert pressure for economic concessions is another question. And later on Labour and Conservative voters changed their minds about the SNP. But in 1974 every party's voters thought SNP victories were good for Scotland.

The SNP closed its last television broadcast before the October election with the words:

Just think back over the last six months. Can you remember a time when Scotland was ever offered so much, so fast, before? . . . as the *Economist* newspaper said 'if that's what Scotland gets with seven nationalists there will be many Scots wondering what it will get with 15 – and willing to use their votes to find out'. It pays to vote SNP. Good night.

To a large extent the SNP hoped to turn the other parties' concessions against them by using concessions as proof of SNP influence or as an admission that Scotland had been badly treated in the past. Once again there is a distinction between the short- and the long-run, between promises and delivery. In the short-run the fact that every party in 1974 promised some form of devolution probably did make the SNP case for change more credible. But in the longer term as devolution plans were worked out in detail the distinction between devolution and the SNP's policy of independence threatened to narrow the potential base for SNP support.

Though they forced a vote of confidence in March 1974 when Wilson's Government was only a fortnight old, the SNP tried to combine a constructive approach to devolution with a continuing commitment to full independence. Some of the results were bizarre: in April SNP MPs backed up by their research officer and a professor of international law submitted their devolution proposals including trade, tax, and oil powers for the Assembly plus seventy-one MPs at Westminster and a continuing seat in the Cabinet for the Scottish Secretary. The first two demands were nationalist in the constitutional sense but the last were Unionist in constitutional terms and only nationalist in pressure-group terms.

The Labour Government's first discussion paper on devolution appeared during the SNP's Elgin conference. They denounced it, with some justification, as a 'mouse of a document' and turned their attention to attacking poverty and the power of highland lairds. But afterwards they reaffirmed their earlier devolution demands – remarkably moderate for a nationalist party and shared, indeed, by a group within the Labour Party.

SNP manifestos, both in February and October, replaced their 1970 emphasis on the EEC with an emphasis on oil or 'mineral wealth'. The October manifesto also stressed their attack on poverty. Both manifestos reaffirmed their policy of full independence and most paragraphs were written in the context of full independence. To bridge the credibility gap between the manifestos and immediate possibilities they also produced a supplement which, in October, even descended to the level of demanding 'inner London weighting allowances' on wages in the Scottish islands and 'outer London weighting' on the mainland. On devolution this supplement repeated their demands for a moderate increase in the powers proposed for a Scottish As-sembly and added that 'it took 633,000 SNP votes at last February's election and the continued advance of SNP support after the election, to extract grudging promises of a Scottish Assembly from the Tory and Labour parties. It will take a further large increase in SNP votes on October 10th to make sure that they do not welsh on their promises.'

They got that further large increase, taking the SNP to 839,617 votes (over 30 per cent) and eleven MPs. The Conservatives who had won over half the vote and thirty-six MPs in 1955 were reduced to less than 25 per cent of the vote and only sixteen MPs. Within a week of the October election the shadow Scottish Secretary, Alick Buchanan-Smith, announced that the Conservatives now accepted a directly elected Assembly and would press the Labour Government to implement its devolution plans with all speed. In 1979 Buchanan-Smith was one of the handful of leading Conservatives who campaigned actively for a 'Yes' vote in the referendum on Labour's Scotland Act.

Chapter 2:

How Far Apart?

So far I have inevitably stressed the Scottish dimension but Scots maintain a dual nationality – Scottish and British at the same time. And politics in Scotland is at once Scottish and British. The Scottish dimension, particularly concern for home rule, is the most distinctive feature of Scots politics but the most distinctive feature may not be the most important. On most issues, and on the most important issues, Scots might still be very close to the English.

I have suggested in the first chapter that whereas the original union bargain was to unite Scotland and England politically but not socially the trend in this century has been towards social integration but political separation. Scots and English have become more alike but within central government the growth of the Scottish Office and Scots committees has tended to separate Scots and English. Politically the two major parties have contributed to this growing separation by playing the Scottish card in their electoral game with each other. And, especially since the SNP victories in the late sixties, Scottish political debate focused on constitutional issues which were largely ignored in England. The Scots mass electorate certainly differed from the English in their 1974 voting behaviour by giving 30 per cent to the SNP and only 25 per cent to the Conservatives while the English voted 39 per cent for the Conservatives and not at all for the SNP. Even if we accept some loose equivalence between the SNP and the Liberals the combined SNP plus Liberal vote was 39 per cent in Scotland but only 20 per cent in England. In strict voting terms Scots and English had grown far apart in October 1974.

But were they far apart in anything except party percentages of the vote? There are well-known differences between Scots and English eating and drinking habits, diseases, standard bed sizes, and the like, but these are not directly relevant to party politics.

In this chapter I want to use two parallel surveys – the British Election Survey (BES) 1974 and the Scottish Election Survey (SES) 1974 – to catalogue and quantify some differences between Scots and English on those political attitudes and aspects of social structure which are particularly relevant to party politics: to discover whether the national differences in 1974 voting behaviour rested on a sure foundation of more general political differences.

These two surveys provide a unique opportunity for measuring Scots–English differences because both asked the same wide range of political questions with only minor additions or adjustments to allow for different national circumstances. The interviewing agency, the briefing systems, and the detailed wording of questions were the same north and south of the border.

THREE PATTERNS OF REGIONAL VARIATION

Since the BES 1974 contains about 2,000 English respondents it is possible to break it down into broad English regions. Sampling problems prevent too fine a subdivision but I have used Greater London, the South excluding London, and the North of England. For simplicity I have excluded the Midlands from the Tables in this chapter.

We can classify the patterns of regional variation into three broad types: first, *national* differences – where the English regions are all fairly similar to each other but different from Scotland; second, *peripheral* North–South trends – where there is a spectrum ranging from London through the South to the North and thence to Scotland; third, what for want of a better word might be called *cultural* North–South trends – where the spectrum runs from the South to the North to Scotland and London lies somewhere in the middle. The South, outside London, is the old idealized England of small villages and ancient churches. London may be the centre of UK administration and the venue of important national events but neither the place nor the people could claim to be at the heart of England.

In addition to these three pure types of regional variation there can be combinations, especially when a national difference operates in addition to one of the North–South trends. Where the national effect augments the trend we should expect a larger difference between Scotland and the North than between the North and South. Where the national effect operates against the North–South trend it will make Scotland as a whole appear like England as a whole despite the existence of a North–South trend within England.

SEPARATE PEOPLES

Britain's population was remarkably segmented along geographic lines. Over 90 per cent of Scots in the 1974 surveys grew up in Scotland and over 90 per cent of the English grew up in England. Even on a more finely drawn set of divisions population stability was impressive. Fully 92 per cent of Scots grew up in Scotland and 89 per cent of Northerners in the North while 84 per cent of Southerners came either from the South or from London. Even within London which acted as a transit camp for incoming foreigners and as the centre of attraction for those moving around the United Kingdom, 78 per cent were raised either in London or in the South.

So while the South of England and especially London did contain significant numbers of incomers, Scotland and the North each had populations made up almost entirely from local stock. It was not always thus. Less than a century before there had been large-scale Irish immigration into Scotland but by the seventies very few Scots electors had been brought up in Ireland though many must still have had Irish grandparents or great-grandparents.

These segmented populations mean that it is reasonable to talk of Scots, Northerners, and Southerners. The terms describe much more than areas on a map or even present residence patterns. To a small approximation they describe separate peoples, born and bred, living and dying in their own areas.

Even geographic proximity did little to mix the Scottish population with that of other areas. London contained a far higher proportion of Scots-born residents than the North of England. The border territories were sparsely populated and had surprisingly well-differentiated populations. Border constituencies on the Scottish side contained only 9 per cent (Berwick and East Lothian), 10 per cent (Dumfries), and 9 per cent (Roxburgh, Selkirk, and Peebles) English born according to the 1971 census. On the English side the percentages born in Scotland were 9 per cent (Berwick-upon-Tweed), 3 per cent (Hexham), and 5 per cent (Penrith). Indeed, the Scottish constituency with the highest percentage born in England, only 12 per cent however, was nowhere near the English border but up in Moray and Nairn where there was a large military establishment. (It returned an SNP MP at both elections in 1974.)

This separation of Scotland's population was particularly striking when compared with Wales. A far higher percentage of Welsh residents were born in England and the highest concentration of English born was on the border. These concentrations ranged very high indeed, so high that the English–Welsh border was in a sense fictitious. Seven of the thirty-six Welsh seats had over a fifth of their population born in England according to the 1971 census: in the south and middle borders Monmouth and Montgomery both had 21 per cent English, while in the north the figures were 22 per cent in Anglesey, 29 per cent in Conway, 33 per cent in Denbigh, 38 per cent in West Flint, and 33 per cent in East Flint. So Wales had a degree of population integration with England which matched its administrative and legal integration just as the separation of Scotland's population reinforced its administrative and legal separation. When Mrs Thatcher spoke on television of the fears felt by Englishmen that they might be 'swamped' by those of an alien culture (i.e. coloured immigrants) she articulated a feeling which might come just as naturally from the Welsh-speaking, Welsh-born population of north Wales who were certainly being swamped by the English. The same fear could not afflict Scotland, not only because Scots and English culture were less visibly different than Welsh and English, but also because neither Scotland as a whole, nor any area within it was in danger of being swamped by English immigration. While this extreme separation of Scots and English populations provided a potential for all sorts of political and other differences it also lowered the political temperature by removing the threat of homogenization by immigration. To Scotsmen, Scotland was still indisputably their own land. It was the acceptable face of Scotland's emigration problem.

SOCIAL STRUCTURE

Social structural variables – class, religion, occupation, vital statistics, mobility, education, and housing – varied across the

regions and nations. All three types of variation – peripheral
North–South, cultural North–South and national – occurred in
one or other aspect of social structure.

First, the peripheral North–South trends, with London at one
extreme and Scotland at the other (Table 2.1). As befits an
administrative capital there were relatively few skilled manual
workers and relatively many junior non-manual workers in
London. When forced to choose a middle- or working-class label
the Londoners opted in relatively large numbers for the middle
class though this was largely the result of the forced choice.
Regional variation in spontaneous identification with class were
entirely different. The centre was also characterized by a much
more transient, or at least recently arrived, population and by
smaller families.

A second cluster of social variables ranged from one extreme in
Scotland to the other extreme in the South, rather than London
(Table 2.2). The self-employed, Anglicans, and those educated
at fee-paying schools were relatively numerous in the South and
sparse in Scotland. Catholics, council tenants, trade unionists,
the unemployed, those working in large establishments or for
public sector enterprises were particularly numerous in Scotland.
These features of social structure define the cultural caricature of
Englishness and are frequently quoted as examples of Scots–
English national differences. But without exception they all
showed marked variation between English regions. Only one of

Table 2.1. Peripheral North–South trends in social structure

	London %	South %	North %	Scotland %
Without children	32	28	28	26
Those with children who have 4 or more children	8	15	19	23
Growing up in area	59(78)	69(84)	89	92
With skilled manual head of household	24	37	39	37
With junior non-manual head of household	40	30	26	25
Middle class (forced choice)	41	36	34	28

Note: figures in brackets for area of origin are the percentages coming from the whole
London plus South area.

Table 2.2. Cultural North–South trends in social structure

	South %	(London) %	North %	Scotland %
RC	4	(9)	13	12
Anglican	52	(32)	43	6*
Self-employed	15	(10)	7	7
Public sector	29	(35)	34	37
In establishments of over 25 workers	63	(74)	69	70
With no family TU connection	66	(64)	52	53
With no family experience of unemployment	94	(93)	89	91
In council housing	20	(21)	36	52*
Educated at fee-paying school	8	(6)	3	4

Notes: (1) London figures are in brackets since the classification does not require them to bear any relation to the North though they must be between the South and Scotland; (2) Asterisks in the Scotland column draw attention to possible national effects in addition to North–South trends.

these variables – Anglicanism – exhibited a larger change between Scotland and the North than between the North and South of England. Indeed, with the exception of council housing, all the other variables changed much more between North and South than between Scotland and the North.

However, a third cluster of social variables did reveal genuinely national differences, with the various regions of England similar to each other but markedly different from Scotland (Table 2.3). The sharpest of these national differences was a direct consequence of history and long-established institutions: 46 per cent of Scots claimed to belong to the Church of Scotland while 46 per cent of the English claimed to belong to the Church of England. Twice as many Scots were educated at the equivalent of English grammar schools and getting on for twice as many Scots lived in council houses. While these differences also depended upon different decisions taken by separate Scottish institutions they were less bound by history since school and housing policy are more recent in origin and can be changed much more quickly and easily than a religious tradition. Two national differences reflected how Scots felt about society and were in no way bound by institutions. Scots were much more willing to identify spontaneously with the working

Table 2.3. National differences in social structure

	South %	London %	North %	Scotland %	England %
Anglican	52	(32)	43	6*	46
No religion	34	(46)	31	26	34
Practising churchmen	27	(25)	30	43	29
Church of Scotland	–	–	–	46	–
Middle class (of spontaneous self-assignments)	42	(40)	40	24	39
In council housing	20	(21)	36	52*	27
Educated at grammar or senior secondary schools	18	(20)	17	35	18

* entries which also appear in Table 2.2.

rather than the middle class. In both Scotland and England less than half our survey respondents identified spontaneously with any class. When those who at first rejected a class label were pressed to make a choice the national difference declined and an objective classification by the occupation of head of household narrowed the gap still further. So the significant point was not just that Scots were a little more working class than the English but that they were much more willing to identify with the working class – and also less willing to identify with the middle class. Scots also declared themselves more religious than the English especially when asked the most subjective of our religiosity questions: 'to what extent would you say you are now a practising member?'

In this third cluster of social variables council housing varied sharply within England as well as between Scotland and England.

COMMUNICATIONS

In the papers they read and the television or radio they listened to, Scots and English broke on national lines but the style of media use varied according to a peripheral North–South pattern (Table 2.4).

The papers, whether high brow or low, which dominated the English market had very few readers in Scotland. The main

Table 2.4. The national pattern of newspaper use

	London %	South %	North %	Scotland %	England %
Mail, Mirror, Sun	48	48	41	10	46
Express	16	15	15	24*	16
Record	–	–	–	27	–
Financial Times, Times, Guardian, Telegraph	20	14	9	3	12
Press & Journal, Courier, Scotsman, Glasgow Herald	–	–	–	20	–
None	15	20	29	13	23

* The *Scottish Daily Express* was a separate edition from the English and took a different editorial line at critical times.

cross-border paper was the *Express* but its *Scottish Daily Express*, though printed in Manchester since 1974, was no ordinary edition of the *Daily Express*. The difference was most evident on the day after the defeat of the guillotine motion on the Scotland and Wales Bill in 1977 when the English edition described the bill as one of the worst ever presented to Parliament while the *Scottish Daily Express* ran a front page headline 'Scotland will never forgive the Devo Traitors' who helped defeat the bill.

In the same way radio and television appear at first to be uniform throughout Britain and in important ways they were: the main lunch-time and early evening radio news and the main late evening television news were uniform throughout Britain. But they also broadcast an increasing volume of Scottish news and current affairs programmes. By 1977 they had begun to suppress London current affairs programmes to find the time for Scottish ones. In this they followed the example of the political parties which, especially in October 1974, broadcast different party political programmes simultaneously in Scotland and England. That, in turn, derived from their decisions in 1950 and regularly since 1959, to issue separate election manifestos in Scotland.

So there was a sharp national division in the electorate's choice of news media, and that choice was not entirely free. Once again national differences at the mass level owed much to institutional differences.

Table 2.5. Peripheral North–South variations in political communication

	London %	South %	North %	Scotland %
Paying very close attention to TV	23	18	19	14
Not understanding prices, EEC, and nationalization issues very well (average)	38	38	40	44
Not much or no interest in politics	27	33	37	45
Rarely talk about politics	32	40	42	48
Never join in or listen to political discussion	18	22	24	28
No political group membership	89	93	91	97
Don't read TU journal	36	34	48	55

But apart from the choice of medium, and hence perhaps of message also, variations in political communication followed a peripheral North–South pattern (Table 2.5). In their attention to television, claimed understanding of the issues, interest in politics, willingness to talk about politics, membership of political groups, and reading of union journals, Londoners were the most involved and Scots the least. A result which is all the more significant since these responses were obtained just after the October 1974 election when according to ORC polls Scottish politics were at their most interesting compared to English, and the turn-out rate was over 2 per cent higher in Scotland than in England. Indeed, it comes as something of a shock to find that at the very time when the SNP drove the Conservatives into third place and the Labour Government was preparing its devolution legislation almost half our Scots respondents said they did not understand issues like prices, the EEC, or nationalization, they had little or no interest in politics, and rarely talked about politics.

Centrality clearly boosted interest in politics while peripherality depressed it. Simply being physically close to Whitehall and Westminster appears to have made people more ready to follow political affairs even on television and in casual conversation – both of which were equally accessible to those who lived far away from Westminster. If a devolved parliament were established in Scotland it would be reasonable to expect a sizeable increase in Scots political interest. If we regard interest and participation as a good thing – and many politicians and pressure-group operators may not approve of too much public interest – then there would be an argument for siting any devolved Assembly in Glasgow rather than Edinburgh so as to interest the maximum number of people.

ECONOMIC AND PSYCHOLOGICAL PERCEPTIONS
AND EXPECTATIONS

We asked BES/SES respondents how happy or unhappy they were, not only about life in general, but about their job, what they could afford, their chances of getting ahead, the parties, politicians, local and national government, today's standards and values, and their own ability to change things (Table 2.6). It

Table 2.6. Happiness in Scotland and England

	% Happy		% Unhappy	
	Scotland	England	Scotland	England
Life as a whole	55	52	3	3
Your job	52	55	3	3
The things you can afford to have	29	30	6	5
The chances of getting ahead in Britain	15	18	13	13
The political parties	8	9	10	11
The politicians in Britain today	7	7	11	9
What your local government is doing	11	13	9	11
What the government is doing for people like you	11	13	15	15
The standards and values of today's society	6	6	29	31
Your chances of changing things you don't like	9	7	26	26
Average	20	21	13	13

Note: respondents were offered a 7-point scale – very happy, happy, satisfied, mixed feelings, unsatisfied, unhappy, very unhappy. The table shows the percentage in the first two and the last two categories.

is a comprehensive list and though Scots seemed a little less happy about their jobs and job prospects they were very nearly as happy and unhappy as the English with each aspect of life, even the most political. Happiness was British!

Scots and English also agreed on their economic expectations about unemployment, inflation, real income, strikes, the effectiveness of voluntary wage agreements, and the general health of the economy. There was only the slightest trace of more pessimism in Scotland (Table 2.7).

Table 2.7. Economic expectations

	Scotland %	England %
Unemployment will go up	70	68
Prices will go on rising	61	57
Income will fall behind prices	77	76
Always will be a lot of strikes	64	62
Voluntary wage agreements effective	71	71
Economy will get worse	45	42
Average	65	63

Perceptions of recent performance varied rather more though not according to a consistent regional pattern. Similar proportions in Scotland and England felt that their own income had drawn closer to the higher or lower paid though 6 per cent more Scots (58 against 52 per cent) felt their income had fallen behind prices in the previous year and 5 per cent more Scots (73 against 68 per cent) felt the economy had declined over the previous six months. A massive 26 per cent more Scots (74 versus 48 per cent) felt that strikes had gone up in the previous six months possibly because the interviewing coincided with some particularly well-publicized Scottish strikes.

A key to more general and evaluative perceptions of British performance is given by two questions which asked whether Britain's government and industry were well or badly run compared with other European countries (Table 2.8). The government was regarded as most successful by Londoners, rather less so by Northerners, and very much less so by the Scots. British industry was generally regarded as unsuccessful but while

Table 2.8. Comparative evaluation of Britain's government and industry (compared to Europe)

	London	South	North	Scotland
Per cent government well run minus per cent government badly run	25	22	21	12
per cent industry well run minus per cent industry badly run	−14	−11	−7	−18

the Scots were again the most critical, this time it was the Northerners who were least critical. Perhaps the North identified with industry and London with government but, if so, Scots rejected both. The industry pattern was a particularly good example of a Scottish national effect running counter to a North–South trend rather than in harmony with it.

POLICY CHOICES

Policy attitudes have a number of dimensions including weight and position. First, how important were the various issues to our respondents when they were making up their mind how to vote? Second, what sort of policy choices did they favour? An extreme Unionist and an extreme home ruler might agree that the constitutional issue was very important while disagreeing on the policy choice. There is a third dimension which the BES/SES surveys did not investigate but commercial surveys did, especially the ORC surveys: what were the important problems facing the Government?

We asked our respondents whether each of a dozen issues was 'the single most important', 'very important', or 'not very important' in helping them decide their vote. In order of the importance assigned to them by our Scots respondents the issues were: prices, wage controls, strikes, unemployment, Scottish government, pensions, North Sea oil, EEC entry, social services, housing, nationalization, and coalition. English respondents were asked about all these issues except for Scottish government but it is reasonable to assume that in 1974 English people were still almost unaware of Scottish government as a party political issue. Certainly, in England, North Sea oil was rated the least

Table 2.9. National differences in issue salience

Issue	% saying issue 'not very important'				
	London	South	North	Scotland	England
Prices	14	16	13	19	14
Wage controls	20	22	19	28	20
Strikes	29	28	26	30	27
Unemployment	27	30	25	32	27
Scottish government	–	–	–	39	–
Pensions	37	40	37	39	38
North Sea oil	54	55	60	44	57
EEC	30	28	31	44	30
Social services	39	42	39	45	40
Housing	37	43	48	51	44
Nationalization	34	32	37	51	35
Coalition	52	52	52	58	52

Notes: (1) The Scottish government question was only asked in Scotland; (2) The issues are ranked from most important to least important according to Scots respondents.

important issue, less important even than the willingness of parties to enter a coalition (Table 2.9).

The weights given to these issues almost always broke along simple national lines. The regions of England had similar views and Scotland differed from them. Scots felt almost all issues were less important than the English, reflecting their lower general interest in politics. The only issues to which the Scots assigned more weight were North Sea oil and probably Scottish government as well. On the rest, an average of 7 per cent more Scots (40 against 33 per cent) described the issues as unimportant. An average of 15 per cent more Scots rejected two issues which sharply divided the London-based parties: EEC membership and the nationalization of industry.

Perhaps I should re-emphasize that our BES/SES issue questions were about 'how important to you (the respondent) when you were deciding about voting was the issue of x?'. ORC found an entirely different pattern of answers to the question 'what do you yourself feel are the most important problems the Government should do something about?' First, Scots were always far *more* willing than the English to name issues like prices and unemployment as important priorities for government action, but far *less* willing than the English to name them as decisive in affecting their own personal voting choice between parties. Second, Scots always named economic issues as the top priority for government and no ORC survey showed more than 10 per cent quoting devolution as an important government priority while 61 per cent told the SES that devolution was important in deciding their vote.

Later polls for ITN and the BBC in 1978 and 1979 again showed that much larger numbers of Scots regarded devolution as an issue which decided their party vote than regarded it as a government priority.

Turning now to the policy preferences of our respondents, there were nine issues on which Scots and English took up very similar positions: nationalization, trade union power, Labour's ties with the unions, big business power, the need to curb communism, workers' control, government control of land, cash for the health service, and foreign aid.

But there were thirteen issues on which Scots and English differed. There were peripheral North–South regional trends on the aims of government and the need to toughen up on crime though the substance of these two trends was somewhat contradictory; there were other peripheral North–South trends on EEC membership and preserving the countryside with Scots less willing to stay in the EEC and less concerned to preserve the countryside. Cultural North–South regional trends were evident on the need to spend on poverty, to redistribute wealth, and decentralize government with northern parts much more favourable to all these. But the gap between attitudes in the North and in Scotland suggests that on decentralization and preserving the countryside a national influence operated in addition to the regional trend (Table 2.10).

Pure national differences appeared on social service cuts, pollution control, comprehensive education, repatriation of immigrants, and would probably have been evident on RC schools and the Scottish Assembly if these questions had been asked in England.

North Sea oil made an interesting contrast with decentralization. It also showed a North to South trend plus a national effect but on oil these effects operated against each other. While the North was most similar to Scotland in wanting decentralization from which it presumably hoped to benefit, it was the area least willing to concede any special Scottish rights over North Sea

Table 2.10. National and North–South differences in issue positions

Most important aim of government?	London % Law & order	South % Law & order	North % Living standards	Scotland % Living standards	England % Living standards
Law and order minus % living standards	1	4	–5	–13	–2 R
Cut social services	40	40	40	34	39 N
Very important to toughen up on crime	72	74	79	82	76 R
Very important to spend on poverty	53	47	55	57	51 R
Very important to control pollution	73	67	71	64	70 N
Stay EEC with or without changes	60	59	56	50	59 R
Very important to preserve countryside	50	42	45	36	45 R+N
Should redistribute wealth	57	49	59	64	55 R
Should not establish comprehensives	42	43	40	32	41 N
Should repatriate immigrants	40	38	41	29	39 N
Very important to decentralize government	12	10	19	36	15 R+N
Should maintain RC schools	–	–	–	22	– N
North Sea oil should be shared equally throughout Britain	75	82	84	31	82 R–N
Favour separate Scottish Assembly	–	–	–	82	– N

Notes: (1) Assembly and RC schools questions were not asked in England; (2) six 'aims of government' were offered – promoting private enterprise, protecting individual liberty, maintaining law and order, protecting the weakest and worst off, achieving greater equality among people, and finally raising everybody's standard of living; (3) issues are ranked from those with the least to those with the greatest difference between Scotland and England as a whole; (4) an R in the last column indicates a regional North–South trend, while an N in the last column indicates that there was a significant purely national effect, i.e. that the difference between Scotland and the North was greater than between the North and either London or the South. R + N means national and regional effects combine, R − N means they conflict.

oil. In this respect the 1974 surveys provided a guide to the way Northerners would behave during the 1974–9 struggles over the Scotland Act.

Some of these regional and national differences were small and could conceivably be due to nothing more than sampling errors, but there were substantial regional and/or national differences that produced a 9 per cent difference between Scots and English on the EEC, on preserving the countryside, redistributing wealth, comprehensive education, and repatriating immigrants. And there were much larger differences on decentralization, oil, the Scottish Assembly, and probably on state-run Catholic schools.

Over-all, Scotland did have a special approach to political issues. The Scots were most clearly set apart by their concern for the special Scottish issues of oil and Scottish government, and by the positions they took up on these issues. But they also differed from the English in a less marked way on a whole range of other issues. Generally Scots rated all the UK-wide issues as less important to themselves and sometimes very much less important than did the English. They were far less antagonistic towards coloured immigrants, possibly for no better reason than that coloured immigration was an English phenomenon. Farther away from the EEC they were less favourable to it than the English. Living in a land superbly well endowed with natural resources per capita they were also more suspicious of the predatory EEC and less concerned to preserve the countryside or control pollution. They were no more attracted to the socialist prescription of nationalizing industry but markedly more favourable to the social democrats' remedies of social services, spending on poverty, redistributing wealth, and establishing comprehensive schools. On several of these issues the distinction was clearly national rather than an extrapolation of a North–South trend and on one critical issue (oil) the national difference sharply reversed a North–South trend. In short, there is evidence that whether they were self-consciously aware of it or not, Scottish politics did exist in the minds of Scots electors as they gave a high level of attention to special Scottish issues and reacted in a distinctive way to more general British issues.

Some of these national differences in the approach to issues might have been expected from a reading of Chapter 1. The tables merely confirm and quantify the fact that devolution was an issue and popular one, for example. Similarly they confirm our expectations that Scots were particularly keen on a redistribution of wealth and less concerned about immigration. But it is a surprise to find more Scots than English – albeit very few more – rejecting the importance of issues like unemployment, the social services, and housing. Perhaps this merely reflected the lower level of political interest in Scotland though it could be the result of these issues being overshadowed by oil and devolution, or yet again it might have reflected a broader party consensus in Scotland that public services were essential to the nation's welfare, thus taking these issues somewhat 'out of party politics' at least by comparison with England.

Lastly, at the end of a four-year rush to extract oil without too much regard for the Scottish landscape, it comes as something of a surprise to find Scots markedly less concerned than the English about avoiding pollution and preserving the countryside.

Not all the national differences fit easily with national caricatures.

THE PARTIES

Given their much greater interest in and desire for decentralization it is also surprising that Scots felt much the same as the English about the attentiveness of MPs and councillors: 33 per cent of Scots and 34 per cent of the English felt they paid little attention to their constituents. Scots and English also agreed very closely on just what Labour and Conservative party policy was on British issues like nationalization or cuts in social services. They agreed too about Conservative EEC policy but not about Labour's EEC policy: 48 per cent of Scots but only 38 per cent of the English thought Labour intended to keep Britain in the EEC.

Fewer Scots than English approved either Labour or Conservative policies on nationalization, the social services, the EEC, or North Sea oil. Fewer Scots thought either Labour or the Conservatives were competent to handle the problems of prices and strikes. Significantly more Scots (27 against 18 per cent) felt they could rarely trust Conservative governments to do what was right.

When respondents were asked to list their likes and dislikes about the parties and given no set of prompted answers more Scots said they liked and disliked nothing about both Labour and

Table 2.11. National likes and dislikes about Labour and Conservative parties

	Like Conservative		Dislike Conservative		Like Labour		Dislike Labour	
	Scot %	Eng %	Scot %	Eng %	Scot %	Eng %	Scot %	Eng %
General judgement	20	23	13	15	8	13	12	10
Leader	10	7	20	25	–	–	–	–
Relationship to middle class	–	–	17	14	–	–	–	–
Relationship to working class	–	–	10	9	34	33	–	–
Relationship to trades unions	–	–	–	–	–	–	16	18
Pensions policy	–	–	–	–	10	10	–	–
Ideological symbols	10	13	–	–	–	–	–	–
Nationalization policy	–	–	–	–	–	–	21	29

Note: Dashes do not mean zero response, but response less than 10 per cent in both countries. Percentages are based on first mentioned like or dislike and exclude 'don't knows'.

Conservative parties (Table 2.11). There was a pro-Labour bias in Scotland because many more Scots liked nothing about the Conservatives (51 versus 42 per cent) and disliked nothing about Labour (33 versus 26 per cent) while only 2 or 3 per cent more Scots liked nothing about Labour or disliked nothing about the Conservatives. But still it was a couple of per cent more, not less. This finding may reflect the notorious inarticulateness of Scots but, if not, then it is further evidence of Scottish withdrawal from the politics of the South. More Scots, 65 per cent, liked the SNP than English liked any English party which suggests that the national pattern of likes and dislikes about Labour and Conservative was not caused by a general Scottish inability to articulate likes and dislikes.

Among those who did volunteer judgements on the parties the pattern of comments was fairly similar on either side of the border. Out of a total of sixty-five categories used for classifying answers, only a handful gained 10 per cent or more respondents in either country. The main reason for liking Labour was that it was a working-class party; the main dislike was its nationalization policy. The Conservative Party was liked for very general reasons and disliked mainly because of Edward Heath, its leader

at the time, and to a lesser extent because it was a middle-class
party.

The two largest Scots–English differences reflected regional
rather than truly national variation. People in the South were the
ones most opposed to the Conservative leader (Heath) and to
Labour's nationalization policy while the Scots were least
opposed but the pattern was essentially regional rather than
national (Table 2.12). Southerners could be expected to be most
opposed to nationalization, given their high level of Conservat-
ism but it is less obvious that they should be the most opposed to
Mr Heath though he certainly failed to conform naturally to the
image of a typical southern Conservative.

Table 2.12. Cultural North–South trends in reasons for disliking
Conservative and Labour

	South %	London %	North %	Scotland %
Dislike Conservative leader	28	23	22	20
Dislike Labour nationalization policy	33	26	26	21

SUPERSCOTS?

In the mid-seventies observers outside Scotland found it difficult
to distinguish between Scots in general and the SNP and its
supporters is particular. Even Scots themselves sometimes
seemed to identify the party with the people. The SES found that
the overwhelming majority of Scottish electors felt the SNP's
existence and electoral successes had been 'good for Scotland'.
That majority included almost all the SNP voters, which is not
surprising, but it also included about three-quarters of Labour
and Conservative voters, which is. In one sense at least Scots in
1974 did tend to identify with the SNP whether they voted for it
or against it.

It is tempting to reverse the logic of this fact and identify the
SNP with Scots, then to go on and assume that the actual SNP
voters were the 'most Scottish' part of the Scottish electorate. A
similar assumption makes some sense in Wales where Plaid
Cymru voters are indeed the most Welsh of the Welsh – in terms
of birth-place, distance from England, and above all language.
On some variables SNP voters were also the most Scottish of Scots.

Table 2.13. SNP voters as superscots or antiscots

Superscots on:	Antiscots on:
TU connections	religion
grammer schooling	house tenure
economic perceptions	class identity
economic expectations	unskilled employment
policy salience (most policies)	self-employed
policy positions (especially on Scottish issues)	small establishments
	public-sector employment
party evaluations (policy competence)	family size
	interest in politics
party perceptions (what policies are)	party dislikes
party likes	

We can call them 'superscots' on those variables but on others SNP voters were what might be called 'antiscots': their characteristics deviated from the Scottish norm towards, not away from, the English norm (Table 2.13).

SNP voters had more links with trade unions and more grammar school (senior secondary) education than even the average Scot but otherwise they were superscots in their economic and political attitudes rather than their social background. Even more than other Scots they felt the economy had got worse in the recent past and was likely to continue to do so in the future. They were more critical of Britain's industry compared to Europe and extremely critical of Britain's governments compared to Europe. On prices, strikes, pensions, housing, social services, and coalitions the average percentage dismissing these issues as unimportant was 36 per cent in England, 40 per cent in Scotland, and 46 per cent among SNP voters, while on oil the figures were 57 per cent in England, 44 per cent in Scotland, and only 24 per cent among the SNP who gave even greater weight to Scottish government. But SNP voters tilted very slightly towards the English view in the importance they assigned to the EEC and nationalization issues.

On the majority of issues SNP voters' *positions* were also superscots but frequently by only a very small margin. There were seven issues where SNP voters differed substantially from other Scots. They were strongly superscot on opposition to EEC membership, on oil revenues, and on decentralization of government, but they merely deviated from a cross-national consensus in their extreme opposition to nationalization and their dislike of Labour's union ties, while their opposition to trade union power and to foreign aid ran at even higher levels than in England.

They were superscots in claiming there was little difference between the parties, in suspecting that Labour intended to keep Britain in the EEC, and in their failure to find anything good to say about the Labour and Conservative parties.

This general tendency for the SNP to be politically superscots contrasts with an equally general tendency for them to lack the distinctive features of the Scottish social character. They were, of course, slightly more Scottish born than average, but in other respects they deviated towards the English norm. They were less religious than the typical Scot. They were so much less Catholic that the English were closer to the Scottish norm than were the SNP. Although their youth prevented them from owning much property, SNP voters were more like the English than other Scots in taking out mortgages. They were less keen to identify with the working class though no more willing than other Scots to link themselves to the middle classes.

On non-class aspects of employment the SNP were so un-Scottish that they looked more like English Southerners than Scots. This was true of the percentages in unskilled manual employment, in public sector employment, and in small establishments (Table 2.14).

Similar background characteristics do not necessarily produce a community of interest, especially when populations are

Table 2.14. SNP voters social characteristics in common with England

	South %	England %	Scotland %	SNP %
In larger establishments (with over 25 workers)	63	68	70	63
In public-sector employment	29	31	37	31
Unskilled manual	15	17	21	16
With 4 or more children	15	15	23	17
Catholic	4	9	12	5
Irreligious	59	56	42	47

segmented. If two men confront a bun, an equally high level of hunger or agressiveness is the very last prescription for consensus on what to do with it. So there is no need to be surprised that SNP voters had a certain Southern English social flavour about them combined with a superscots approach to politics.

HOW FAR APART?

How far apart then were the Scots and the English in 1974? First, there were some genuinely national differences which cannot be explained away as part of a regional trend. These were most marked where Scottish institutions or the special Scottish issues of oil and self-government were involved but they extended to other matters as well. The Scots were a separate people by birth and upbringing, they attended separate Churches, they read separate newspapers, and their education and housing systems were very different from those in England. They had a strong interest and a highly deviant position on North Sea oil and Scottish government. All these differences are strongly linked to the existence of separate Scottish organizations and institutions. But there were also sizeable national differences in religiosity, in class identification (more than in class itself), evaluation of industry's and government's performance, the weight given to most general British political issues, and the positions taken on a few of them.

Second, there were various North–South trends which put Scotland at one extreme and either London or the South at the other. Analytically these are regional rather than national differences though the distinction may be too subtle for a nationalist politician attacking the 'London' government or contrasting Scottish living and working conditions with those in the South East or even for a Scots Labour politician talking about the English 'coffin'. Scotland differed substantially from both London and the South on such regionally varying factors as family size, mobility, trade union links, and interest in politics, as well as on those variables which split on genuinely national lines.

The surveys also revealed national similarities on economic expectations, the nature of likes and dislikes about the Conservative and Labour parties, and on happiness with many aspects of life.

Over-all, Scottish–English differences were large only where they flowed from separate Scots institutions or involved the two special Scots issues. But there were moderate differences on a wide range of other variables and these owed more to genuinely national divisions than to regional variation.

Chapter 3:

The Demand for Devolution up to 1974

TIME TRENDS BEFORE 1974

Since the day when the Treaty of Union was signed in haste as the signatories fled before the Edinburgh mob a substantial body of Scots have hankered after some form of separate assembly or parliament. A typical comment in late Victorian times appears in Grant's *Illustrated Guide to Edinburgh*:

During the period (from 1710 to 1866) the revenue of England increased 800 per cent while that of Scotland increased 2,500 per cent thus showing that there is no country in Europe which has made such vast material progress [a seemingly Unionist sentiment, but it goes on] but it is doubtful if those who sat in the old Parliament House on that 25th March 1707, least of all such patriots as Lord Banff, when he pocketed his [English bribe of] £11 2s od could, in the wildest imagery, have foreseen the Edinburgh and the Scotland of today . . . generations went to their grave ere the long-promised prosperity came . . . the departure of the King to London in 1603 caused not the slightest difference in Edinburgh but the Union [of parliaments] seemed to achieve the irreparable ruin of the capital and the nation (p. 165).

Unfortunately there is no way of quantifying the Scottish public's attitude to a separate parliament before the First World War, and before the advent of universal suffrage mass attitudes were less relevant to politics anyway. We do know that on every occasion after 1893 when the question has been put to a vote in the House of Commons, a majority of Scottish MPs – usually a very large majority – has voted for a separate parliament. These votes occurred in 1893, 1894, 1908, 1911, 1912, 1913, 1920, 1976, and 1977. Various Scots MPs put forward home rule motions or bills at other times though they did not get as far as a vote. But this is no more than indicative, however, because we know full well that MPs' attitudes on issues like capital punishment do not represent or even come near to popular attitudes.

The earliest mass surveys on devolution were run by the two mass circulation newspapers, the *Scottish Daily Express* and the *Daily Record*. In 1932 they both produced straw polls, with no pretence at systematic sampling, showing overwhelming majorities in favour of a Scottish parliament. The *Express* found 112,984 in favour of home rule with only 4,596 against (27 September 1932). Once again the evidence is not conclusive because the samples, though large were almost certainly biased. Similarly organized polls based on write-in coupons were published by the *Scotsman* in 1969 and the *Record* in 1976 and show an enormous bias towards independence compared with contemporary results using standard sample survey techniques. The 1969 *Scotsman* poll put support for full sovereign independence at 50 per cent and the 1976 *Record* poll at 44 per cent though quota and random samples suggest it was really less than half these figures. In the 1969 *Scotsman* poll 57 per cent of respondents intended to vote SNP – another indication of the enormous bias in such polls.

After the Second World War MacCormick's breakaway faction from the SNP organized the signing of a Scottish Covenant petition in favour of home rule and claimed two million signatures. Once again there is evidence that a large number of Scots had an emotional commitment to some kind of parliament or assembly for Scotland. But once again the unscientific nature of the evidence prevents any real attempt to quantify home rule support.

Opinion polls based on standard quota or random sampling techniques began to appear in the sixties. At first the *Scotsman* published weekly (not monthly!) Gallup polls but they were simply Britain-wide polls covering Britain-wide issues and voting intentions. However, SNP by-election successes stirred the media's interest in purely Scottish political attitudes and voting intentions. So between 1968 and 1970 especially, and again after 1974, the news media commissioned a large number of Scottish polls and there were also a few by academics, the parties, and the Kilbrandon Commission.

Unfortunately each poll asked about constitutional change in its own way which makes them only approximately comparable. The options of full independence and the status quo were the easiest to define and the most comparable from one survey to another but even their meanings changed according to whether any intermediate categories, or how many intermediate categories, were offered to respondents. Obviously, if they were offered a straight choice between independence and the status quo support for both extremes would be greater than if there were a variety of federal, devolution, or just better government options on offer as well. Most surveys offered at least one intermediate option.

Most answers could be classified under one of four headings – independence, status quo, some form of devolved assembly or federal system, and finally some form of change which did not imply a Scottish parliament in any sense (more Scots MPs at Westminster, more understanding by the London government, etc.). The Royal Commission on the Constitution used what has become known as the Kilbrandon question. It allowed five different answers:

1. leave things as they are at present
2. keep things much the same as they are now but make sure the needs of Scotland are better understood
3. keep the present system but allow more decisions to be made in Scotland
4. have a new system of governing Scotland so that as many decisions as possible are made in the area
5. let Scotland take over complete responsibility for running things in Scotland.

Of these options (1) and (5) can be identified with the status quo and independence, option (2) with 'other changes' and option (4) with 'devolution'; but option (3) is apparently self-contradictory and it is not obvious whether it should be treated as another devolution option or not. In Table 3.1 all surveys using the Kilbrandon question have been analyzed with this central option treated both ways.

Two points emerge from Table 3.1. First, there is very little evidence of any trend at all, despite the enormous swings to and from the SNP in the period from 1965 to 1974. Over-all the average figures were:

full independence	22 per cent	
devolution or more	63 "	(including 22 per cent for independence)
less than devolution	37 "	(including 15 per cent for the status quo)
status quo	15 "	

Table 3.1. Support for home rule 1965–October 1974

Survey Organization and date	% for full independence	% for some form of devolution (inc. those in Col. 1)	% for other changes or no change (inc. those in Col. 4)	% for status quo
Strathclyde University March 1965 (Craigton only)	–	58/64	42/36	24
Express February 1968	–	61	39	–
Dundee University May 1968 (Dundee only)	35	–	–	–
BBC May 1968	18	67	34	11
Express May 1968	–	63	37	–
Herald June 1968 (Glasgow only)	21	59	41	14
Gallup September 1968	33	60	40	–
Express April 1969	20	54	47	–
NOP/*Record* December 1969	26	74	–	26
Herald Feb. 1970 (Glasgow only)	11	59	40	–
Kilbrandon Summer 1970	23	47/73	51/25	6
MORI February 1974	21	46/70	53/29	8
ORC April 1974 Q. 1	18	41/61	58/34	14
Q. 2	18	59/79	42/22	22
ORC September 1974	21	64/75	37/22	22
System Three October 1974	17	–	–	7

Table 3.1 continued

Survey Organiza-tion and date	% for full independence	% for some form of devolution (inc. those in Col. 1)	% for other changes or no change in Col. 4)	% for status quo
SES Oct–Nov 1974				
Q. 1	21	65	34	8
Q. 2	–	82	18	–

Notes: (1) ORC April 1974: Q. 1 was the Kilbrandon question ranging through choices such as 'more understanding by the government in London', i.e. it included non-constitutional options, while Q. 2 offered a set of four specific constitutional changes, or the status quo. (2) SES Oct–Nov 1974: Q. 1 was a modified version of the Kilbrandon question while Q. 2 asked for approval (or not) of the 'Scottish Assembly' – advocated by all four parties at that time, though with different meanings.

In 1965, before the first wave of SNP electoral successes, devolution support was close to the over-all average, just as it was after their rout in 1970 and after their victories in 1974. A more precise test is shown in Table 3.2 which shows results from three surveys using the same Kilbrandon questions each time.

If anything, support for independence was lower, and for the status quo higher after the SNP successes in 1974 than it was after the SNP rout in 1970, but the main feature of Table 3.2 as of Table 3.1, is the stability of levels of devolution support over the years up to 1974. It raises but does not answer the question whether devolution attitudes were themselves stable, that is,

Table 3.2 Trends on the Kilbrandon Question

	Kilbrandon Answer				
	1 (status quo)	2 (more understanding)	3 (more decisions, same system)	4 (new system)	5 (complete responsibility)
Kilbrandon Summer 1970	6	19	26	24	23
MORI February 1974	8	21	24	25	21
ORC April 1974	14	20	24	23	18

whether it was the same group of people who favoured independence at different times, or merely the same quantity of people.

However, it clearly makes more sense to regard support for
devolution as a constant rather than a variable. Party voting
successes then depend upon their success in raising or lowering
the salience of devolution as a party issue and on the success or
failure of their appeals to pro- or anti-devolutionist groups of
electors rather than raising or lowering support for devolution
itself.

How real was this Scottish demand for home rule? The 1970
Kilbrandon survey asked similarly worded devolution questions
throughout Britain but substituted the names of English regions –
Yorkshire, West Midlands, etc. – in place of Scotland. While
Scots took the devolution and independence options more
frequently than people in other parts of Britain they did so only
very marginally more than people in the South of England. So
Kilbrandon's survey analysts concluded that 'interest in complete regional responsibility in Scotland is not much more
widespread than in some English regions'. The problem with this
interpretation is whether it is reasonable to equate 'East Anglia
should completely run its own affairs' with 'Scotland should
completely run its own affairs'. My own view is that both East
Anglians and Scots would instinctively put a much wider
interpretation on 'Scotland's own affairs' than 'East Anglia's own
affairs'. So though the wording was the same the responses were
not truly comparable.

But there was other direct evidence that Scots demands for
home rule were qualitatively different from those in the regions of
England. Kilbrandon found that when people were asked to say
spontaneously what they themselves would like to see done to
improve things in their 'region' about 20 per cent of Scots
spontaneously mentioned home rule but practically no one in the
English regions suggested regional government. Earlier in Budge
and Urwin's Craigton survey in 1965 they found that 36 per cent
spontaneously mentioned home rule as a means of improving
Scottish government. Again, in the SES of October 1974, when
we asked people to tell us in their own words what they liked and
disliked about the SNP they mentioned a parliament or assembly
about as frequently as general 'good for Scotland' or 'puts
Scotland first' type comments. Over-all 10 per cent liked the SNP

for its oil policy, 33 per cent because it was 'good for Scotland', and 32 per cent for its home rule policy. Amongst SNP voters the balance tilted more strongly towards constitutional affairs: 51 per cent mentioned home rule against 47 per cent who mentioned general Scots interests and 16 per cent who mentioned oil. (Up to four likes were recorded and classified into one or other of sixty-five categories.)

So home rule was introduced spontaneously by Scots respondents when discussing what could be done to improve their area or what they liked or disliked about the parties.

While opinion polls which asked about the most important problems for government action never found more than 10 per cent of Scots choosing devolution, those that asked which issues had been important when deciding about voting found much higher percentages stressing the importance of home rule. In our 1974 SES, for example, it ranked fifth: 81 per cent said prices were important, 72 per cent wage controls, 70 per cent strikes, 68 per cent unemployment, and 61 per cent Scottish government. Home rule was not regarded as a major problem facing the government but was reported to be one important factor in deciding how to vote.

COHERENCE

As well as being highly stable over time, support for devolution was impressively stable across a wide range of questions. The 1974 SES asked several different questions with a bearing on devolution (Table 3.3). I shall take as the basic question for analytical purposes a modified Kilbrandon question, modified to remove the self-contradictory middle category. In the SES version there were four possible answers to the question.

Q. 'There has been a lot of discussion recently about giving more power to Scotland. Which of these statements comes *closest* to what you yourself feel should be done?'
(SQ) Keep the governing of Scotland much as it is now.
(MU) Make sure the needs of Scotland are better understood by the government in London.
(MD) Allow more decisions to be made in Scotland.
(SG) Scotland should completely run its own affairs.

Since I will be making intensive use of this question I will

Table 3.3. Coherence of devolution attitudes

| | Per cent in favour of | |
	Devolution (MD+SG)	Independence (SG)
Q. Shifting power from London to regions and local authorities.		
Very important that it should	82	34
Fairly important that it should	67	15
Doesn't matter either way	50	14
Fairly important that it should not	38	11
Very important that it should not	35	13
Q. People have different views about the need for a separate Scottish Assembly. How about you? Which of these views comes closest to what you yourself feel?		
Very much in favour of a separate Scottish Assembly	89	44
Somewhat in favour of a separate Scottish Assembly	63	10
Somewhat against a separate Scottish Assembly	30	3
Very much against a separate Scottish Assembly	26	6
Q. And when you were deciding about voting, how important was the general question of the form of government for Scotland?		
The most important single thing	89	61
Fairly important	71	18
Not very important	52	9
Q. Is there anything in particular that you like about the SNP? (unprompted answers, but coded as below)		
Good for Scotland	73	24
More say for Scotland	77	21
Scottish Assembly	88	29
Independence, home rule	92	66
Q. Is there anything in particular that you dislike about the SNP? (unprompted)		
Independence	63	10
All respondents	66	22

abbreviate these answers to status quo (or SQ); more under-standing (or MU); more decisions (or MD); and self-government (or SG). Further, I shall identify the total of MD plus SG responses as the total 'devolution' response and when I wish to distinguish between devolution and independence I shall use MD as 'narrowly defined devolution'.

One related question was so worded as to obscure its connection with Scottish devolution as much as possible. It asked whether power should be shifted from London to the regions and local authorities. Within Scotland the word region meant Strathclyde, Tayside, Lothian, Highland, etc. – the areas which had regional councils. Respondents had voted in regional council elections about six months before the SES interview. What 'region' did not usually mean within Scotland was Scotland-as-a-whole. Despite this there was a very strong relationship between answers to the shifting power question and the basic devolution question; comparing those who felt it was very important to shift power from London with those who took the opposite view, the power shifters were 47 per cent more in favour of devolution and 21 per cent more in favour of independence.

A third question asked about Scottish Assembly proposals which in one form or another were backed by all parties in the autumn of 1974 but were linked most closely with the Labour Government. Again, comparing those who were very much in favour of the Assembly with those who were very much against, the pro-Assembly people were 63 per cent more in favour of devolution and 38 per cent more in favour of independence. Two factors make this result far from obvious. First, the question wording used the term '*separate* Scottish Assembly' which was reputed to frighten off moderate devolutionists. It did not. Second, it would be a logically justifiable position to favour independence but reject half-measures like the Scottish Assembly. Indeed, Labour presented the Assembly as a bulwark against independence. Yet very few of those who wanted independence (or voted SNP) did reject the Assembly. Of those who wanted independence 97 per cent were in favour of the Assembly, and 77 per cent were very much in favour – and that of a policy designed to destroy the SNP. Five years earlier the *Scotsman* (6 February 1969) referendum, biased sample though it was, had shown that federalism was the almost universal second choice of pro-independence people but that the converse was not true.

Those who wanted full independence did not take the view

that nothing less was worth having, or the still more extreme position that the status quo was actually preferable to half measures which might reduce support for full independence. They were willing to take as much as they could get. Devolution might, or might not, be half-way down the 'slippery slope' towards independence which some Unionists feared but it was clearly half-way to satisfying those who wanted independence. Some nationalist activists may have had a more sophisticated or intransigent view but the mass electorate did not.

The only lack of coherence, if that is what it is, found in the SES was a lack of correlation between devolution and independence attitudes on the one hand and feelings that MPs and councillors did or did not pay enough attention to ordinary citizens on the other. This emphasized the national or corporate nature of Scottish devolutionary demands.

One pattern which is probably misleading is the apprently sharp relationship between pro-devolution, and especially pro-independence, attitudes and the importance given to the question of Scottish government. Among those who said it was the single most important thing, 61 per cent wanted independence, but among those who called it unimportant only 9 per cent were for self-government. It is very natural to describe as unimportant a proposed change which we do not want. The chain of argument goes: unimportant, not a priority, no immediate action, postpone indefinitely. Certainly among the politicians some of the most passionate debaters on devolution were those like Dalyell or Sproat who opposed it. Consequently all the measures of the importance of devolution probably underestimate it since those who reacted most strongly against it tended to deny its importance. Yet anti-devolution views were, as we shall see later, a prime determinant of SNP voting in the negative sense of preventing an SNP vote.

There was a more plausible link between respondents' own attitudes on devolution and the unprompted reasons they gave for liking the SNP. Those who thought the party was good for Scotland, protected Scottish interests, or even gained more say for Scotland in her own affairs, were only a little more pro-devolution than average, and no more in favour of independence, while those who specifically mentioned a parliament, assembly, home rule, or self-government were very much more pro-devolution and pro-independence according to my basic measure of devolution attitudes.

Thus, although my analysis of the patterns of pro-devolution and independence support is based on the modified Kilbrandon question it does show a high degree of correlation with other measures of devolution support. It was possible to remove or insert words like Scotland or like 'separate' in the question, or to ask about highly specific devolution proposals, and still find much the same people at the pro- and anti-devolution ends of the spectrum. And it was a spectrum: to the electorate, independence was a super-devolutionary position while devolution was diluted independence. Except in terms of the degree of extremism there was not much point in distinguishing devolution from independence. To the mass electorate they were not the two distinct and opposed categories they could so reasonably have been.

RELATIONSHIP TO OTHER ISSUES

Attitudes on devolution and independence correlated with the special Scottish issue of North Sea oil, with attitudes towards the EEC which was not peculiarly Scottish but was especially significant in Scotland, with general evaluations of British government and industry, and finally with social welfare attitudes that were in no way specific to Scotland.

Comparing those who wanted all the oil benefits for Scotland with those who would share them evenly throughout Britain oil nationalists were 33 per cent more pro-devolution and 53 per cent more pro-independence (Table 3.4). Similarly those who thought the oil issue 'most important' were 16 per cent more pro-devolution and 32 per cent more pro-independence. On both questions oil attitudes were linked far more closely to independence than devolution. Indeed, part of the oil effect was to encourage a trade-off between independence and devolution (narrowly defined). Those who took a more 'British' view on oil were both more favourable to the status quo and to narrowly defined devolution at the expense of pro-independence attitudes.

The relationship to EEC attitudes was similar but less extreme (Table 3.5). Those who wanted to leave the EEC were 17 per cent more pro-devolution but 26 per cent more pro-independence than those who wanted to stay. Those who felt it 'most

Table 3.4 Devolution and oil

	Per cent in favour of	
	Devolution	Independence
Q. People have different views about the benefits from North Sea oil. Which of these comes closest to what you feel should be done with the benefits from North Sea oil?		
Scotland should get all the benefits	81	60
Scotland should get by far the largest share of the benefits	74	32
Scotland should get a somewhat larger share than the rest of Britain	71	15
The benefits should be shared equally by Britain as a whole	48	7
Q. When you were deciding about voting how important was the question of North Sea oil?		
The most important single thing	75	46
Fairly important	72	24
Not very important	59	14

Table 3.5. Devolution and the EEC

	Per cent in favour of	
	Devolution	Independence
Q. It is sometimes said that Britain should try to change the terms of entry into the Common Market and if this is not successful get out. Which of the following statements comes closest to what you yourself feel should be done? If you haven't a view on this, just say so.		
It is all right for Britain to stay in the Common Market on the present terms	52	5
Britain must stay in the Common Market but should try hard to change the terms	64	17
Britain must change the terms and should leave the Common Market unless they improve	73	27
Britain should get out of the Common Market no matter what	69	31
Q. When you were deciding about voting how important was the question of Britain and the Common Market?		
The single most important thing	79	37
Fairly important	66	21
Not very important	64	19

important' were 15 per cent more pro-devolution but 18 per cent more pro-independence than those who felt it unimportant.

People who thought Britain was relatively badly governed were 11 per cent more in favour of devolution or independence, but there was no correlation between general evaluations of British industry and either independence or devolution (Table 3.6). Further investigation shows that there was also no correlation with expectations about the future success of the economy. Looking backwards, those who felt the economy had recently got better in 1974 (yes, better!) were 8 per cent more pro-independence and 10 per cent more pro-devolution than those

Table 3.6. Devolution and evalutions of British government and industry

	Per cent in favour of	
	Devolution	Independence
Q. Compared with other European countries do you feel Britain is		
Relatively well governed	64	19
About average	64	18
Relatively badly governed	75	30
Q. Compared with oother European countries do you feel that British industry and commerce is		
Relatively well run	66	24
About average	66	18
Relatively badly run	67	23

who thought it had got worse. Clearly the evaluation of general government performance and perceptions of recent economic successes were very different things.

We asked three questions relevant to the social welfare dimension: did respondents favour government spending to eliminate poverty? did they favour the redistribution of income and wealth? and did they favour workers control? – which last might be called redistribution of power in the language of social democracy or industrial devolution in the language of nationalism. All three issues correlated with devolution and independence views. Comparing extremes on the five-point scales in Table 3.7, the pro-social welfare category was 7 per cent, 22 per cent, or 18 per cent more pro-independence when social

Table 3.7. Devolution and social welfare

| | Per cent in favour of | |
	Devolution	Independence
Q. Spending more money to get rid of poverty in Britain?		
Very important that government should	68	25
Fairly important that government should	68	16
Doesn't matter either way	48	23
Fairly important that government should not	52	13
Very important that government should not	64	18
Q. Redistributing income and wealth in favour of ordinary working people?		
Very important that government should	69	31
Fairly important that government should	65	19
Doesn't matter either way	68	21
Fairly important that government should not	64	14
Very important that government should not	53	9
Q. Giving workers more say in the running of the place where they work?		
Very important that government should	74	34
Fairly important that government should	70	20
Doesn't matter either way	56	18
Fairly important that government should not	58	13
Very important that government should not	59	16

welfare was measured in terms of public expenditure, income redistribution, and workers' control respectively.

DEVOLUTION AND SOCIAL ALIGNMENTS

Surprisingly, perhaps, there was little or no correlation between devolution attitudes and being self-employed, working in a small plant, or working in the private or public sector (Table 3.8). But devolution attitudes did follow a strong occupational class pattern no matter whether class was defined by self-identification or by head-of-household occupational grades. The middle class were very much less keen on independence but rather more favourable to devolution of some kind than the working class. This paradox is explained by middle-class devotion to moderation. Working-class people were more favourable to both independence and the status quo, while the middle class were particularly in favour of the more decisions option, i.e. devolution contrasted with independence. Table 3.9 illustrates this in more detail for the first and last social grades.

Table 3.8. Devolution, class and employment status

| | | Per cent in favour of | |
		Devolution	Independence
Subjective class			
Spontaneous middle		69	16
Forced middle		65	15
Forced working		65	23
Spontaneous working		66	25
Head of household social grade			
A higher managerial	1	73	8
B lower managerial	2	68	10
Cl A higher non-manual	3	62	19
Cl B lower non-manual	4	67	23
C2 skilled manual	5	68	27
D unskilled manual	6	64	27
TU: Respondent		69	26
Other member of family		66	22
No family connection		64	19
Respondent Self-employed		63	24
Not self-employed		67	22
Respondent In private sector job		66	21
In public sector job		69	23
Respondent In small establishment		70	21
In large establishment		66	23

Table 3.9. Senior managers and unskilled workers attitudes to devolution and independence

| | Per cent in favour of | | | |
	status quo	more understanding	more decisions	run own affairs
Senior managers	8	19	65	8
Unskilled manual workers	10	26	38	27

Both independence and devolution had more support in younger age groups and among men rather than women, but other social patterns were more complex. Those who had had the minimum of education, or who belonged to no Church were, like the lowest social grades, the most inclined to independence but only because they opted for independence as an alternative to more moderate devolution. It was the highly educated and Church of Scotland members who gave most support in total to the combination of devolution and independence (Table 3.10).

One finding would have surprised may commentators in Scotland who knew the pattern of SNP party support: Catholics were almost as pro-devolution and pro-independence as Protestants yet they gave relatively little support to the SNP.

Table 3.10. Devolution, age, sex, religion, education and house tenure

| | | Per cent in favour of | |
		Devolution	Independence
Age:	Under 25	75	30
	25–29	67	26
	30–34	69	29
	35–44	69	19
	45–54	62	19
	55–64	65	16
	65–74	58	14
	75 plus	55	19
Sex:	Male	72	25
	Female	61	19
Religion (sect):			
	Church of Scotland	68	19
	RC	63	20
	None	65	30
	Anglican	56	15
Religiosity:			
	Very much so	63	16
	To some extent	68	16
	Not really	67	22
Education:			
	Academic further	68	10
	Other further and academic school	78	20
	Other further	69	23
	More than minimum	63	23
	Minimum	61	23
Tenure:	Owned	62	20
	Mortgaged	73	21
	Private rented	70	20
	Council	63	22

Table 3.11 Devolution and media usage

| | Per cent in favour of | |
	Devolution	Independence
Main morning paper:		
None	63	24
Express	69	15
Record	63	25
(Glasgow) *Herald*	72	13
(Edinburgh) *Scotsman*	68	18
(Aberdeen)*Press and Journal*	67	30
(Dundee) *Courier*	72	28

DEVOLUTION AND MEDIA USE

For a morning newspaper there were three popular choices – the *Express*, the *Record*, or nothing (Table 3.11). Of these three groups *Express* readers in 1974 were the least favourable to independence but the most favourable to devolution. Four papers combined a high-brow and a single-city appeal – the *Glasgow Herald*, Edinburgh *Scotsman*, the Aberdeen *Press and Journal*, and the Dundee *Courier*. Our samples of their readers are small but they appear to show little variation in devolution support among the four, though all four papers' readers were more pro-devolution than average. This similarity masked sharp differences in support for independence ranging from only 13 per cent of *Glasgow Herald* readers to 30 per cent of *Press and Journal* readers.

DEVOLUTION AND PARTISANSHIP

Party identification was measured in the SES by the standard Michigan question, 'Generally speaking, do you think of yourself as Conservative, Labour, Liberal, Scottish Nationalist, or what?' together with a probe to find the inclinations of the don't knows and another to find out whether respondents identified very strongly, fairly strongly, or not very strongly with their chosen party.

There was a steady rise in support for independence across the spectrum from strong Conservative identifiers (7 per cent pro-independence) through weak identifiers to strong Labour identifiers (19 per cent pro-independence). However, strong Labour and Conservative identifiers were less pro-devolution than weaker identifiers. SNP identifiers were 58 per cent pro-independence and 91 per cent pro-devolution which is certainly no more than we might expect, but Liberal identifiers were only 10 per cent pro-independence and less than average in their support for devolution, which might not be expected from supporters of an avowedly federalist party.

Categorizing respondents by how they remembered voting in 1970, February 1974, and October 1974 reveals significant trends. If we could assume as a very crude approximation that memories were accurate and that individual respondents' devolution attitudes had been the same in 1970 as in 1974 (which they certainly were in aggregate), then Table 3.12 could be interpreted as showing that in 1970 the SNP vote had been no more or less pro-independence than in 1974, but that 1970 Conservative

Table 3.12 Devolution and party identification

		Per cent in favour of	
		Devolution	Independence
Con identification			
strong		42	7
fairly		65	8
not very		60	11
Lab identification			
not very		57	10
fairly		61	15
strong		55	19
Lib identification		61	10
SNP identification		91	58
Voted SNP	in 1970	90	47
	in February 1974	91	47
	in October 1974	89	48
Voted Con	in 1970	63	13
	in February 1974	60	9
	in October 1974	55	6
Voted Lab	in 1970	62	22
	in February 1974	59	18
	in October 1974	59	17
Voted Lib	in 1970	67	15
	in February 1974	61	17
	in October 1974	60	10

voters had been 7 per cent more pro-independence and 1970 Labour and Liberal voters 5 per cent more pro-independence than in 1974, which suggests that the pro-devolution wings were indeed the ones that defected in 1974.

CONCLUSION

In this chapter I have shown that the demand for devolution was sufficiently strong to be raised spontaneously and to be sustained at a fairly constant level for at least a decade before 1974. It was also coherent; those who favoured specific policies like shifting power from London or establishing a Scottish Assembly were those who were at or near the pro-independence end of our very generalized Kilbrandon-style question on devolution. So were those who named a Scottish Assembly or Parliament rather than protection of Scottish interests as the feature they most liked about the SNP. There was, however, no correlation between our measure of devolution demand and feelings that MPs did not pay attention to their constituents, nor with economic expectations, nor with personal or nation-wide perceptions of economic failures, though there was a link between pro-devolution attitudes and a generalized feeling that British government did not work very well.

Devolution attitudes correlated fairly strongly with anti-EEC positions and still more with Scottish oil positions. For some few people in special localities it might be that consideration of these issues turned them into pro-devolutionists but since our survey of trends pointed to fairly stable devolution attitudes over time while EEC attitudes were notoriously unstable and oil was a very recent issue altogether it seems at least as likely that attitudes on oil and EEC entry were shaped by attitudes to devolution rather than the reverse. There were overtones of this in SNP propaganda which admitted the oil could only be Scottish if an independent Scotland existed. If oil discoveries turned Scots towards independence then they would be canny Scots indeed, even venal, but they would also have to be far more pro-independence after 1970 than before and there is no evidence for that whatsoever. Oil wealth might make them feel safe to indulge a preference they already possessed, but no more than that. Conversely, it was natural for those already committed to independence to claim the oil revenues.

But there were other correlations with devolution attitudes that cannot be explained as other variables responding to devolution attitudes. First, social structural variables. Obviously pro-independence attitudes could not make people younger, nor male, nor is it likely that they caused people to switch their religious categories or social grades.

Men and young people were both pro-independence and pro-devolution. We may guess that these social groups are more restive, more adventurous, more willing to accept or demand change.

The irreligious, the uneducated, and the lower social grades were markedly pro-independence but more at the expense of moderate devolution views than anything else. They showed a tendency to adopt extreme positions rather than pro-devolution attitudes as such. We might explain that by the social isolation of the irreligious and the distance between the uneducated or lower social grades and the nervous, naturally hesitant, and incremental business groups; or perhaps they found the subtleties of Kilbrandon's intermediate categories of devolution attitude a mite too clever.

Whatever the details of our explanations it seems reasonable to set social structure down as a cause rather than an effect of devolution attitudes.

That leaves the relationship between devolution, party identification, and social welfare attitudes. We could suppose that party identification caused devolution attitudes. Clearly that is false at least for SNP party identification since it grew rapidly up to 1974 while pro-independence attitudes did not. Moreover, the patterns in Table 3.12 suggested that the Labour and Conservative parties had shed some of their most pro-independence followers to the SNP between 1970 and 1974, indicating that devolution affected partisanship. There is clear evidence, which I shall come to later, that partisanship affected attitudes towards the Scotland Act during the 1979 referendum campaign, but in 1974 and on the general issue of devolution rather than the specifics of the Scotland Act, devolution attitudes appear to have affected voting, not the reverse.

In addition Table 3.12 shows that while the strongest Conservative identifiers were the least pro-independence, the strongest Labour identifiers were the most pro-independence. In other words, strong identification with a British party on balance made people neither more nor less pro-independence.

This range of increasing pro-independence attitude from strong Conservatives through to strong Labour roughly matched the correlation between independence and social welfare attitudes. Perhaps the link was nothing more than a desire to meddle: Margo MacDonald, the SNP's brief victor in Govan, kept describing the SNP as the 'only identifiable party of change'. Those who wished to change the world might not have been too choosy about the direction of change (provided their various policies were not flagrantly self-contradictory). There was also a very specific historical tradition of 'socialism in one country' derived from the feeling that it would be easier to achieve a socialist victory and impose socialist solutions in a separate Scotland than in a united Britain. By the seventies that tradition was at least fifty years old and according to one's interpretation of events perhaps considerably older than that. In particular it was older than the bulk of the current electorate. So in the 1974 electorate the notions of social welfare and independence might have been linked at a subconscious, tradition-based level.

Chapter 4:

Party Images in Scotland

Before moving on from the demand for devolution or other policies to the act of voting, I want in this chapter to consider the question of supply: what was on offer? Or, more significantly, what did ordinary Scots electors *think* was on offer when they went to vote in October 1974?

First, I want to look at pure value-free perceptions especially on Scottish issues: what did people think Labour's policy was on devolution? Had all the vacillations and U-turns earlier in 1974 left ordinary folk without any clear idea at all about the parties' devolution policies? Second, I want to look at public evaluations of the parties: did they think Labour had done a good job on prices? or would the Conservatives have done better? Which party did they think had the best policy on oil? And so on. Last, what was the public image of the relationship between the parties? Was there much difference between them? Was the SNP closer to Labour or the Conservative Party?

Generally, pure perceptions of the parties on British issues were remarkably similar in Scotland and England but evaluations somewhat less so. And on special Scots issues – the EEC, oil and devolution – Scots both perceived and evaluated the parties in a distinctive way.

Only 10 per cent of Scots thought the Conservative party favoured more nationalization despite their recent experience of Rolls Royce and Upper Clyde Shipbuilders, and 39 per cent even thought Conservative policy was one of active denationalization. By contrast 96 per cent thought Labour would nationalize more firms. About half our respondents had no idea what Liberal and SNP policy was on nationalization but among those who claimed to know 26 per cent thought the Liberals would agree to more nationalization and 46 per cent thought the SNP would do so too. On the Labour, Conservative, and Liberal parties these were typical of the responses in England. The interesting Scots feature was that Scots were fairly evenly divided on their view of the SNP and nationalization.

Forty-one per cent thought Conservative policy was to cut the social services, compared with 24 per cent the Liberal Party, 7 per cent Labour, and 11 per cent the SNP. Once again about half confessed ignorance of Liberal and SNP policy but among those with a view twice as many associated a large increase in social spending with the SNP as with Labour.

Liberals had campaigned in favour of some form of EEC at least since the early fifties: I described the SNP's virulent and imaginative anti-EEC campaign at some length in Chapter 1. Yet in 1974, 46 per cent denied any knowledge of Liberal policy on the EEC and 40 per cent had no idea about SNP policy. Two-thirds of those with views thought the Conservatives would stay in Europe on the terms Heath had negotiated and most of the rest thought the Conservatives would go no further than ask for some changes. Most Scots thought Labour wanted to renegotiate the terms and half of them thought Labour would threaten to quit the EEC if it could not get enough changes. Even among those with a view the Liberal image was fuzzy: about half thought the Liberal Party favoured some changes but a quarter thought it did not and a fifth thought it favoured a threat to withdraw. Once again these were fairly general British views of the parties except that Scots thought Labour a bit more pro-EEC than did the English. Among the 60 per cent of Scots who volunteered an opinion on SNP policy, the overwhelming majority thought the party favoured leaving the EEC without any attempt at renegotiation. So the SNP campaign against the EEC had been at least partially successful in identifying the SNP as the only party of outright opposition to membership.

As I noted in Chapter 1, the various parties' policies on North Sea Oil in October 1974 were as follows: the SNP wanted all the revenues for Scotland, the Liberals wanted 50 per cent, the Conservatives had promised a Scottish Development Fund specifically financed by the oil revenues, while Labour had a rather ambiguous position – in some documents it stressed that oil was a British resource but in its election broadcast it described its Scottish Development Agency as being backed by the oil revenues. However, these oil policies had been very recently adopted and many leading politicians – including Heath and

Ross – had made self-contradictory statements about oil revenues within a year or two of each other. So it is not totally surprising that mass perceptions of the oil policies did not match the manifesto promises (Table 4.1).

Eighty-two per cent thought the SNP wanted all the oil revenues for Scotland and most of the rest thought it wanted the lion's share. Few Scots thought any of the other parties would concede all the revenues but many thought they would agree to some Scots bias. Despite the Conservatives' Oil Development Fund only 19 per cent of Scots believed the party would give special benefits to Scotland while 36 per cent thought Labour would. The Liberal Party suffered again from ignorance – 39 per cent claimed not to know its oil policy and of those who claimed to know only half thought it favoured any Scots bias. Very few indeed believed that the Liberal Party favoured a large Scots bias in the oil revenues despite the fact that English Liberal leaders

Table 4.1. General images of party polices on the EEC and Oil

Oil revenues for Scotland	Perceived policy of party					(% DK)
	Brit. share	More	Most	All		
Perceived Con policy	81	15	3	1	100%	(17)
" Lab "	64	26	9	2	100%	(16)
" Lib "	50	32	16	2	100%	(39)
" SNP "	1	2	14	82	100%	(6)

EEC Membership	Stay	Stay & Change	Change or leave	Leave		
Perceived Con policy	68	27	2	2	100%	(13)
" Lab "	5	43	42	10	100%	(14)
" Lib "	26	47	20	7	100%	(46)
" SNP "	5	10	14	72	100%	(32)

Note: Percentages based on all respondents with a view. See text for variations of perception across party groups, etc.

like Thorpe had explicitly backed Scotland's claim to 50 per cent of the oil.

Significantly, Labour and Conservative voters had a relatively pro-Scots view of their own party: 35 per cent of Scots Conservative voters thought the Conservative Party would give Scotland some special oil benefit; and 48 per cent of Labour voters but only 35 per cent of Conservative voters thought the Labour Party would. Strangely enough the SNP's own voters were markedly less inclined to believe their party wanted all the oil for Scotland. Only 75 per cent of SNP voters compared to 86 per cent of Labour and Conservative voters thought the SNP wanted all the oil.

The parties had been least consistent on constitutional questions. Until the sixties Labour had been generally more sympathetic to the idea of political devolution but the Conservatives had delivered much more in terms of administrative devolution. In the late sixties Heath and Home had persuaded the Conservatives to propose a form of Scottish Assembly but failed to deliver after the 1970 election. Labour had adopted a rigidly anti-devolution line from 1968 until the day after the February 1974 election but then had embraced devolution with enthusiasm. Scots electors could be forgiven if they claimed not to know party policies on devolution. But apart from the usual exception of the Liberal Party, Scots electors felt quite able to assign devolution policies to the parties though they were significantly less able to specify the devolution policies of candidates in their local constituencies.

First of all we asked respondents to associate each party with one or other of the four Kilbrandon options – the status quo, more understanding, a new system for more decisions, or self-government (Table 4.2). Half our respondents thought the Conservative Party favoured the status quo and another quarter felt it offered nothing more than more understanding of Scots problems by the government in London. Labour succeeded remarkably well in establishing itself as the party of devolution. Recall that its devolution policy was only finally adopted by the Dalintober conference in mid-August 1974 and that it had fought the February election as the only anti-devolution party in Scotland. Naturally it failed to convince everyone that it was now a devolutionary party. But 40 per cent thought it was and only 25

Table 4.2. General images of party policies on devolution

Devolution spectrum	Perceived policy of party					(% DK)
	SQ	MU	MD	SG		
Perceived Con policy	50	27	21	1	100%	(12)
" Lab "	25	32	40	2	100%	(12)
" Lib "	18	28	48	6	100%	(32)
" SNP "	2	1	5	93	100%	(5)

Assembly position	Very much against	Somewhat against	Somewhat for	Very much for		
Perceived Con policy	18	37	39	6	100%	(18)
" Lab "	10	26	53	12	100%	(17)
" Lib "	8	21	58	14	100%	(35)
" SNP "	3	1	2	95	100%	(8)

Candidate strongly for assembly?	No	DK	Yes		% do not know his name
MP	24	44	32	100%	(21)
Con candidate	26	60	17	100%	(55)
Lab "	29	48	23	100%	(39)
Lib "	13	56	31	100%	(80)
SNP "	0	9	91	100%	(57)

Note: Percentage based on all respondents with a view on party policy and all respondents who knew a candidate's name. See text for variations of perception across party groups, etc.

per cent thought it still favoured the status quo. Almost everyone knew that the SNP was a party of independence, and the only party of independence. That was a significant change since 1968 when Gallup found almost a third of Scots thought the SNP stood for devolution rather than independence. But a third of Scots had no idea about Liberal policy and despite its century-old commitment to federalism only slightly over half of those with a view thought it favoured any constitutional change. Despite winning six Scots constituencies in the sixties and holding three in the seventies the Scots Liberal Party had a public policy profile so fuzzy as to be almost invisible.

We also asked a more specific question on whether each party was in favour of a Scottish Assembly and whether it was 'very much' or only 'somewhat' for or against it. Despite the fact that Labour and Conservative Assembly plans had been drawn up partly or even mainly to dish the SNP almost everyone thought the SNP as a party was very much in favour of an Assembly. Clearly the party had been completely successful in picturing itself as moderate in style though extremist in its ultimate ambitions. No one saw the SNP as an intransigent nationalist party out to wreck moderate plans for constitutional change. On balance electors thought the Conservative Party was against an Assembly while two-thirds thought Labour was in favour. About a fifth thought the Conservatives were very much against but few thought Labour was either very much in favour or very much against. Apart from the usual 35 per cent who knew nothing about the Liberal position the general view of the Liberal Party Assembly policy was close to people's view of Labour.

We also asked whether people knew their MP's name and if so whether he had been strongly in favour of an Assembly. Then we repeated these questions about the local constituency candidate for each party. Four-fifths knew the name of their MP but half of them knew nothing about his Assembly policy. By only 32 to 24 per cent they thought their local MPs were strong supporters of an Assembly. Labour candidates – probably because so many were elected – were the best known: 61 per cent knew their Labour candidate, about 44 per cent knew the Conservative and SNP candidate, and only 20 per cent knew the Liberal. Among those who knew their candidates' names, SNP candidates were almost universally recognized as strong Assemblymen but over half the respondents did not know the views of their Conservative, Labour, or Liberal candidates. On balance they thought Liberal candidates were strongly pro-Assembly but Labour and especially Conservative candidates were not.

Over all, therefore, the electors overwhelmingly identified the SNP and its candidates as strong supporters of an Assembly. They had hazy ideas about the Liberals. They thought that neither the Labour Party, the Conservative Party, nor Labour and Conservative candidates were strongly in favour of an Assembly. But on balance they thought Labour was at least somewhat favourable to the idea while the Conservative Party was not.

For its own voters each party had a more pro-Assembly, pro-devolution, or pro-independence image than it had in the eyes of the electorate generally. Though half our respondents thought the Conservative Party favoured the status quo, only 27 per cent of Conservative voters thought so. Similarly only 18 per cent of Labour voters and 8 per cent of Liberals thought their own parties favoured the status quo. And in contrast to the pattern on oil-policy images, a slightly higher percentage of SNP voters thought their own party committed to outright independence – it could not possibly have been much higher because so many people in every voting group knew it as the party of independence.

On the specific proposal of an Assembly 70 per cent of Conservative voters, 73 per cent of Labour, 88 per cent of Liberals, and 97 per cent of SNP voters thought their own parties favoured an Assembly. By contrast, only 32 per cent of Labour voters thought the Conservative Party was pro-Assembly, though as many as 62 per cent of Conservatives admitted the Labour Party was so.

People's own attitudes to devolution had much less effect than their partisanship on their perceptions of the parties' devolution policies: 46 per cent of status quo respondents thought the Conservative Party was pro-Assembly while 41 per cent of pro-independence respondents thought so. The corresponding figures for Labour policy were 54 and 69 per cent. Thus there was no consistent tendency for respondents to pull perceptions of all the parties into line with their own devolution views though there was a very strong tendency for them to see their own party as particularly pro-devolution.

So far I have dealt with perceptions that were superficially value free and non-evaluative, though the patterns on devolution in particular suggested that people did consider it a mark of approval when they associated a party with a devolution policy. But we also asked explicitly evaluative questions.

On prices and strikes we asked whether Labour had handled the issue well and whether the Conservatives would have handled it well. Both in Scotland and England Labour was ahead on both issues. On prices Labour was ahead by 10 per cent in both countries but in Scotland that was because both parties got about 8 per cent less approval than in England. On strikes Labour was ahead by a margin of 16 per cent in Scotland but even that was considerably less than in England.

Labour was also ahead on unemployment, pensions, and housing by an average of 22 per cent in Scotland but on these issues Labour's lead in Scotland was close to twice as large as in England.

On six issues we simply asked which party had the best policy and let our respondents choose any of the four parties or 'don't know'. Two were the ideological issues of nationalization and public spending on the social services; one the contemporary question of wage controls; and three were the special Scots issues of EEC membership, oil, and devolution.

Significantly more people had a party preference on devolution than on the other issues where between 35 and 40 per cent replied 'don't know'. Among those with a preference the Conservatives had a three-to-two lead on nationalization balanced by a Labour lead of three to two on public spending for social services. On wage controls Labour had only a marginal lead over the Conservatives (Table 4.3).

Table 4.3. Party preferences on selected issues

	Party preferred on issue					
	Con	Lab	Lib	SNP	DK	
Nationalization	35	22	4	5	35	100 %
Social services	22	32	2	5	39	100 %
Wage controls	28	31	3	3	35	100 %
EEC membership	20	31	3	9	37	100 %
Oil	13	17	3	26	40	100 %
Devolution	15	21	7	30	27	100 %

On all these Britain-wide issues only a handful of Scots preferred the SNP. Perhaps that was only to be expected on this old Labour – Conservative battleground but the SNP must have been disappointed that less than one Scot in ten preferred the SNP on EEC policy after all their intensive campaigning since 1970 and all their constituency polls showing popular support for the nationalists' EEC policy.

However, the SNP came out top on the more distinctively Scots issues of North Sea oil and devolution. And this was somewhat paradoxical. Overwhelmingly, Scots saw the SNP as a party that wanted all the oil revenues and full independence for Scotland. Yet relatively few Scots themselves wanted these policies. The most popular devolution policy was devolution itself, not independence, and the most popular oil policy was for only a modest Scots bias in the oil revenues. Only a fifth of Scots wanted independence and only a tenth wanted all the oil. So their stated SNP preference on oil and devolution must have depended upon a comparison with the other parties and a comparison that involved trustworthiness as well as policy differences. Devolution was a Labour policy, not an SNP one, yet in 1974 the SNP could be relied upon to press for devolution while Labour had still to prove its trustworthiness on the issue.

At the most general level the 1974 SES asked slightly different evaluative questions about the different parties which makes comparison difficult. But while 18 per cent said they could 'rarely' rely on Labour governments to do what was right, and 27 per cent could 'rarely' rely on the Conservatives, only 16 per cent felt that SNP election successes had been bad for Scotland. There was a climate of general approval for the SNP on everything to do with Scotland. After 1974 that climate changed dramatically.

SNP votes had gone up from 11 per cent in 1970 to over 30 per cent in October 1974. Naturally, people were a little slower to identify with the SNP than to vote for it. Using Michigan's identification question, 'generally speaking, do you think of yourself as Conservative, Labour, Liberal, Scottish Nationalist, or what?' and excluding a very few respondents who did not identify with any party, we found that in the three months after the October 1974 election the percentages identifying with each party were: Labour 41, Conservatives 31, SNP 20, and Liberals 8. If Labour and the Conservatives were worried by the fact that many of their 1974 voters preferred the SNP on Scottish issues they could take heart from the fact that many SNP voters still thought of themselves as Labour people or Conservative people. By coincidence party identification percentages just after the 1974 election almost exactly equal the party shares of the vote at the 1979 election.

Roughly a third of Scots saw a 'great deal' of difference between the parties while another third saw 'not much': the remaining third saw 'some'. Compared to the English, the Scots claimed to see rather less difference between the parties despite the fact that one of their major parties was compaigning for the break-up of the Union. Possibly, in answering the question, both

Scots and English were focusing on the two great parties of government.

Like the English, about four times as many Scots thought the Liberal Party was nearer to the Conservatives as thought it nearer to Labour. Only a quarter were unable to answer the question. When they were asked about the SNP, however, almost half our respondents were unable to place it nearer to one party than the other, but by 37 to 17 per cent the remainder placed it nearer Labour. This matched their views of party policy on all the Scottish issues and on welfare spending (Table 4.4).

Table 4.4. Perceived party differences

	% Perceiving party as closer to			
	Con	DK	Lab	
Perception of Liberal Party	57	28	15	100%
Perception of SNP	17	46	37	100%

	Second choice				
	Con	Lab	Lib	SNP	(% would not vote)
Second choice of Liberal voters	46	25	–	30	100% (19)
Second choice of SNP voters	31	35	33	–	100% (14)

It is also matched the pattern of second choices for voting. In Scotland as in England Liberal voters favoured the Conservatives rather than Labour as their second choice. Indeed, in Scotland the bias was greater because many Liberals had the SNP as a second choice and compared to England this appears to have been mainly at the expense of Labour. Conversely, the second choices of SNP voters split roughly equally between Labour, the Conservatives, and the Liberals though Labour was top and the Conservatives bottom. Finally, we asked people whether there was any party which they actually preferred but for various reasons, like the fear of a wasted vote, they had not voted for. About 8 per cent of Scots preferred the SNP, but had failed to vote for it and slightly more English felt the same way about the Liberals. But while these potential English Liberals had actually split their votes between Labour and Conservatives, the potential SNP voters had actually cast mainly Labour votes. Labour's close connection with the SNP was thus a source of danger.

Chapter 5:

Voting – I: Introduction, Social, and Partisan Alignments

For the first ten years after the War, third parties did badly at elections. And increasingly badly. So that by 1955 97 per cent of both Scots and English votes went either to Labour or the Conservatives. Moreover, throughout these ten years the Labour–Conservative balance in Scotland was almost the same as in England with just a hint of a Conservative advantage in Scotland.

But after 1955 Scots and English voting patterns diverged. National differences were moderate till 1970 but large in 1974 and 1979. According to our choice of measure the largest national difference was either in October 1974 or 1979. In 1974 the SNP took 30 per cent of Scots votes and Labour beat the Conservatives by 10 per cent more in Scotland than in England. In 1979 the SNP share of the vote fell to only 17 per cent but

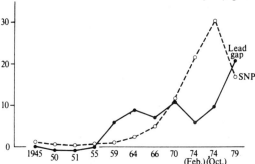

Notes: (1) Continuous line shows difference between the Labour per cent lead over the Conservatives in Scotland and England. Positive values indicate that Labour did better in Scotland. On purely social class grounds Scotland could be expected to have a Labour lead about 8 per cent higher than in England; (2) hatched line shows SNP per cent of Scots vote; (3) in addition the level of turn out in Scotland was 4½ per cent below the English level in 1945 and stayed lower until 1964. In 1970, October 1974 and 1979 Scottish turnout was 1 or 2 per cent higher than in England

Fig. 5.1. Two measures of the difference between Scots and English Voting, 1945–79

Table 5.1. Scots votes and MPs elected since 1945

	Per cent of vote					MPs elected				
	Con	Lab	Lib	SNP	Turn-out per cent	Con	Lab	Lib	SNP	Other
1945	41	48	5	1	69	27	37	–	–	7
1950	45	46	7	0	81	31	37	2	–	1
1951	49	48	3	0	81	35	35	1	–	–
1955	50	47	2	1	75	36	34	1	–	–
1959	47	47	4	1	78	31	38	1	–	1
1964	41	49	8	2	78	24	43	4	–	–
1966	38	50	7	5	76	20	46	5	–	–
1970 Feb	38	45	6	11	74	23	44	3	1	–
1974 Oct	33	37	8	22	79	21	40	3	7	–
1974	25	36	8	30	75	16	41	3	11	–
1979	31	42	9	17	77	22	44	3	2	–

Notes: (1) The 7 'other' MPs in 1945 were 1 Communist, 3 ILP, 2 Independent Liberals, and 1 Independent Conservative. In addition the Combined Scottish Universities elected an independent; (2) the 'other' in 1950 was elected as an Independent Liberal but joined the Conservative allied Liberal Unionists; (3) the 'other' in 1959 was an Independent Conservative; (4) Labour contested 68 seats in 1945 but the full 71 thereafter. The Conservatives and allies contested 68 in 1945 and 1950, 70 in 1951, 1959, and 1970 but the full set in other years. This means that Conservative support relative to Labour was underestimated by the votes in 1950, 1951, 1959, and 1970; (5) the Liberals contested as few as 5 seats in 1955 and as many as 68 in October 1974. The SNP had 8 candidates in 1945 but never more than 5 in the fifties rising to 15 in 1964, 23 in 1966, 65 in 1970, 70 in February 1974, and 71 thereafter. Source: *British Electoral Facts* (Craig).

Labour beat the Conservatives by a huge 21 per cent more in Scotland than in England, or to put it another way Labour won by 10½ per cent in Scotland and the Conservatives by 10½ per cent in England (Fig.5.1).

So, as Table 5.1 shows, national voting differences grew from nothing in the early post-war years and exploded in the mid to late seventies.

But while true, that way of looking at Scots and English voting is misleading. As I shall show in Chapter 8 there is good reason to expect on purely social-class grounds that Labour should beat the Conservatives by about 8 per cent more in Scotland than in England. And over the full span of elections from 1923 to 1979 Labour had just that margin on the average. Before the First World War, the Liberal Party usually had an even larger Scottish advantage than Labour enjoyed after 1923. Quite simply, Britain-wide uniformity in the class–partisan relationship implied that Scotland should be somewhat less Conservative and more Labour than England.

Viewed from this standpoint Table 5.1 suggests that, relative to England, Scotland gave Labour a 'normal' margin of votes from 1959 to 1974. After allowing for the effect of class differences, truly Scottish national effects on Labour–Conservative voting were only large in 1945–55 and in 1979 – pro-Conservative in the first decade after the War and pro-Labour in 1979.

In October 1974 Labour did only a little better than could be expected in Scotland. The really distinctive elements of Scots voting in October 1974 were the larger vote given to third parties – 39 per cent in Scotland against 20 per cent in England – and the fact that over three-quarters of the Scots third-party vote went to the SNP instead of the Liberals. Indeed, with the exception of three Liberal-held seats and one near miss in a former Liberal seat, Scots Liberals averaged only 6 per cent and they lost sixty-one of their deposits.

Without too much of a distortion the analysis can be simplified by treating the Scottish vote in the autumn of 1974 as a three-way Con–Lab–SNP split. I will compare that with the three-way Con–Lab–Lib split in England.

Tables 5.2 and 5.3 show that even at times when third parties could expect to do particularly well – in the parliamentary mid-term – Scotland usually had no more than a three-way split. Neither Liberals nor Nationalists saved a deposit at a by-election until the Liberal John Bannerman stood for Inverness at the very end of 1954. From then until the end of 1961 there was usually a third option – a Liberal candidate – at Scots by-elections and he could expect around a quarter of the votes: a substantial but unprofitable level of support. Bannerman himself marked the end of this period with 41 per cent at Paisley – almost, but not quite enough to win the seat. Four years later David Steel won the Roxburgh by-election but by then a Liberal success at a by-election or even a Liberal candidate was quite exceptional. From the end of 1961 to the end of 1963 SNP candidates appeared twice as often as Liberals and gained rather more votes.

During the 1966–70 parliament only one Liberal fought a by-election and he got less than 2 per cent of the vote, while SNP candidates fought every by-election and got between 20 and 46 per cent. The next Liberal by-election candidate did not appear

Table 5.2 Scots by-elections since 1945

Year	Month	Constituency	% swing to Con	% Lib	% SNP	
1945–50 Parliament						
1945	March	Edinburgh East	−2.0	–	–	
1946	Feb.	South Ayrshire	−2.3	–	–	
	Feb.	Cathcart	−1.1	–	10.4	
	Aug.	Bridgeton	ILP held seat, this time with Labour opponent			
	Nov.	Aberdeen South	2.6	–	–	
	Dec.	Kilmarnock	−4.2	–	7.8	
1947	Nov.	Edinburgh East	1.4	10.1	5.0	
1948	Jan.	Camlachie	Labour re-took seat by intervening against ILP			
	Feb.	Paisley	Lab. held against MacCormick who had Con, Lib and Scottish Convention support			
	Sep.	Gorbals	Intervening Communist took 17%, no Lib, no SNP			
	Oct.	Stirling Burghs	3.0	–	8.2	
	Nov.	Hillhead	5.9	–	–	
1950–51 Parliament						
1950	Apr.	Dunbarton West	0.4	–	–	
	Oct.	Scotstoun	1.5	–	–	
1951–5 Parliament						
1952	July	Dundee East	−6.5	–	7.4	
1954	Aug.	Edinburgh East	−3.6	–	–	
	Apr.	Motherwell	−1.3	–		Communist 4.3%
	Dec.	Inverness	5.1	36.0		Lib Intervention
1955	Jan.	Edinburgh North	0.6	–	–	
1955–9 Parliament						
1955	Dec.	Greenock	−2.3	–	–	
1957	May	Edinburgh South	−10.2	23.5	–	Lib intervention
1958	Mar.	Kelvingrove	−8.6	–	(7.6)	Unofficial Home Rule candidate
	Jun.	Argyll	−7.1	27.5	–	Lib intervention
	Nov.	Aberdeen East	−7.8	24.3	–	Lib intervention
1959	Apr.	Galloway	−3.7	25.7	–	Lib intervention

Table 5.2 continued

Year	Month	Constituency	% swing to Con	% Lib	% SNP	
1959–64 Parliament						
1960	May	Edinburgh North	−2.1	15.5	–	Lib intervention
1961	Apr.	Paisley	−8.8	41.4	–	Lib intervention
	Nov.	East Fife	−9.4	26.1	–	Lib intervention
	Nov.	Bridgeton	−5.0	–	18.7	
1962	Jun.	West Lothian	−9.5	10.8	23.3	
	Nov.	Woodside	−6.1	–	11.1	
1963	Nov.	Kinross	−4.6	19.5	7.3	SNP had 15% at 1959 general election
	Nov.	Dundee West	−4.9	–	7.4	
	Dec.	Dumfries	−7.2	10.9	9.7	
1964	May	Rutherglen	−7.6	–	–	
1964–66 Parliament						
1965	Mar.	Roxburgh	0.2	49.2	–	Lib had 39% at 1964 general election.
1966–70 Parliament						
1967	Mar.	Pollock	5.3	1.9	28.2	
	Nov.	Hamilton	6.7	–	46.0	
1969	Oct.	Gorbals	8.8	–	25.0	
1970	Mar.	South Ayrshire	3.0	–	20.4	
1970–4 Parliament						
1971	Sept.	Stirling Burghs	−5.9	–	34.6	SNP had 15% at 1970 general election.
1973	Mar.	Dundee East	−0.8	8.3	30.2	
	Nov.	Edinburgh North	−0.5	18.4	18.9	
	Nov.	Govan	2.7	8.2	41.9	
1974 Parliament						
1974		No Scots by-elections				

Note: See also Table 1.1 on local government elections in the late sixties and early seventies. Source: *British Electoral Facts* (Craig)

Table 5.3. Voting   intentions   in   Scottish
opinion polls 1967–74

Survey organization and date		Voting percentages			
		Con	Lab	Lib	SNP
NOP	Nov. 1967	25	41	9	24
Express	Feb. 1968	35	23	5	37
Gallup	Mar. 1968	31	30	6	33
BBC	May 1968	30	22	4	43
Express	May 1968	31	29	4	35
Gallup	Sept. 1968	36	28	5	31
NOP	Jan. 1969	34	39	6	21
Express	Mar. 1969	40	32	2	26
Express	Apr. 1969	43	31	4	22
Gallup	Mar. 1970	43	38	7	13
ORC	9 Feb. 1974	40	36	9	15
MORI	13 Feb. 1974	40	34	9	17
ORC	23Feb. 1974	32	38	11	18
ORC	Apr. 1974	29	39	7	24
System Three	Apr. 1974	26	36	7	30
System Three	June 1974	28	39	7	25
System Three	Aug. 1974	25	43	8	23
ORC	20 Sept. 1974	24	41	12	23
System Three	27 Sept. 1974	25	39	6	30
ORC	27 Sept. 1974	22	38	11	28
ORC	5 Oct. 1974	23	43	10	25
System Three	5 Oct. 1974	22	33	8	36

Note: The September 1968 Gallup survey is particularly interesting because it asked three voting intention questions that produced
very different responses:

Q: Which party would you support?	Con	Lab	Lib	SNP
(1) in a by-election	32	27	6	35
(2) at a general election	36	28	5	31
(3) if your vote might decide which party formed the government for the next five years	45	40	2	13

in Scotland until English Liberals had already won by-elections
at Rochdale and at Sutton. But in 1973, despite equalling a poor
SNP performance in Edinburgh North, Scots Liberals could
come nowhere near their English colleagues. While English
Liberals won five seats and did very well in several others, Scots
Liberal candidates averaged only 12 per cent of the vote.

Scots opinion polls in the late sixties and again in 1974
frequently put the SNP in first or second place but never gave the
Liberals more than 11 per cent of voting preferences.

To a reasonable approximation Scots voting split only three ways in 1974, as it usually had done in the past. And the three-way split excluded the Liberals as it usually had for the previous ten years.

Even a three-way split presents some problems of analysis. The traditional method is to look at the pattern of Labour versus Conservative support, then move on to a separate discussion of the minor party or parties. Unfortunately the SNP was not a minor party in 1974: it had beaten the Conservatives into third place by a margin of 6 per cent. Moreover, Scots voters were faced with a three-way choice, not a sequence of more restricted choices. Some of their voting alignments were indeed Labour versus Conservative or SNP versus the rest, but others were not. In any case it is vastly preferable to let the evidence tell us what the political nature of alignments was in 1974 rather than impose our preconceptions on the data.

So I will make use of a special technique for the analysis of three-party systems. It may look unfamiliar at first but the method has been around for a long time. What was missing until the seventies was a genuinely three-way split to analyze. In the period from 1931 to 1970 British elections were so much a two-party battle that there was little need to use three-way methods. The minor parties were minor and were more interesting for their effects on the two-party balance than for any other reason. None of this was true for Scotland in the seventies.

The basic tool of analysis is a symmetric representation of election outcomes in three-party systems. If we take an equi-lateral triangle and label the corners Lab, Con, SNP, then we can use points within the triangle to represent three-way splits of votes (Fig. 5.2). Any possible division of 100 per cent into a Labour, Conservative, and SNP percentage (assuming for the moment that no other candidates get any votes at all) can be represented by a point within the triangle. Conversely any point within the triangle can be interpreted as a specific three-way split.

Points near to the middle of the triangle correspond to voting splits close to 33 per cent Lab, 33 per cent Con, and 33 per cent SNP. Points near one of the corners correspond to voting splits in which one party gets nearly all the votes. Points near to a side of the triangle correspond to splits in which two parties get sizeable votes but the third does not. Figure 5.2 illustrates this triangular

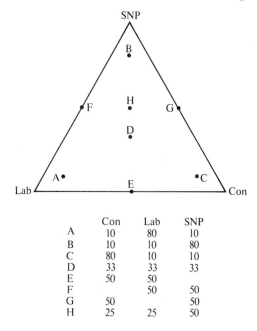

	Con	Lab	SNP
A	10	80	10
B	10	10	80
C	80	10	10
D	33	33	33
E	50	50	
F		50	50
G	50		50
H	25	25	50

Fig. 5.2 Triangular representation of three-way voting splits

representation by showing the points corresponding to half a dozen different voting splits. Technical details of this method are given in the Appendix but readers can follow the text without troubling themselves with technical details.

The next step is to develop a 'political compass' which can be used to measure the difference between one election outcome and another.

Two different election results correspond to two different points within the triangle. The difference between those election results has two properties: *size* and *direction*. First how big is the difference between the two results? How different are they? This is what is meant by *size* and it is measured by the length of the line joining the two points in the triangular diagram. Second, what sort of difference is there between the two election results? Did the SNP make a gain at the expense of both other parties? Did one party score a gain primarily at the expense of just one other party? This is what is meant by the political *direction* of a difference between two election results and it is measured by the angle of the line joining the two election points in the triangle.

Angles can only be measured and understood when they are angles relative to some particular, easily interpretable direction. One of the properties of the triangular representation is as follows: any gain by one of the three parties which is balanced by equal losses from both the other two corresponds to a movement perpendicularly away from one of the sides of the triangle. By contrast, any gain by one party which is completely balanced by a loss from just one of the other two parties corresponds to a movement parallel to one of the sides of the triangle.

Figure 5.3 shows the point near the centre of the triangle which corresponds to the actual October 1974 election result. Radiating from it are a dozen arrows showing how that point would move if the three parties made various gains and losses. For example, if the SNP gained 20 per cent more than in October and both

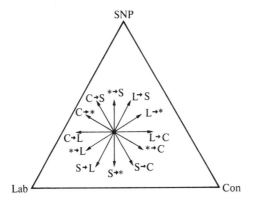

The central point in the political compass represents the three way voting split that occurred throughout Scotland as a whole, i.e. Con 25, Lab 36, SNP 30. Each arrow represents a single party gaining 20 per cent more votes either entirely from one other party or equally from both other parties (which then each lose 10 per cent). Symbols S→C mean 'SNP loss to Conservative', etc. and * stands for 'both other parties'. So that *→C means Labour and the SNP each losing 10 per cent and the Conservatives gaining 20 per cent. For England, the letter R is used for Liberal voting

Fig. 5.3. Deviations from the over-all Scots voting pattern of October 1974: the political compass

Labour and Conservative dropped by 10 per cent each, then the point would move vertically upwards. We should call such a change a *unipolar* SNP gain. On the other hand, if the SNP vote went up by 20 per cent and the Conservative vote down by 20 per cent, leaving the Labour vote unchanged, the point would move upwards and to the left. We should call that a *bipolar* SNP gain from the Conservatives. Symbolically we write such a bipolar change as C→S, while a unipolar SNP gain can be written * →S where * stands for 'both others'.

Altogether there are twelve bipolar or unipolar changes. They occur at intervals of 30° round the political compass and are described by the symbols shown in Fig. 5.3. These are the 'points' of our political compass like north, south, east and west on the geographic compass. Very few actual political changes or political differences will be in directions which are exactly on one of the points of our compass just as very few ships sail due east. But the points of the compass help us to interpret the directions of those political changes that do occur. The Appendix shows how to calculate the size and direction of any difference between election results in an approximately three-party system. The size is calculated as a percentage. When one party gains entirely at the expense of just one of the other parties this measure of size equals the traditional Butler measure of swing, i.e. it equals the percentage gained by one party and lost by the other. The direction is calculated in degrees. In terms of Fig.5.3 zero degrees (and 360°) is vertically downward; 90° is to the right, 180° vertically upwards, and 270° is to the left.

For my initial overview of voting patterns I shall measure the difference between the voting split in some subgroup of BES/SES respondents and the over-all voting split in the whole sample. So, if some group of senior managers were more Conservative than average, but no more or less SNP, then the *direction* of their political deviance would be at 90°, and its *size* would depend upon just how politically deviant they were. The tables show the size (in per cent) and the deviation (in degrees) of each group's political deviance from the overall Scots average. To help interpret that direction, the Tables also show the nearest point on the political compass to the direction of the deviance. And as a further guide, I will also give the full party shares of the vote for selected subgroups of respondents.

I do not want to get into the complexities of statistical calculations of standard errors but two points are necessary for proper interpretation of the Tables. First, the reliability of both size and direction calculations depends upon sample size. This is true for any survey data, even simple percentages. Calculations based on small sub-samples of respondents – senior managers for example – are necessarily subject to a lot more sampling error than those based on large sub-samples – the manual working class for example. The second statistical point is unique to three-way calculations and it is this: the realiability of *direction* calculations is inversely proportional to the *size*. Thus when groups deviate *very little* from the average voting pattern the *direction* of that deviance is statistically insignificant. We should only pay attention to estimates of the direction of political deviance when that deviance is relatively large.

THE BRITISH DIMENSION

While Conservative and Labour parties fought the election throughout mainland Britain, the SNP was restricted to Scotland (though it had English branches and occasionally threatened to put up candidates in England). How then can we compare voting patterns in Scotland and England? We could treat the Labour versus Conservative division as the only point of comparison between the nations, but it was surely more than coincidence that produced simultaneous surges of support for the English Liberals and the SNP in February 1974. While it would be false to suggest that English Liberal and SNP votes were exact equivalents they had enough in common to make comparison worth while. That comparison reveals both similarities and differences.

So when comparing Scots and English voting in October 1974 I will treat the English vote as a three-way split between Conservative, Labour, and Liberal and construct an English political compass in which the English Liberal votes take the place of SNP votes. It is necessary to remember however that the point in the triangle representing the over-all English voting split is displaced downwards and to the right compared to the over-all Scottish voting split because the English gave 14 per cent more votes to the Conservatives, only 4 per cent more to Labour, and 10 per cent less to the English Liberals than the SNP. That made

England much more Conservative and less 'third party' than Scotland even when the only 'third party' counted in the Scots analysis is the SNP.

CLASS ALIGNMENTS

Peter Pulzer's famous claim that 'the basis of British politics is class – all else is embellishment and detail' looked a little out of date in 1974, especially in Scotland. Nationalism and the SNP were far more than 'embellishment and detail'. But the nationalist dimension was superimposed on Scots voting alignments without destroying old cleavages. Political divisions simply became more complex. Class remained a very powerful predictor of Scots political partisanship.

Table 5.4 and Fig. 5.4 display the patterns of class voting in Scotland and England using the three-way split technique. Let

Table 5.4. Patterns of class voting in Scotland and England

Deviation from over-all national voting patterns by:	Size (%)		Direction (degrees)		Approx. direction (nearest point)	
	Scot.	Eng.	Scot.	Eng.	Scot.	Eng.
Class identification:						
spontaneous middle	15.5	14.6	93	101	L → C	L → C
forced middle	22.0	20.9	84	92	L → C	L → C
forced working	4.3	3.4	224	261	C → S	C → L
spontaneous working	16.4	22.2	277	281	C → L	C → L
Head of household social grade:						
1. Higher managerial	21.7	29.4	90	101	L → C	L → C
2. Lower managerial	19.0	14.5	103	112	L → C	L→*
3. Supervisory non-manual	15.9	17.5	93	91	L → C	L→C
4. Lower non-manual	6.5	6.6	96	74	L → C	* →C
5. Skilled manual	10.3	12.8	253	270	C→*	C→L
6. Unskilled manual	18.0	15.5	289	289	* →L	* →L

	Scotland				England		
Full voting patterns:	Con	Lab	Lib	SNP	Con	Lab	Lib
In households of higher managers	46	15	12	27	64	10	26
" " " unskilled workers	14	61	2	24	27	59	14

me use them both to exemplify the method and describe class alignments.

The first two columns in Table 5.4 show the size of class effects in Scotland and England. Naturally there was not complete agreement, but the similarities were more obvious than the differences. Despite the impact of the SNP and special Scottish issues, class effects in the two nations were broadly similar in size. Though a little larger in England than Scotland the important point is that class effects were large in both nations in 1974.

The third and fourth columns show the political directions of class effects. Again very similar in the two nations. Neglecting the 'forced working' and 'lower non-manual' entries, where the size of effects was small and directions consequently indeterminate, directions never differed by more than 17°. The last two columns show the nearest compass point and are just a rough but easily understood approximation to columns three and four.

Figure 5.4 illustrates Table 5.4. Notice that the point from which English class deviances are measured is not the same as for Scotland since the over-all English voting split was more Conservative, less 'third party', than in Scotland. Broadly

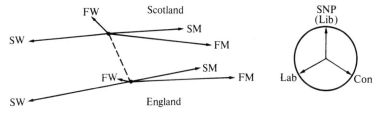

(a) Effects of class identification (F=forced choice, S=spontaneous)

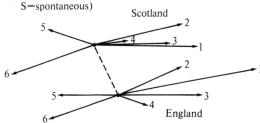

(b) Effects of social grade (1=senior managers, 6 =unskilled manuals)

Fig. 5.4. Class alignments

speaking, the English pattern of class voting looked very much like the Scottish, but the whole pattern was displaced downwards and to the right.

Now let us go through Table 5.4 in more detail. Self-identification with the middle class made respondents more Conservative and less Labour while self-identification with the working class had the opposite effect. However, class identification made little difference to respondents' tendencies to vote SNP or English Liberal. Hence the approximately horizontal lines in Fig. 5.4 and the L→C or C→L directions in Table 5.4. In both countries those who were reluctant to accept a class label but opted for 'middle' when forced to make a choice were the most Conservative group. By contrast, the most Labour were those who spontaneously identified with the working class.

Generally the four non-manual social grades were pro-Conservative and anti-Labour and manuals were the reverse. But in both countries unskilled manual workers were purely pro-Labour: they did not support the SNP in Scotland nor the Liberals in England as much as the national average. Hence the * →L entries in Table 5.4 and the arrows which point downwards as well as to the left in Fig. 5.4.

In England, middle-class categories – particularly the top two social grades and middle-class identifiers – deviated more to the Liberals than their counterparts in Scotland deviated to the SNP. Hence the steeper angles in Table 5.4 and Fig. 5.4. Conversely, skilled workers in Scotland deviated towards the SNP as well as Labour while their English equivalents did not deviate towards the Liberals.

The fact that class effects were a little larger in England than Scotland can also be seen from Fig. 5.4. The English diagrams are a little larger, more spread out from left to right. But the difference is relatively small.

OTHER OCCUPATIONAL INFLUENCES

As I have argued at length elsewhere the basis of class, or at least 'class' as it affects British partisanship, is the division between employers and managers on the one side and non-managerial or even anti-managerial groups on the other. However, several other occupational variables also relate to party choice without necessarily being closely linked to the managerial–non-managerial division.

Trade union membership is perhaps the most closely connected to class but there are also divisions between the self-employed and employees, between public and private sector employment, divisions according to size of establishment and experience of unemployment (Table 5.5).

As a trade union party Labour could expect to get a particularly high vote among trade unionists though many unions affiliated only to the TUC and not to the Labour Party. Self-employed people could be expected to vote for a party which stressed self-reliance, though whether that would be the Conservatives or the SNP was an open question. Public-sector

Table 5.5. Voting and occupational variables in Scotland and England

Deviation from over-all national voting patterns by	Size		Direction		Approx. Direction	
	Scot.	Eng.	Scot.	Eng.	Scot.	Eng.
T.U. connection						
Respondent in TU	13.1	17.7	267	280	C → L	C → L
Other family in TU	7.5	9.5	218	253	C → S	C → *
No TU connection	9.4	10.4	76	93	* → C	L → C
Self-employed						
Respondent self-employed	30.9	29.9	105	87	L → C	L → C
Respondent employee	4.4	3.9	258	267	C → L	C → L
Respondent employed in private sector	4.4	3.2	220	292	C → S	* → L
Respondent employed in public sector	7.6	6.4	292	243	* → L	C → *
Size of establishment: small	11.5	9.7	139	94	L → S	L → C
large	7.1	6.0	280	275	C → L	C → L
All those with job	4.5	3.9	256	269	C → L	C → L
Respondent or family have been unemployed.	14.8	16.5	227	266	C → S	C → L

Full voting patterns	Scotland				England		
	Con	Lab	Lib	SNP	Con	Lab	Lib
Workers in small establishments	27	25	10	38	48	32	20
Workers in large establishments	20	47	6	28	33	48	19
With experience of unemployment	8	43	9	39	23	57	20

employees should favour Labour as the party of public expenditure. People in small workshops might be less socialized into accepting trade union norms and, like the self-employed, favour one or other of the parties of self-reliance. While the Conservatives claimed to have the policies to promote growth and reduce unemployment, Labour had a fairly long-established image as the party more sympathetic to those without a job and in need of immediate help. But Labour's concern for the unemployed was being challenged in 1974 by the SNP who claimed Scots oil could eliminate Scots poverty.

Trade union connections, or the lack of them, had somewhat larger effects in England than Scotland. Directions were similar except that in addition to the main Labour versus Conservative pattern there was a smaller pro-SNP tendency among Scottish trade unionists which had no parallel in England.

The self-employed deviated strongly in a pro-Conservative, anti-Labour direction, though in Scotland they also had a slight pro-SNP tendency as well. Workers in large plants deviated pro-Labour, anti-Conservative by similar amounts in both countries. But while those in small plants deviated against Labour everywhere they were pro-Conservative in England but pro-SNP in Scotland.

Differences between public- and private-sector workers were small in both countries, especially if we allow for the fact that workers as a whole deviated a little in a pro-Labour, anti-Conservative direction.

Respondents who had themselves been unemployed or whose family had been unemployed were fairly strongly anti-Conservative in both countries but pro-SNP in Scotland while pro-Labour in England.

So the SNP, in contrast to the English Liberals, gained both in those groups that might be expected to favour self-reliance and in the group which most needed state help: the self-employed, workers in small establishments, and also those with experience of unemployment. None of these characteristics made people very strongly SNP, but they went with higher than average SNP votes.

RELIGIOUS AND SECTARIAN ALIGNMENTS

Catholics were the most politically deviant religious group in both countries. They were strongly pro-Labour at the expense of

Table 5.6. Voting and religion in Scotland and England

Deviation from over-all national voting patterns by	Size		Direction		Approx. direction	
	Scot.	Eng.	Scot.	Eng.	Scot.	Eng.
Church of Scotland	6.3	–	104	–	L→C	
RC	30.1	14.8	301	298	*→L	*→L
None	8.2	7.2	237	293	C→*	*→L
Anglican	21.3	6.5	81	97	L→C	L→C
English Nonconformist	–	14.6	–	165		*→R
Religiosity: very much	5.7	8.2	7	129	S→*	L→*
some	8.5	8.1	71	95	*→C	L→*
not really	3.3	0.6	213	185	C→S	–
none	8.2	7.2	237	293	C→*	*→L

Full voting patterns	Scotland				England		
	Con	Lab	Lib	SNP	Con	Lab	Lib
RC	11	75	2	12	30	59	12
Religiosity 'very much'	29	41	8	22	41	39	20
Religiosity 'none'	16	43	8	34	34	50	16

all other parties. In Scotland the direction of the Catholic effect was almost exactly the same as in England but the size was twice as great (Table 5.6).

On both sides of the border the Established Churches deviated a little in a pro-Conservative, anti-Labour direction, but Scottish Anglicans much more so. In addition Scottish Anglicans were biased against the SNP while English Anglicans tilted a little towards the Liberals.

English nonconformists had no real Scottish equivalent but they deviated so much towards the Liberals and against both other parties, especially Labour, that the three-way split in their votes looked very like the Church of Scotland voting pattern except for the substitution of Liberal votes for SNP.

The irreligious were relatively anti-Conservative but while they were pro-SNP in Scotland they went against the Liberals in England.

The link between English religious nonconformity and Liberal voting had its roots deep in history. And Labour's support for both the class interests of Irish immigrants and the cause of Irish home rule explains what is an anomaly in a European context: massive Catholic support for a socialist party.

But the special feature of religious alignments in Scotland and in 1974 was the pattern of support for the SNP – at its highest among the irreligious and its lowest among the Catholics: two groups that in England had the same pro-Labour tendencies. Since Catholics had much the same attitudes towards devolution as non-Catholics it seems unlikely that the religious pattern of SNP support was derived from special hopes and fears about SNP policy. Nor is it likely that Catholics and the irreligious differed greatly in socio-economic characteristics. That leaves the possibility of social integration. A new party, rapidly gaining support and with a generally popular policy, might be best able to turn sympathy for policy into voting support among the least integrated, most atomized, least organized, sections of society. Conversely supporters of an old party going through a phase of unpopularity would be more likely to stay loyal to it if they had a high level of social contact with other supporters. It would be more difficult for a new party to win flash support from a socially and politically integrated group than from a collection of individuals.

Certainly there was a steady rise in SNP support across the religiosity spectrum from 22 per cent among those to whom religion meant 'very much', through 25 and 32 per cent in the intermediate

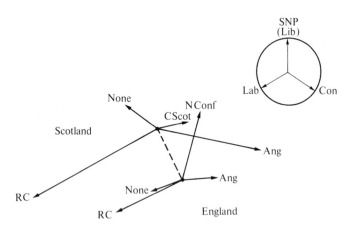

Fig. 5.5 Religious alignments

religiosity categories to 34 per cent among the irreligious.

AGE, SEX, EDUCATION, HOUSE TENURE

The young were anti-Conservative and the old were pro-Conservative in both nations but age effects were twice as powerful in Scotland and it was the SNP rather than both non-Conservative parties that did well among the young and badly among the old (Table 5.7).

Table 5.7. Age, sex, education, house tenure and voting in Scotland and England

Deviation from over-all national voting patterns by:	Size		Direction		Approx. direction	
	Scot.	Eng.	Scot.	Eng.	Scot.	Eng.
Age: Under 25	14.3	10.0	210	258	C → S	C → L
25–30	10.2	9.7	178	188	* → S	* → R
30–35	7.8	0.8	183	173	* → S	* → R
35–45	3.6	2.3	253	245	C → *	C → *
45–55	4.8	2.3	34	271	S → C	C → L
55–65	6.6	5.2	3	51	S → *	* → C
65–75	13.2	3.9	25	65	S → C	* → C
Over 75	10.9	14.8	54	47	* → C	* → C
Age: Under 45	7.5	4.4	202	228	C → S	C → *
Over 45	7.8	3.6	23	45	S → C	* → C
Sex: Male	4.6	2.8	204	327	C → S	R → L
Female	4.2	2.7	24	147	S → C	L → R
Education: Academic further	12.8	14.2	116	127	L → *	L → *
Minimum	14.9	10.8	300	282	* → L	C → L
Tenure: Owner	27.0	15.1	16	86	S → C	L → C
Mortgager	15.7	9.9	125	123	L → *	L → *
Private tenant	8.3	4.4	98	276	L → C	C → L
Council tenant	15.0	21.5	276	284	C → L	C → L

Full voting patterns	Scotland				England		
	Con	Lab	Lib	SNP	Con	Lab	Lib
Aged under 25	10	37	10	42	28	50	22
All aged under 45	19	37	8	36	34	43	23
All aged over 45	33	40	7	20	43	41	17
Aged over 75	37	32	12	20	55	37	8

Sex differences, though small, were also twice as large in Scotland and the direction was sharply different. Men were pro-SNP and anti-Conservative in Scotland but pro-Labour and anti-Liberal in England.

Educational comparisons are not possible in the middle range of education because of the different educational systems and the difficulty of comparing English grammar schools with Scottish senior secondaries. But at the extremes comparison is possible. Those with further education of an academic nature deviated against Labour while those with only the minimum statutory education deviated towards Labour by similar amounts in both countries.

Scottish council tenants appeared to deviate much less than English in a pro-Labour, anti-Conservative direction while Scottish mortgagors deviated more than English away from Labour but this pattern reflected the sheer numbers of Scottish council tenants. Apart from generally greater support for the SNP than English Liberals, council tenants and mortgagors split their votes similarly in Scotland and England. The tenure groups that behaved very differently in the two countries were the house

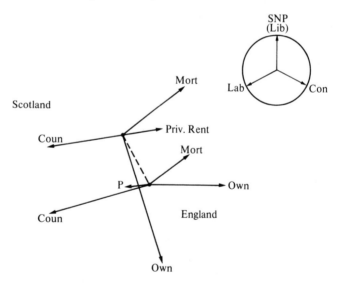

Fig. 5.6. House tenure and voting

owners and those who rented their house from a private landlord. Private tenants deviated to the Conservatives and away from Labour in Scotland but deviated in exactly the opposite way in England. English house owners were pro-Conservative and anti-Labour but the distinguishing mark of Scottish house owners was their enormously large bias against the SNP. House owners were, of course, much older than mortgagors.

Once again, the patterns of voting support on these background variables probably reflect variations in the susceptibility of different sections of society to the penetration of new parties. The more adventurous sections – male and, above all, young – had switched more strongly to the SNP. Young people were a little more Liberal than their elders in England but English Liberal voting was a less adventurous option than SNP for two reasons: first, it was more of a revived old party and less of a new one and, second, it was associated with a lack of extreme Labour and Conservative policies rather than with an extreme policy of its own.

MEDIA USE

Express readers were pro-Conservative, anti-Labour and *Record* or *Mirror* readers were the opposite in both countries. But *Scottish Express* readers were only half as deviant as English *Express* readers, reflecting the much greater market penetration of the *Scottish Daily Express* (Table 5.8).

Among the smaller circulation newspapers the *Glasgow Herald*

Table 5.8 Voting and media use

Deviation from over-all national voting patterns by:		Size		Direction		Approx. Direction	
		Scot.	Eng.	Scot.	Eng.	Scot.	Eng.
Papers read: None		1.8	5.8	334	215	S→L	C→R
	Express	10.3	19.1	104	78	L→C	L→C
	Record (*Mirror* in England)	17.4	19.7	283	268	C→L	C→L
	Courier (Dundee)	9.3	–	157	–	L→S	–
	Herald (Glasgow)	30.7	–	75	–	*→C	–
	P. & J. (Aberdeen)	2.2	–	167	–	*→S	–
	Scotsman (Edinburgh)	11.7	–	119	–	L→*	–

had a very pro-Conservative readership while the *Scotsman* was moderately anti-Labour.

PARTY IDENTIFICATION

As anyone would expect, those who identified very strongly with either the Labour or Conservative Party deviated very strongly towards that party and against all others. But we might have expected that weak identifiers with either party would have been inclined to vote for third options, yet that expectation was not supported by the evidence. Weak identifiers deviated towards their own party and against the other major party. The size of weak identifiers' deviations were relatively weak – only around two-thirds that for very strong identifiers. But they did not deviate towards the Liberals or SNP. The most that can be said is

Table 5.9 Party Identification and voting

Deviation from over-all national voting patterns by:	Size		Direction		Approx. Direction	
	Scot.	Eng.	Scot.	Eng.	Scot.	Eng.
Very strong Con identifiers	57.1	51.4	67	74	*→C	*→C
Fairly ″ ″	48.8	46.4	74	76	*→C	L→C
Not very ″ ″	32.1	37.7	97	85	L→C	L→C
Not very strong Lab identifiers	40.1	33.5	296	281	*→L	C→L
Fairly ″ ″ ″	45.4	44.6	298	284	*→L	C→L
Very strong ″ ″	47.3	50.5	299	288	*→L	*→L
SNP identifier (Lib in England)	56.8	51.9	175	197	*→S	*→R
Voted Lib in 1970	18.0	43.3	162	180	L→S	*→R
Voted SNP in 1970	49.3	–	176	–	*→S	–

Full voting pattern	Scotland 1974				England		
	Con	Lab	Lib	SNP	Con	Lab	Lib
Remembered vote in 1970							
1970 Conservatives	68	5	6	21	76	8	16
1970 Labour	2	78	3	17	6	82	12
1970 Liberals	8	10	48	35	14	16	70
1970 SNP	2	8	5	86	–	–	–
1970 Did not vote	16	34	10	40	32	43	26
1970 Too young	9	33	14	44	30	47	24

that weak Conservatives failed to deviate either for or against the Liberals and SNP, though weak Labour identifiers, deviated in much the same direction as strong Labour identifiers (Table 5.9).

Americans have traditionally been willing and able to change their vote without changing their sense of identification with a party. But Britons have a less detached and enduring sense of party identification. They do not register as supporters of a particular party. They also have a lot less voting to do than Americans so they have less opportunity to indulge in split voting, less opportunity and less need to separate their sense of party identity from their most recent parliamentary vote.

Large numbers of Liberal and SNP voters who must previously have voted for other parties or grown up in Labour and Conservative households reported a Liberal or SNP identification in 1974. So the only party identification groups which showed a strong voting bias in favour of the Liberals or SNP were their own party identifiers.

One party-defined group which did deviate to the SNP, without being defined in terms of previous support or current identification with the same party, was the group who remembered voting Liberal in 1970 (according to their 1974 reports of the 1970 vote). In fact the Liberals still took 48 per cent of their votes in 1974 but the SNP took 35 per cent. By comparison the SNP gained only 21 per cent of 1970 Conservatives and 17 per cent of 1970 Labour voters.

Memories of past voting must be treated with some scepticism but the SNP clearly did especially well among all the groups that had not voted for major parties in 1970: according to our respondents' memories 35 per cent of 1970 Liberals, 40 per cent of 1970 abstainers, and 44 per cent of those too young to vote in 1970 voted SNP in 1974. With English Liberals the pattern was less dramatic but they too won higher than average votes among those who were either too young or abstained in 1970. Naturally enough, those people were less committed by their own past behaviour to voting Labour or Conservative and hence much more likely to respond to the appeals of a newly popular third party.

CONCLUSIONS

The most powerful social and partisan influences – class alignments and Labour/Conservative party identification – were broadly similar in size and partisan direction both north and south of the border.

But there were many national differences among less powerful effects, mainly due to patterns of SNP support. Managers tended towards the Liberals in England but only junior managers plus skilled manual workers tended towards the SNP in Scotland. The SNP captured some of the otherwise pro-Conservative tendencies among the self-employed and those in small establishments plus some of the otherwise pro-Labour tendencies among those with family experience of unemployment. In England the irreligious inclined against the Liberals but in Scotland they inclined towards the SNP. While English Liberals did somewhat better among the young, the SNP did very much better still especially among the very young.

Some of these differences reflected different SNP policies – strongly in favour of independence, uniquely able to offer a remedy for poverty. Some reflected the SNP position as a more adventurous party than the Liberals, something very different from a 'middle way'. Some simply reflected a newer and more successful party penetrating further into those sections of society that were weakly committed to old-established parties.

But only the sharper SNP age profile and the divergent religiosity effects showed great differences between social effects on voting in Scotland and England. Above all, class remained powerful in Scotland despite the rise of the SNP and class effects on Scots voting were generally similar to class effects on English voting. Class effects were overlaid, but not seriously attenuated by the rise of a nationalist dimension in Scots voting.

Chapter 6

Voting – 2: Balanced Attitudes, Scottish Issues, and Amplification Effects

UNIMPORTANT ISSUES

It may seem strange to concentrate attention on the issues which voters dismissed as 'not very important' in their voting choice. Yet there was a small but consistent correlation between SNP voting and rejecting many of the traditional issues of British politics. Not only did SNP voters stress special Scottish issues; they also rejected the great issues of Labour versus Conservative politics. Their stress on special Scottish issues in no way required them to reject other issues as unimportant. They could avoid labelling an issue as 'most important' or 'very important' and still call it 'fairly important', yet often they went further and described it as 'not very important' or 'does not matter either way'.

In the BES there were four traditional economic management issues – prices, unemployment, strikes, and wage controls. Those who denied the importance of unemployment were pro-Conservative, anti-Labour in both countries. There was less similarity on the other issues, especially prices where accepting the issue in England seems to have become confused with accepting Labour's record on the issue.

The next three issues – pensions, housing, and social services – were more 'position' issues. While few people argued the case for more unemployment there were genuine disagreements about what the proper levels of social services, social housing, and state pensions should be. To deny the importance of these issues was in a sense to refuse to take sides. On the other hand, arguments about levels in the mid-seventies were about the need for more government expenditure versus no more, rather than less. To assert the importance of these issues was almost to take the side of more public expenditure, that is, to take the Labour side. So it was natural that those who denied the importance of these issues should be biased against Labour. But on all three issues, especially social services, they were pro-SNP in Scotland though pro-Conservative in England. To the extent that they refused to take either a Labour or Conservative position on these issues Scots were SNP but the English did not go Liberal.

There were three purely social issues: position issues that had little to do with expenditure – comprehensive education, immigration, and crime. Those who denied the importance of tougher measures against crime were relatively few in number but very strongly Labour. In Scotland their Labour bias was at the expense of both other parties, in England only at the Conservatives' expense. Those who rejected the importance of comprehensive schooling were anti-Conservative but pro-Labour in England while pro-SNP in Scotland. Rejecting immigration as an issue inclined Scots towards the SNP and English (very slightly) towards the Liberals.

Four issues were related to socialist or social democratic ideals – nationalization, workers' control, spending on poverty, and redistribution of wealth. Nationalization was an unpopular word used more in Conservative propaganda than Labour. Labour voters denied its importance, Conservatives stressed it. Workers' control however was phrased in a more neutral way as 'giving workers more say'. Respondents who said that did not matter tended towards the Conservatives. Those who thought public spending on poverty was important tended to Labour. The question on redistributing wealth was particularly valuable. It allowed five options for answers ranging from 'very important that it should be done' through to 'very important that it should not'. Those who opted for the central category, 'does not matter either way' had an anti-Labour bias with, in Scotland, a strong pro-SNP bias as well.

EEC membership was a much more live issue in England and those who did not accept its importance were highly deviant to Labour in England but hardly deviant at all in Scotland.

Finally, there was oil and decentralization plus, in Scotland, devolution. English respondents who denied the importance of these were fairly typical of English voters as a whole but not so in Scotland. Denying any of these in Scotland went with a strong anti-SNP bias, least strong on decentralization, strongest on devolution.

Table 6.1 Unimportant issues and voting

Deviation from over-all national voting patterns when issue described as unimportant was:	Size		Direction		Approx direction	
	Scot.	Eng.	Scot.	Eng.	Scot.	Eng.
Economic management issues:						
Wage controls	4.9	3.2	88	231	L→C	C→*
Prices	6.5	23.2	150	109	L→S	L→*
Strikes	2.6	7.6	176	252	*→S	C→*
Unemployment	6.4	9.3	101	104	L→C	L→C
Public expenditure issues:						
Pensions	9.1	9.7	144	96	L→S	L→C
Housing	5.6	3.4	141	89	L→S	L→C
Social services	6.7	6.1	161	95	L→S	L→C
Pure social issues:						
Comprehensives	4.3	6.6	199	261	C→S	C→L
Repatriation of immigrants	4.1	1.1	191	199	*→S	C→R
Tougher crime prevention	17.4	19.7	304	258	*→L	C→L
Social democratic issues:						
Nationalization	8.1	17.9	278	266	C→L	C→L
Workers' control	8.5	5.5	33	58	S→C	*→C
Public expenditure on poverty	11.3	14.3	117	97	L→*	L→C
Redistributing wealth	9.4	9.2	191	125	L→S	L→*
Scottish issues:						
EEC membership	1.4	16.5	89	305	L→C	*→L
North Sea oil	10.5	1.5	353	195	S→*	*→R
Scottish government	14.8	–	5	–	S→*	–
Decentralization from London	8.5	1.9	8	248	S→*	C→*

Table 6.1 contains a welter of detail. But in summary, there are fourteen British issues plus four more or less specially Scottish issues. Out of the fourteen, denying the importance of the issue went with an anti-SNP bias only twice (crime, workers' control) but with a pro-SNP bias nine times. In England, denying the importance of these fourteen issues went with an anti-Liberal bias once (on the EEC) but with a pro-Liberal bias only four times. So denying the importance of traditional British issues was a much more significant feature of SNP voting than English Liberal voting.

Conversely, denying the importance of decentralization, oil, or devolution – the special Scottish issues – went with large anti-SNP bias every time. This also provided a contrast with the pattern of English Liberal votes and it was not entirely obvious that it should do so. The BES did not measure English attitudes to Scottish devolution but it did ask the same decentralization question as in Scotland and the English Liberals were officially regionalist and federalist. Yet there was almost no link between Liberal voting and the importance attached to decentralization.

Over all, Table 6.1 suggests we should look more closely at two aspects of issue voting – special Scottish issues, and the concept of neutrality, refusal to take sides, or balance.

BALANCE AND THIRD-PARTY VOTING

Three factors might explain a significant part of the growth of third-party voting in 1974: attraction, repulsion, and balance. First, the Liberals and Nationalists could have attracted votes in a positive way by having policies or personalities with a special appeal to the elector. There is some evidence that Jeremy Thorpe gained votes for the Liberals in England by being more popular than Heath, if not Wilson, and though the SNP was deeply hostile to any personality cults within the party and stressed policy rather than personality, it had policies which attracted at least some Scots.

The ideas of repulsion and balance are mixed together in the notion of a 'protest vote'. Electors who wished 'a plague on both your houses' to Labour and Conservative would be driven, rather than attracted, to the SNP or the Liberals. But repulsion and balance are two very different things and they interact in a complex way. Deep hostility towards one of the old parties could prevent rather than encourage defections to a rising new party if that hostility was unbalanced. We should talk of a politically polarized situation which left no opportunity for third parties. The man with a passionate hatred of nationalization would be so keen to keep Labour out of office by voting for its main UK opponent that he would be unlikely to split the anti-socialist vote by switching to the SNP. Conversely, warm approval of the existing parties might not keep voters loyal to those parties if that approval was balanced. The man who thought that both Heath and Wilson would make excellent prime ministers had no need to consider voting in such a way as to affect the outcome between them. He was free to indulge even mild nationalist tendencies if he had them.

There is a fundamental difference between balance on the one hand and attraction or repulsion on the other. A balanced relationship to old parties facilitates rather than causes defection. Balance breaks constraints, permits freedom of movement, and amplifies change but that does not necessarily give any impetus to change. Some forms of balance – such as those described as 'cross-pressure' situations – may be an active cause of abstention if not third-party voting, but other forms of balance – like an equally high level of trust in both old parties – are clearly insufficient reasons in themselves for defection to third parties.

I will consider eight types of balance between Labour and Conservatives as it affected voting in 1974:

(1) Balanced ratings of party leaders: respondents were asked to give Heath and Wilson 'marks out of 10'. Marks from zero to 3 were taken as 'low', 7 or above as 'high', the rest as medium.

(2) Balanced ratings of the parties themselves: respondents were asked to give the parties 'marks out of 10' and also to say whether they could trust them in government 'usually', 'sometimes', or 'rarely'. That gave two ways of constructing very general indicators of balanced attitudes to the parties.

(3) Balance on valence issues: some issues like unemployment or inflation incorporated a generally agreed 'good'. Few admitted liking unemployment or inflation. But the parties could be seen as equally good at 'handling the problem of unemployment'.

(4) Balance on ideological issues: on some issues there was little doubt that the parties stood for opposing policies – for example, on redistributing wealth. But respondents could be in a balanced position on such an issue if they said that, to them, it 'did not matter' whether the government redistributed wealth or not.

(5–8) Class contradictions: these were relatively uncomfortable forms of balance in which the respondent had some attribute which would tend to link him with the opposite class party – classic examples of cross-pressures.

(5) Class-contradicted ideology: for example, working-class respondents who disapproved the redistribution of wealth and middle-class respondents who approved it.

(6) Class-contradicted party rating: a respondent's class could be contradicted by, for example, his failure to trust his natural class party or by trust in the opposite class party.

(7) Class-contradicted previous voting: a respondent could have had a father who voted for the opposite class party, or might have done so himself prior to 1974.

(8) Class-contradicted class: a respondent could have grown up in a family of the opposite class, or might subjectively feel that he belonged to the class opposite to the one defined by his head of household's occupation.

In each of (5)–(8) the respondent's own class was defined by the occupation of his head of household – manual occupations being working class, non-manual being middle class.

The first three lines of Table 6.2 show that where rating of Labour and Conservative leaders was balanced and low the SNP or English Liberals gained very much more than average votes. But where ratings were high but balanced third parties did not

Table 6.2 Voting by Balanced ratings of party leaders

Deviation from over-all national voting patterns		Size		Direction		Approx. dir.	
		Scot.	Eng.	Scot.	Eng.	Scot.	Eng.
Rating of Heath	Rating of Wilson						
HI	HI	1.8	2.4	300	55	* →L	* →C
MED	MED	21.7	24.2	161	142	L→S	L→R
LO	LO	19.3	30.0	171	177	* →S	* →R
HI	MED	40.9	41.6	79	85	L→C	L→C
MED	HI	28.5	31.0	288	277	* →L	C→L
MED	LO	32.9	36.9	100	102	L→C	L→C
LO	MED	22.9	23.8	206	239	C→S	C→*
HI	LO	39.9	48.8	86	78	L→C	L→C
LO	HI	37.6	42.3	291	282	* →L	C→L

Note: A direction of 0 degrees or 360° indicates a totally anti-SNP or anti-Liberal tendency. A direction of 180° indicates a totally pro-SNP or pro-Liberal tendency. Generally directions between 90° and 270° are pro-SNP or pro-Liberal while those less than 90° or greater than 270° are anti-SNP or anti-Liberal.

suffer a corresponding disadvantage. It was unbalanced ratings that damaged the third parties most. In both Scotland and England the worst combinations for third parties were high ratings for Wilson, combined with low or medium ratings for Heath, and high ratings for Heath combined with low or medium for Wilson.

We might think that this pattern was entirely obvious – strong Conservatives would rate Heath high and Wilson low, strong Labourites would do the opposite, and neither group would vote Liberal or SNP. But this reverse causation model cannot explain why those who rated both Heath and Wilson highly included so many SNP or Liberal voters – in Scotland 28 per cent of them

Table 6.3: Voting by trust in Conservative and Labour governments and by ratings of parties

Deviation from over-all national voting patterns		Size		Direction		Approx.direction	
		Scot.	Eng.	Scot.	Eng.	Scot.	Eng.
Trust Con	Trust Lab						
Usually	Usually	3.9	2.2	321	342	S→L	R→L
Sometimes	Sometimes	5.6	8.7	161	168	L→S	*→R
Rarely	Rarely	21.4	21.6	170	192	*→S	*→R
Usually	Sometimes	41.5	37.0	78	82	L→C	L→C
Sometimes	Usually	28.9	41.2	282	278	C→L	C→L
Sometimes	Rarely	32.1	41.0	101	85	L→C	L→C
Rarely	Sometimes	29.7	38.5	277	273	C→L	C→L
Usually	Rarely	54.1	48.1	67	76	*→C	L→C
Rarely	Usually	39.0	46.5	294	285	*→L	C→L
Difference be-	A great deal	7.0	3.7	350	44	S→*	R→C
tween parties:	Not much	6.6	4.1	180	232	*→S	C→*

Full voting patterns		Scotland				England		
Trust Con	Trust Lab	Con	Lab	Lib	SNP	Con	Lab	Lib
Usually	Usually	27	44	2	27	39	44	17
Rarely	Rarely	15	20	14	51	22	34	44
Usually	Rarely	89	5	2	5	92	2	6
Rarely	Usually	0	84	7	10	1	93	6

voted SNP and in England 18 per cent voted Liberal, well up to the over-all votes for these parties.

This analysis can be repeated using attitudes towards the parties rather than their leaders. The top three lines in Table 6.3 show the effect of increasing, but balanced, distrust in Labour and Conservative. Clearly the SNP gained enormously from balanced distrust, but it lost remarkably little in the face of balanced trust. The last two lines of the table show the effect of extremely unbalanced trust. A high level of trust in Labour combined with a low level of trust in the Conservatives naturally helped Labour, but it damaged the SNP almost as much as the Conservatives. Similarly, the opposite trust combination hurt the SNP almost as much as Labour. Moderately unbalanced trust – represented by the four lines in the middle of Table 6.3 – neither helped nor hurt the SNP (see also Fig. 6.1). An analysis using party 'marks out of 10' shows a similar but less pronounced pattern.

Instead of computing the respondent's degree of balance we could use the simple question: 'would you say there is a great deal of difference between the parties?' Respondents seem to have interpreted this as applying to Labour and Conservative; those who saw a 'great deal' of difference deviated against the SNP, those who saw 'not much' favoured the SNP.

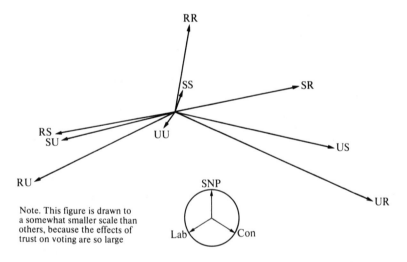

Note. This figure is drawn to a somewhat smaller scale than others, because the effects of trust on voting are so large

Fig. 6.1. Voting by trust in Labour and Conservative governments

Table 6.4. Voting by balance on valence and ideological issues

Deviation from over-all national voting patterns	Size		Direction		Approx direction	
	Scot.	Eng.	Scot.	Eng.	Scot.	Eng.
Valence issue:						
Parties' handling of unemployment						
Con much better	43.0	42.4	75	75	* → C	* → C
Con somewhat better	33.9	40.1	81	83	L → C	L → C
Same	11.2	12.0	138	146	L → S	L → R
Lab somewhat better	17.6	26.5	260	270	C → L	C → L
Lab much better	35.4	43.9	290	286	* → L	* → L
Ideological issue:						
Redistribution of wealth						
Very important that govern- ment should	17.8	29.1	275	279	C → L	C → L
Fairly " " "	4.0	11.7	268	261	C → L	C → L
Does not matter either way	9.4	9.2	161	125	L → S	L → *
Fairly important that govern- ment should not	25.6	27.4	96	88	L → C	L → C
Very important that govern- ment should not	29.5	32.4	78	81	L → C	L → C

Full voting patterns	Scot.				Eng.		
	Con	Lab	Lib	SNP	Con	Lab	Lib
Very important to redistribute wealth	9	58	6	27	13	73	15
Does not matter either way	22	29	13	37	43	31	26
Very important not to redistribute wealth	59	14	6	22	74	13	13

Balanced attitudes to valence or position issues had a similar effect on third-party support: those in the centre of the issue spectrum, whether valence or ideological, deviated towards the SNP in Scotland or the Liberals in England by roughly similar amounts in each country. Those at the extrimities naturally favoured Labour or Conservative (Table 6.4, Fig. 6.2).

Finally, contradictions between respondents' class on the one hand and their ideology, party rating, parental voting, family class, or subjective class on the other, all produced a tendency to vote SNP. But such class contradictions were a much less powerful influence towards Liberal voting in England. Out of the twenty lines in Table 6.5 there are fifteen lines producing a pro-

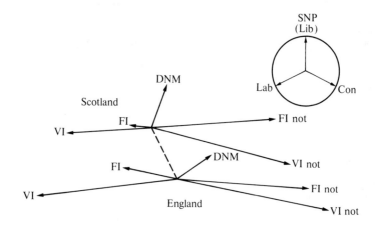

Fig. 6.2. Redistribution of wealth and vote

Table 6.5. Voting by balance on class contradictions

Deviation from over-all national voting patterns	Size		Direction		Approx. direction	
	Scot.	Eng.	Scot.	Eng.	Scot.	Eng.
Class contradicts ideology:						
MC – Nationalize a lot more industries	21.6	49.3	271	287	C → L	* → L
MC – Nationalize a few more industries	7.8	21.4	240	259	C → *	C → L
WC – Nationalize no more	3.5	4.8	211	236	C → S	C → *
WC – Denationalize some	20.2	21.3	153	102	L → S	L → C
MC – More social services needed	9.9	5.5	209	203	C → S	C → R
WC – Cut social services a lot	7.0	9.2	181	100	* → S	L → C
MC – Should redistribute wealth	3.8	7.4	142	228	L → S	C → *
WC – Should not ” ”	13.9	13.6	101	97	L → C	L → C
Class contradicts party trust:						
MC – Distrust Con	11.9	28.3	243	265	C → *	C → L
MC – Trust Lab	10.2	23.1	246	283	C → *	C → L
WC – Distrust Lab	20.0	28.5	141	84	L → S	L → C
WC – Trust Con	22.5	18.1	56	72	* → C	* → C

Table 6.5 continued

Deviation from over-all national voting patterns	Size		Direction		Approx. direction	
	Scot.	Eng.	Scot.	Eng.	Scot.	Eng.
Class contradicts previous vote:						
MC – Voted Lab 1970	23.4	30.6	277	269	C → L	C → L
WC – Voted Con 1970	33.1	28.4	91	92	L → C	L → C
MC – Father Lab	7.3	2.9	200	177	C → S	* → R
WC – Father Con	13.8	11.0	140	103	L → S	L → C
Class contradicts class:						
MC – WC family	8.3	8.0	133	106	L →*	L →*
WC – MC family	7.9	2.0	159	96	L → S	L → C
MC – Feel WC	7.6	1.5	147	109	L → S	L →*
WC – Feel MC	5.3	1.0	167	123	* →S	L →*

Full voting patterns	Scot.				Eng.		
	Con	Lab	Lib	SNP	Con	Lab	Lib
MC respondent from WC family	28	28	10	34	45	33	22
WC respondent from MC family	26	33	4	38	41	40	20
MC resp. wants more social services	15	38	10	38	34	41	25
WC resp. wants big cut in social services	21	34	9	36	47	32	21

SNP deviation and only one anti-SNP: but for England, there are only seven pro-Liberal lines and two anti-Liberal. The majority of class-contradiction situations had little effect on Liberal voting. Half the entries show that the direction of political tendencies was over 30° different in Scotland from England and in every case the Scottish reaction to a class contradiction was directed more towards a straight third-party gain (see Figs 6.3 and 6.4).

BALANCE AND PROTEST

Taking the relationship between SNP voting and trust in Labour and Conservative governments we can calculate the relative power of balance and protest as factors influencing a high SNP vote (Table 6.6). The influence of protest or disaffection can be measured by comparing the SNP vote among those who rarely

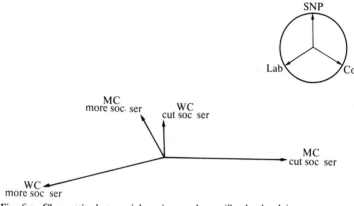

Fig. 6.3. Class, attitude to social services, and vote (Scotland only)

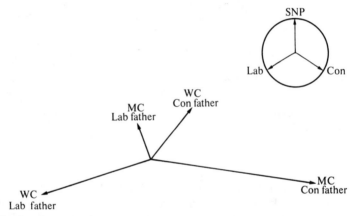

Fig. 6.4. Respondent's class, father's partisanship, and vote (Scotland only)

trusted either old party and those who usually trusted both. That gives a 'protest effect' of $(50.6 - 26.6) = 24$ per cent.

The influence of balance can be gauged by comparing the levels of SNP voting among those with the most unbalanced trust and those with perfectly balanced trust. That gives a 'balance effect' of

$$(26.6 + 32.5 + 50.6)/3 - (4.5 + 9.6)/2 = 29.5 \text{ per cent}$$

which is somewhat larger than the index of protest effect. The two effects could be calculated in other ways but then balance would appear even more powerful compared to protest.

Table 6.6. Voting, political attitudes and parental vote by trust

Trust Con	Trust Lab	SNP % Oct. 74	% SG	% SG+MD	% All oil	% All + largest share	Father's vote % Lib
Usually	Usually	26.6	15.9	75.0	9.4	28.3	9.1
Sometimes	Sometimes	32.5	19.2	66.1	6.3	31.7	13.3
Rarely	Rarely	50.6	38.5	78.2	24.7	44.9	16.2
Usually	Sometimes	20.7	13.0	60.8	2.3	21.8	8.3
Sometimes	Usually	22.8	16.9	63.7	10.4	39.6	9.0
Sometimes	Rarely	36.5	15.2	68.2	8.5	36.5	15.5
Rarely	Sometimes	26.2	30.8	71.0	9.8	41.8	11.4
Usually	Rarely	4.5	6.7	46.7	10.2	20.4	21.4
Rarely	Usually	9.6	27.9	57.4	19.0	53.2	16.2

SCOTTISH ISSUES

Membership of the EEC was an issue on the borderline between British and Scottish. The SNP attacked Britain's membership of the EEC for making Scotland a periphery of a periphery. They suspected the Europeans of coveting Scotland's oceanic resources – fish and oil. At the same time they realized that European institutions could only gain sovereignty or political authority at the expense of the Westminster parliament and since they looked forward to the day when they might gain a majority of Scottish MPs and then try to negotiate independence with Westminster, anything that reduced Westminster's authority was in the interests of the SNP. They resolved these contradictions during the EEC referendum campaign by demanding a separate Scottish negotiation with the EEC followed by a separate Scottish referendum on EEC membership.

But the SNP were not Scotland. The EEC stood out as a mark of Scottish–English differences because so many *fewer* Scots thought EEC membership an important issue. No doubt they did so because they were a periphery of a periphery but their reaction was more marked by apathy than antagonism.

EEC attitudes produced less political deviation in Scotland than in England (Table 6.7). In addition, the general direction of the EEC axis was different. In England, despite the Liberal Party's ideological commitment to Europe, respondents' views

Table 6.7. EEC attitudes and voting

Deviation from over-all national voting patterns by	Size		Direction		Approx. direction	
	Scot.	Eng.	Scot.	Eng.	Scot.	Eng.
Respondent's view on EEC:						
Stay on present terms	29.8	33.3	70	82	* → C	L → C
Stay but try to change	7.1	5.4	82	112	L → C	L →*
Change or leave	8.9	16.0	256	271	C → L	C → L
Leave	11.4	16.1	242	279	C →*	C → L
Importance: Most	11.6	8.9	257	279	C → L	C → L
Fairly	1.2	1.2	130	143	L →*	L →*
Not very	1.4	1.7	89	60	L → C	* →C

on EEC membership produced Labour versus Conservative deviations (roughly horizontal lines in Fig. 6.5) but in Scotland it produced a Conservative versus the rest pattern (lines tilted up to the left and down to the right).

North Sea oil was undoubtedly a special Scottish issue in the sense that one of the main arguments concerned how much benefit Scotland should get from oil revenues. But there were other aspects, principally the rate of extraction, the degree of state participation, and whether to use the revenues to finance consumption or investment. English respondents were asked for

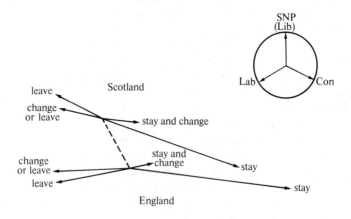

Fig. 6.5. EEC attitudes and voting

Table 6.8. Voting and oil attitudes

Deviation from over all national voting patterns by: Respondent view	Size		Direction		Approx. direction	
Scotland all	18.5	15.3	219	219	C → S	C → R
Largest	9.4	2.2	203	272	C → S	C → L
More	2.2	8.6	90	152	L → C	L → R
Equal	12.2	1.3	19	333	S → C	R → L
Importance:						
Most important	24.8	2.7	185	353	* → S	R → *
Fairly	6.2	1.3	162	21	L → S	R → C
Not very	10.5	1.5	353	195	S → *	* → R

their view on the importance of this whole complex of oil issues, and their opinions on Scotland's right to the oil (Table 6.8).

In Scotland attitudes to the Scottish share of the revenues went with substantial voting variations along a Conservative versus SNP axis. Attitudes towards oil revenues were not related to Labour voting in Scotland. In England pro-Scottish attitudes to oil revenues went with Liberal voting.

Scots votes were strongly related to respondents' views on the importance of North Sea oil. Those who thought the issue important showed a strong tendency to vote SNP; those who thought it unimportant deviated against the SNP (Fig. 6.6). In

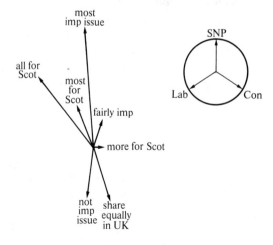

Fig. 6.6. Oil attitudes and voting (Scotland only)

England there was a double contrast: the importance of oil was only weakly related to voting but what pattern there was showed the Liberals doing best among those who thought oil unimportant.

Devolution still more than oil was primarily if not exclusively a Scottish issue. The 1974 surveys did not ask the English respondents for their views on a Scottish Assembly but did ask the general question about the importance of 'shifting power from London to the regions and local authorities'. Scottish respondents were asked this question plus specific questions about the need for constitutional change, about the proposed Assembly, and about the importance of Scottish government in deciding their vote.

Of these, constitutional change and the importance of Scottish government were the most strongly linked to voting patterns – much more strongly than oil attitudes or other devolution attitudes – and produced SNP versus the rest variations. Attitudes to the Assembly proposals produced Conservative versus SNP variations. Ironically, since the Conservatives at that time were proposing an Assembly and the SNP were not, it was the pro-Assembly respondents who tended towards the SNP and against the Conservatives.

Our only point of comparison with attitudes in England is by means of the decentralization question. Attitudes towards shifting power from London were less strongly related to voting in England than in Scotland but not by a large margin. In both countries the Conservative Party suffered among decentralizers and did specially well among centralizers. But in Scotland, the SNP did well among decentralizers while the English Liberals did not (Table 6.9, Fig. 6.7)

BALANCED TRUST, DEVOLUTION ATTITUDES, AND SNP
VOTES: THE AMPLIFICATION EFFECT

So three factors influenced Scots to vote SNP – the SNP's attraction on Scottish issues, disaffection with the other parties, and a balanced attitude towards the other two parties. There is a danger, however, that we are analysing the same phenomenon twice over: perhaps those who distrusted both old parties were simply those who wanted Scottish independence, or all the oil revenues.

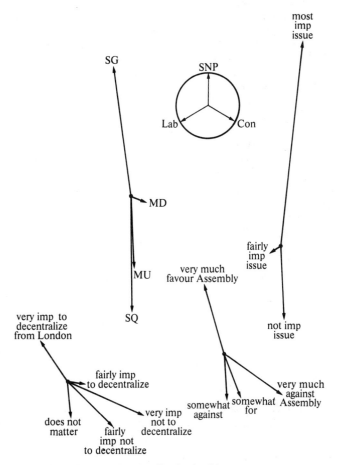

Fig. 6.7. Devolution attitudes and voting (Scotland only)

Table 6.9. Devolution and voting

Deviation from over-all national voting patterns by		Size		Direction		Approx Direction	
		Scot.	Eng.	Scot.	Eng.	Scot.	Eng.
Respondent's view:	SQ	23.4	NA	3	NA	S→*	NA
	MU	13.9	”	4	”	S→*	”
	MD	3.4	”	68	”	*→C	”
	SG	27.1	”	190	”	*→S	”

Table 6.9 continued

Deviation from over-all national voting patterns by	Size		Direction		Approx Direction	
	Scot.	Eng.	Scot.	Eng.	Scot.	Eng.
Very much for Assembly	15.0	NA	199	NA	C→S	NA
Somewhat for	9.3	"	23	"	S→C	"
Somewhat against	9.5	"	7	"	S→*	"
Very much against	14.6	"	57	"	*→C	"
Importance: Most	42.0	"	175	"	*→S	"
Fairly	2.4	"	304	"	*→L	"
Not very	14.8	"	5	"	S→*	"
Very important to decentralize	9.7	11.9	216	260	C→S	C→L
Fairly " "	3.4	0.3	74	217	*→C	–
Doesn't matter	8.5	1.9	8	248	S→*	C→*
Fairly important not to	13.5	12.5	48	111	*→C	L→*
Very " "	17.7	13.6	68	54	*→C	*→C

Full voting patterns	Scot.			
	Con	Lab	Lib	SNP
Devolution attitude: SQ	39	49	12	0
MU	34	45	10	12
MD	29	35	10	26
SG	7	29	4	61

Table 6.6 showed that this was not the case. While trust combinations predicted SNP voting fairly well they did not correlate nearly so well with either constitutional or oil attitudes, nor with a family background of third party voting. For example, the extremely unbalanced category 'rarely trust Conservative, usually trust Labour' was the second lowest on SNP vote, but the third highest on support for independence, the top for wanting Scotland to get at least the largest share of the oil revenues, and the second highest for a family background of third-party voting – all of which should imply a high rather than low SNP vote.

The interactions between trust combinations and devolution attitudes are set out in Table 6.10, which shows the relationship between SNP votes and devolution attitudes within each trust combination. Within seven of the nine trust combinations the

Table 6.10. SNP Vote by trust combination and devolution attitude

Trust Con	Trust Lab	Status quo	More understanding	More decisions	Self government
Balanced trust:					
Usually	Usually	0	17	14	71
Sometimes	Sometimes	0	15	26	76
Rarely	Rarely	0	27	35	80
	Average	0	20	25	76
Moderately balanced:					
Usually	Sometimes	0	5	26	50
Sometimes	Usually	0	13	28	31
Sometimes	Rarely	0	13	40	56
Rarely	Sometimes	0	5	22	57
	Average	0	9	29	49
Extremely unbalanced:					
Usually	Rarely	0	0	13	0
Rarely	Usually	0	7	13	21
	Average	0	4	13	11

Scot voting patterns among those who rarely trusted both Conservative and Labour governments and whose constitutional preferences were:

	% LIB	% SNP
SQ	75	0
MU	27	27
MD	27	35
SG	4	80

Note that this inverse Lib–SNP pattern occurred despite the Liberal Party's official advocacy of federalism.

level of SNP voting increased monotonically from the status quo to the self-government end of the devolution spectrum, and the two exceptions were almost certainly no more than sampling errors. But there was a clear division between the balanced, moderately unbalanced, and extremely unbalanced trust combinations. The SNP's vote among those who wanted self-government averaged 76 per cent in the balanced trust categories, but only 49 per cent in the moderately unbalanced categories, and 11 per cent in the extremely unbalanced categories. Thus although there was a completely general tendency for increased SNP votes towards the self-government end of the devolution spectrum, this tendency was heavily damped by unbalanced trust and amplified by balanced trust.

OTHER AMPLIFYING FACTORS

So balanced trust in Labour and Conservative governments had a major effect in amplifying the relationship between devolution attitudes and SNP vote. Trust and devolution each made a contribution to SNP voting but it would be meaningless to describe their contributions as independent. Perhaps the best analogy is that of a drum of petrol and a lighted match: neither produces an explosion by itself. It is not a matter of adding two factors which produce two small explosions to get one big one but of finding the critical combination. This is the key to further analysis of SNP voting: to see how other variables interacted with devolution attitudes to produce SNP votes.

With oil, like trust, the amplification effect was clear, though far less strong (Table 6.11). In every category of oil attitude SNP votes went up towards the self-government end of the devolution spectrum but in the more pro-Scottish oil categories the increase was sharper. Compare the extremes – all the oil for Scotland versus a British share-out. There was no difference between SNP votes in these oil categories among status quo respondents, but a 15 per cent difference among those who wanted more understanding, 17 per cent among those who wanted more decisions, and 25 per cent among those wanted self-government.

Young people were twice as likely to vote SNP as old people, but only a little more favourable to devolution and self-

Table 6.11. Oil as amplifier

	% SNP Vote			
Oil attitude	SQ	MU	MD	SG
All	0	20	38	65
By far largest	0	13	42	62
More	0	17	21	58
Share equally	0	5	21	40
First row minus last row	0	15	17	25

Table 6.12. Social background as amplifier

	%	SNP % among				% favouring
	SNP	SQ	MU	MD	SG	MD or SG
Age: young (<35)	40	0	21	26	74	71
middle (35–55)	27	0	15	29	63	66
old (>55)	18	0	1	24	36	61
Religion:						
C. of S.	30	0	11	27	67	68
RC	12	0	0	10	40	63
None	34	0	19	30	56	65

government. Catholics were only a third to a half as likely to vote SNP as other Scots, but, paradoxically they had fairly typical devolution attitudes. The irreligious were pro-SNP without being specially pro-devolution (Table 6.12).

The paradoxes here – of which that concerning Catholics is the most startling – are explained by amplification patterns. Old people and Catholics were only a little less pro-devolution than others but were far less likely to convert their desire for devolution or self-government into an SNP vote. The more they favoured self-government, the more they voted SNP but the relationship was relatively muted. Class had no amplification effect and religiosity only a small one, but religious sect and age had large amplification effects.

We should interpret the presence of amplification effects as evidence for unusually strong or weak constraints on vote switching. Young people, Protestants, the irreligious, those who felt North Sea oil was Scottish, and those who had balanced trust, and especially a balanced distrust of the old parties all shared one thing in common: they were, for a variety of reasons, less bound by the ties of traditional political behaviour. Conversely, old people had become set in their ways; Catholics lived in a highly integrated sub-culture that would be resistant to new party fashions as, to a lesser extent, would practising religious people of all sects; those who felt the oil was British had to take a less optimistic view of a separate Scottish economy; and those with extremely unbalanced trust in the old parties had to give high priority to the balance of forces at Westminster – all factors that made it harder to indulge their self-government attitudes by voting SNP.

So the nature of facilitating influences towards third-party voting was radically different in Scotland from what it was in England. South of the border they simply and directly cut the ties of loyalty to the old parties but in Scotland they operated in an interactive combination with attitudes to devolution.

Chapter 7

Voting – 3:   Scottish Electoral Geography

In almost any political system the spatial distributions of votes and opinions are important but they are especially significant under the British electoral system based, as it is, on first-past-the-post voting in single-member territorial constituencies. Under this system nation-wide patterns of voting may be only loosely related to the election of MPs. In this chapter I want to look at some of the properties of the electoral system in Scotland, at the concentration process which played so vital a part in turning SNP votes into SNP seats in Parliament, and finally at environmental influences on attitudes and their relation to votes.

THE ELECTORAL SYSTEM

Most electoral systems discriminate in favour of larger parties and especially in favour of the largest single party. The first-past-the-post system discriminates more than others. Typically, a small party could expect less than half the share of seats that it won in votes and the top party could expect up to one and a quarter times as large a share of seats as votes. Let us consider how that might happen in a British election. Suppose that at one election nearly all the votes were split equally between two parties – as they were in 1955. Then, other things being equal, we would expect each of these two parties to get half the seats and each of them would have a seats to votes ratio just slightly over 1.0. Indeed this is exactly what happened in 1955.

Now suppose that a third party took 10 per cent of votes from both the major parties giving a 40:40:20 per cent voting split and suppose that the third party's appeal was fairly diffuse and its vote fairly evenly spread. Then we should expect much the same division of seats as before – the third party would be unlikely to gain any seats with only 20 per cent of the vote – but since the two major parties now had only 40 per cent of the vote their seats-to-

Table 7.1. Ratio percentage seats to percentage votes

	Scotland				England		
	Con	Lab	Lib	SNP	Con	Lab	Lib
1955	1.01	1.03	.74	0	1.14	.90	.15
1959	.93	1.15	.34	0	1.24	.87	.09
1964	.83	1.24	.74	0	1.16	1.11	.05
1966	.75	1.30	1.04	0	1.00	1.17	.13
1970	.85	1.39	.77	.12	1.18	.98	.05
1974	.90	1.54	.53	.45	1.29	1.22	.08
1974	.91	1.59	.51	.51	1.26	1.23	.08
1979	.99	1.48	.50	.16	1.26	1.07	.09

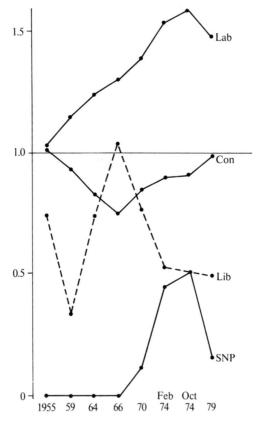

Fig. 7.1. Seats-to-votes ratio in Scotland, 1955–79

votes ratio would rise from 50:50 = 1.00 to 50:40 = 1.25. This is very much what happened in England in 1974.

But in Scotland the ratios of seats to votes ranged far beyond the norm (Table 7.1, Fig. 7.1). At every election from 1955 to October 1974 Labour's seats ratio increased until it stood at 1.59 – Labour took 58 per cent of Scottish seats with only 36 per cent of the vote. Meanwhile the Conservatives' seats ratio dropped no further than 0.91 even though they dropped to third-party status, but the SNP only got half as many seats as votes despite breaking through to second place in terms of votes. Scottish Liberals got so few votes or seats at all times that their treatment is unimportant but, for the record, they did far better than such a minor party could expect and far better than their English counterparts. Indeed, in 1966 the system discriminated in favour of the Liberals despite the fact that they won only 7 per cent of the vote. The explanation of this unusually favourable treatment is that Liberal votes consisted of a handful of large, personal votes which elected MPs, coupled with a uniformly very low level of support elsewhere.

More difficult questions are these: first, why did the system favour Labour so much? And second, why did it treat the SNP more harshly than the Conservatives even when the SNP became the larger party? I will consider several possible explanations: namely the effects of

(1) constituency electorate sizes
(2) turn-out
(3) tactical voting
(4) patterns of candidature
(5) the spatial distribution of votes
(6) accidents
(7) size and fractionalization in combination.

Constituency Electorates

One party could be specially favoured if its MPs represented smaller constituencies since they would then need smaller votes to get elected. Scotland had two sorts of small constituency – decaying urban centres which elected Labour MPs and sparsely populated rural areas which elected MPs of all four parties. One way of measuring this effect is to calculate the percentage of each

Table 7.2. Cumulative percentage of parties' seats with electorates under x thousand

		Size of Electorate (thousands)										Index of Con advantage
		20	30	40	50	60	70	80	90	100	110	
1955	Lab	0	3	3	44	88	100	——	——	——	——	
	Con	0	6	23	70	100	——	——	——	——	——	61
1970	Lab	2	9	25	39	64	91	96	98	100	——	
	Con	0	4	34	51	73	86	100	——	——	——	24
1974 (Oct.)	Lab	0	5	15	32	71	95	97	100	——	——	
	Con	0	6	19	44	82	100	——	——	——	——	36 over Lab
	SNP	0	9	27	54	72	100	——	——	——	——	31 over SNP
1979	Lab	2	7	18	29	56	88	95	97	97	100	
	Con	0	0	18	45	77	100	——	——	——	——	51

party's seats which had electorates less than 20,000, then less than 30,000 etc. Table 7.2 shows the cumulative percentages of seats whose electorates were less than x thousand. It shows that a higher percentage of Conservative seats had smaller electorates. A useful over-all summary of the Conservative advantage can be derived from the difference between the cumulative distributions of Conservative and Labour seats – the shaded area in Fig. 7.2. This shaded area showed a Conservative advantage with an index of 61 in 1955 which fell to only 24 in 1970 as the population in Labour's city centre seats declined while the Conservatives more rural seats maintained their populations. After the 1974 redistribution of constituency boundaries the Conservative advantage rose to 36 against Labour (31 against the SNP) and by 1979 the Conservative advantage was up still further, to 51. The spread of 1979 Labour electorates from tiny Glasgow Central with under 20,000 to Midlothian with over five times that number was larger than the spread of electorates in Conservative-held areas, but the balance of advantage was decisively in favour of the Conservatives at all times. This helps to explain why the system helped the Conservatives against the SNP but it makes it all the more difficult to explain Labour's large and increasing seats-to-votes ratio.

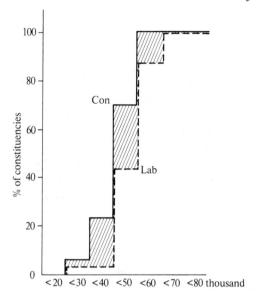

Fig. 7.2. Cumulative percentage of parties' seats with smaller electorates (1955)

Turn-out

If turn-out was low in a party's seats it could once again win with relatively few votes. Thus if Labour represented areas which had low turn-outs its seats-to-votes ratio would be spuriously inflated, rather more by a technical lack of votes than a genuine lack of support. Turn-out is highly dependent upon such pure technicalities as the accuracy of the register which in turn depends upon the rate of removals out of the constituency. In large cities people frequently move the few miles necessary to take them out of the constituency. So perhaps Labour represented low turn-out areas. It certainly represented some – like Glasgow Central or Maryhill both of which had under 60 per cent turn-outs in 1974 – but it also held Lanark, Berwick, Kilmarnock, and others with over 80 per cent turn-outs. On average the turn-outs in Labour, Conservative, and SNP seats in October 1974 were exactly the same. In 1979 Labour seats averaged 1 per cent less turn-out than Conservative and in 1955, 1½ per cent more, but differential turn-out provides no explanation of Labour's huge seats ratio.

Tactical Voting

There is some evidence for what could be interpreted as Labour
supporters casting tactical votes for the SNP in some rural seats
from February 1974 onwards. If this happened on a large scale,
and only applied to Labour it would mean that the number of
Labour votes seriously underestimated the level of Labour
support and hence spuriously inflated Labour's seats-to-votes
ratio. However, the October survey showed that while 12 per
cent of Conservatives and 18 per cent of Labour had thought of
voting SNP, only 9 per cent of SNP had thought of voting
Conservative and 8 per cent Labour. Over all, there is scant
evidence that Labour was especially unsuccessful in converting
support into votes.

Patterns of Candidature

In recent years Labour has contested every seat at every election
and the Conservatives only missed one – Greenock in 1970. But
the Liberals only once came near to a full slate of candidates
when they put up 68 in October 1974. They fought half in
February 1974 and 1979, a third in 1964, 1966 and 1970, and
very few in 1955 and 1959. It could be argued that if they had
contested more they would have gained more votes though that
would have stretched their campaign resources further and in the
three elections in 1974–9 their votes remained almost unchanged
despite doubling, then halving their number of candidates. The
SNP also varied its candidatures from 2 in 1955 to 5, 15, 23, 65,
and 70 at subsequent elections reaching 71 only for the elections
of Oct 74 and 1979. So in the earlier years the lack of Liberal and
SNP candidates probably cut these parties' votes, hence inflated
the Labour and Conservative vote and depressed the big parties'
seats-to-votes ratio.

Though there were 26 Liberals and 15 SNP in 1964 there
were only 4 seats where they fought each other. So it is not
unreasonable to group them together as a third force which got
10 per cent of votes in 37 seats. If they had jointly contested all 71
it is unlikely that their total vote would have exceeded 20 per
cent. If that had happened and both Labour and Conservative
received 5 per cent less, then the Conservative seats-to-votes ratio
would have risen from 0.83 to 0.95 and the Labour seats ratio

from 1.24 to 1.39. If the total third-force vote had been much less than 20 per cent these ratios would have risen correspondingly less.

So increasing candidatures by Liberals and Nationalists – as opposed to increased support – only explains a part of the growth in Labour's seats-to-votes ratio.

The Spatial Distribution of Votes

In February 1974 the English Liberals and the SNP received 21.3 and 21.9 per cent of votes respectively. Moreover, the English Liberals contested proportionately fewer seats; so that their votes per candidate were 24.3 per cent compared with the SNP's 22.2 per cent. Yet the English Liberals' seats-to-votes ratio was 0.08 compared with the SNP's 0.45. If English Liberals had converted votes into seats as efficiently as the SNP they would have had fifty seats in England instead of just nine. Part of the reason lies in the greater fragmentation of the Scottish votes but most is to do with the far more efficient spatial distribution of SNP votes. English Liberals, despite a higher average vote per candidate, exceeded 30 per cent of the vote in only 14 per cent of English seats while the SNP beat that vote share in 18 per cent of Scottish seats. And the difference was even more marked at higher levels: the SNP had over 40 per cent of the vote in 10 per cent of Scottish seats while the English Liberals reached 40 per cent in only 2½ per cent of English seats.

But how efficient was the SNP's vote distribution compared to its main rivals, Scottish Labour and Conservative? In a pure two-party system the most efficient distribution is one in which a party gets either zero or 51 per cent in every constituency. Votes less than 50 per cent are completely wasted by defeat while those much over 50 per cent entail an element of waste through unnecessarily large majorities. With an ideal distribution a party with 51 per cent of the national vote could win 100 per cent of the seats, with 26 per cent of the votes it could win over half the seats. Whatever its national vote, big or small, this ideal distribution guarantees a seats-to-votes ratio of 2.0. Note that it is not a question of having a uniform or non-uniform spread of votes – small parties would benefit from a very non-uniform distribution while large parties would benefit from a highly uniform spread of votes. All that matters is that the party's votes be divided into groups large enough to win seats, but no larger, and that it wastes no votes in seats it does not win.

Now in multi-party contests like 1974 it is impossible to calculate the most efficient distribution by a purely arithmetic procedure. We need to know the operating characteristics of the system. In particular the relationship between votes and victories becomes a matter for observation rather than calculation. Obviously, every vote over 50 per cent won a seat, but so did most votes in the range 40–50 per cent and a good many of the votes in the range 30–40 per cent. In October, Dunbarton East was won by the SNP on a vote of only 31 per cent, and every vote over 42 per cent won a seat.

Taking votes in bands of 10 per cent, the probability of victory was zero for votes under 30 per cent and total for votes over 50 per cent. For votes in the range 30–40 per cent the probability of

Table 7.3. Vote distributions and system characteristics February and October 1974

	No. of constituencies where vote was in the range:						
	0–10	10–20	20–30	30–40	40–50	50–60	60–70%
February							
Lab	5	11	8	9	27	10	1
Con	1	8	20	24	15	3	0
SNP	3	34	21	6	5	1	1
Lib	44	18	5	2	0	1	1
Winners	0	0	0	10	43	15	3
Totals	53	71	54	41	47	15	3
Fraction successful	0	0	0	0.24	0.91	1.00	1.00
October							
Lab	6	9	8	13	23	11	1
Con	5	26	15	18	7	0	0
SNP	0	6	33	19	11	1	1
Lib	57	9	2	1	1	1	0
Winners	0	0	0	19	37	13	2
Totals	68	50	58	51	42	13	2
Fraction successful	0	0	0	0.37	0.88	1.00	1.00

victory was 0.24 in February 1974 and 0.37 in October; for those in the range 40–50 per cent the probabilities were 0.91 in February and 0.88 in October. Thus the operating characteristics of the system in 1974 were fairly stable but very different from what they had been in the mid-fifties. Between February and October the main change was that greater fractionalization gave votes in the range 30–40 per cent a higher chance of victory in the autumn (Table 7.3).

Now we can calculate the probable seats-to-votes ratios if a party had all its votes in one band of 10 per cent. Let me take a concrete example. The October SNP vote was 30 per cent nationally. Divided into a set of constituency votes of 45 per cent it could be spread over exactly two-thirds of the constituencies. The likely percentage of SNP seats won on this vote distribution would be

$$\frac{30}{45} \times 0.88 \times 100\%$$

i.e. fraction of seats with non-zero votes times probability of victory times 100 per cent. And the seats-to-votes ratio would then be

$$\frac{30}{45} \times 0.88 \times 100 \div 30 = \frac{88}{45} = 1.96$$

Table 7.4 shows the likely seats-to-votes ratios for a variety of different vote distributions.

Only the entries for bands 30–40 per cent and 40–50 per cent differ between February and October and then not by much. Clearly by far the most efficient vote distribution for a party would be one in which all its votes were parcelled out so as to give 40–50 per cent votes in as many constituencies as possible. Votes in the range 50–60 per cent would be only a little less efficient but

Table 7.4. Likely Seats-to-votes ratios, February and October 1974

System Operating characteristics *as in*	Likely seats-to-votes ratio if all constituency votes are either zero or in the range									
	0–10	10–20	20–30	30–40	40–50	50–60	60–70	70–80	80–90	90–100%
Feb 1974	0	0	0	0.69	2.02	1.82	1.54	1.33	1.18	1.05
Oct. 1974	0	0	0	1.06	1.96	1.82	1.54	1.33	1.18	1.05

anything else would be wasteful. Votes under 30 per cent would be a complete loss, votes over 60 per cent would entail quite unnecessarily large majorities. Votes in the 30–40 per cent range though ultra efficient when they won the seat, involved a high risk of failure and a high vote penalty when failure occurred.

We can now evaluate the distributions of party votes in 1974 shown in Table 7.3. Taking February first, Labour had less than 4 per cent more votes than the Conservatives but a far more efficient vote distribution. There were twenty-seven Labour votes in the 40–50 per cent range compared to only fifteen Conservative. Labour had twice as many votes under 20 per cent as the Conservatives – which wasted few Labour votes. Conversely, the Conservatives had two and a half times as many as Labour in the ultra wasteful 20–40 per cent range.

Uniform votes were not necessarily a bad thing in February 1974 but they were bad for a party like the SNP whose votes clustered around 20 per cent. If any party had achieved a national vote of 45 per cent then it would have gained enormously from a uniform spread of votes but for parties with around 30–35 per cent or less – which applied to all the Scottish parties – a uniform spread of votes was disastrous.

For each party we can calculate the number of seats implied by its distribution of votes by noting how many votes it got in a certain range, then multiplying by the probability that votes in that range won seats. For example, there were nine seats where Labour had a 30–40 per cent vote and the probability of such votes winning seats was 0.24; so Labour could expect $9 \times 0.24 = 2.16$ seats from that source; from its twenty-seven votes of 40–50 per cent with a 0.91 probability of winning it could expect another $27 \times 0.91 = 24.57$ seats, and so on. Proceeding in this way we calculate the statistically expected number of seats for each party, given the parties' distribution of votes. The results for February are:

	Lab	Con	SNP	Lib
Statistically expected	38	22	8	3
Actual	40	21	7	3
Discrepancy	+2	−1	−1	0

The discrepancies between what actually happened and the statistical implications of the distributions of votes are so small that there is nothing left to explain about February 1974. Labour did so well and the SNP so badly in converting votes to seats because Labour's combination of a larger and less uniformly distributed vote produced a more efficient conversion of votes to seats.

But when we repeat the calculations for October 1974 this simple explanation no longer holds. Indeed, it would be surprising if it did because between February and October the SNP and Conservatives swapped places in terms of the popular vote but the parties seats-to-votes ratios changed very little. It was quite normal for the SNP as third party in February to suffer the worst seats ratio but quite pathological for it to continue to suffer in that way after breaking through into second place in October.

Helped more by their national increase in votes than by a redistribution of their vote, the SNP in October had twelve votes in the 40–60 per cent range while the Conservatives had only seven. And the SNP also had more votes in the 30–40 per cent and 60–70 per cent ranges than the Conservatives. The efficiency of the SNP's vote distribution was roughly equal to the Conservatives' and their higher vote should have won them more seats. The statistically expected numbers of seats for October, given the vote distributions are as follows:

	Lab	Con	SNP	Lib
Statistically expected	37	13	19	2
Actual	41	16	11	3
Discrepancy	+4	+3	−8	+1

In contrast to February, therefore, the parties' vote distributions do not fully explain the numbers of seats won. Both Labour and the Conservatives should have taken several seats less than they did, and the SNP should have gone into second place with nineteen seats instead of only eleven.

Accidents

There could be several reasons for the failure of parties' vote distributions to explain seats won. It might be necessary, for example, to take account of the interaction between those distributions. High SNP votes could have occurred where the two other parties were evenly balanced, in which event the high SNP votes would have won many seats, or they could have occurred in the so-called 'safe' seats where Labour and Conservative were extremely unbalanced, in which case even relatively high SNP votes might not have won seats.

But another possible cause for the failure of vote distributions to predict seats won is accidents or 'stickiness at the margin'. A party could suffer from an unusually high percentage of 'near misses'. If those near misses arose from a combination of previous voting distributions and uniform national swings we could describe them as 'accidents'. On the other hand, if the near misses were seats which should have changed hands on national swings but did not, then it is evidence of 'stickiness at the margin' caused perhaps by special efforts by parties to retain their marginals or by a special reluctance of voters in marginal seats to switch their votes, knowing that they were likely to defeat the local incumbent party.

The numbers of seats held on very small margins grew significantly in 1974 and, as Table 7.5 shows, the relationship with party changed. In 1955 and 1970 Labour held more of its seats than the Conservatives on small majorities, but by October 1974 three-quarters of Conservative seats were held by less than 10 per cent.

We can calculate the effects of accidents at the margin by taking all the seats that would switch between a pair of parties on swings of up to 5 per cent either way: then divide this set of seats equally between the two parties rather than according to the possibly unequal division that occurred in practice. Clearly this adjustment would benefit the Conservatives in 1955 and 1970

Table 7.5. Percentage of each party's seats held by majority of under 10 per cent

	Con	Lab	SNP
1955	19	32	–
1970	17	27	–
Feb. 1974	24	25	57
Oct. 1974	75	29	55

but the calculation is more complex for the multi-party elections of 1974 when we must consider all six pairwise combinations of the four parties.

In February these calculations on accidental effects showed they were fairly small, but together with the parties' distributions of votes they predicted seats won with a very high level of accuracy – to within one seat for each party:

	Lab	Con	SNP	Lib
Seats implied by vote distributions	38	22	8	3
Plus accident effects	41	20	8	2
Actual	40	21	7	3

In October, however, there were an unusually large number of Conservative super-marginals against Labour and very many Labour super-marginals against the SNP: 5 per cent swings between Labour and the SNP would have given Labour only one gain in one direction but eleven losses in the other. Over all therefore, these accidental effects cost the SNP a net five seats and benefited Labour and the Conservatives equally. Thus we get:

	Lab	Con	SNP	Lib
Seats implied by vote distributions	37	13	19	2
Plus accident effects	40	15	14	2
Actual	41	16	11	3

Together, vote distribution plus accident effects, predict October seats won to within one seat for each of Labour, Conservative, and Liberals but still over-predict the number of SNP seats. This remaining discrepancy may be attributed to the placing of high SNP votes in relatively safe seats. There were four places – Govan, Kinross, Stirling Burghs, and West Lothian – where the party got over 39 per cent of the vote but failed to take the seat because of the extreme imbalance between the other parties.

How accidental were these accidents in October 1974? Although Labour's vote declined fractionally and the SNP's went up by over 8 per cent, the SNP failed to gain any seats from Labour. On uniform swings it should have taken at least Govan and Stirling Burghs and been very close to victory in West Lothian. Similarly Labour, on uniform swings, should have taken Cathcart and Aberdeen South from the Conservatives. There was evidence of stickiness at the margins between Labour and both other parties. But there was no evidence of a similar effect on the margin between the SNP and the Conservatives. In sum, this stickiness had no net effect on Labour seats, helped the Conservatives, and damaged the SNP, despite the fact that there was no direct Conservative–SNP stickiness effect.

CONCLUSIONS ON THE ELECTORAL SYSTEM

In 1974 Labour did so well in the seats-to-votes ratio primarily because of the distribution of party votes. The party owed nothing to an unfair distribution of electoral sizes. In October but not in February, Labour's seats ratio was inflated by its luck in holding onto a large number of seats on small majorities but this was not the result of deviant swings so much as the prior distribution of party votes. Labour did so well because it was the largest party and it had an efficient spatial distribution of votes. While no other party in Britain has enjoyed such a high seats ratio since the War, the British electoral system was functioning quite normally as far as Scottish Labour was concerned.

The Conservatives suffered from a smaller vote – though only a little smaller than Labour's in February – coupled with a less efficiently distributed vote. But they hung on to some seats against the swings in October.

SNP votes were badly distributed in February – far too uniformly distributed for such a small national total. Their vote distribution matched their higher over-all vote rather better in the autumn. But in the autumn a combination of accidents, stickiness at the margin, and the imbalance in their opponents' votes in seats where the SNP vote was high, all conspired to give the SNP a pathologically low seats ratio and prevented it taking second place in seats as well as votes.

None the less, the SNP's appeal was not to spatially distributed social classes but to those who favoured a greater measure of self-government. So to many observers the main surprise was that the SNP achieved as efficient a spatial distribution of votes as it did. Unless attitudes to self-government were spatially distributed – favourable in some areas, unfavourable in others – then even with 30 per cent of the vote the SNP could expect to win very few seats at all. Its chances of victory would be limited to the few places where Labour and Conservatives split their votes almost equally. Yet, as we shall see, attitudes towards self-government were remarkably uniform throughout Scotland, and the seats the SNP won were not Labour/Conservative marginals. So I will now consider the processes by which the SNP vote was concentrated as efficiently as it was. That level of efficiency was far less than total, far less than Labour's, but much greater than the distribution of attitudes to self-government might lead us to expect.

SPATIAL VARIATIONS IN POLITICAL ATTITUDES

Some political attitudes vary between one part of the country and another while others do not. We can measure that variation by dividing survey respondents according to the area in which they live. Given the over-all size of the typical survey it would be unwise to break the sample into more than three parts: further division makes the results far too dependent upon sampling errors. This trichotomy can be done in several different ways.

First, and most obvious, is a breakdown by physical geography. I will use:

(1) West Central: Strathclyde region minus Argyll.
(2) East Central: the regions of Fife, Lothian, the county of Stirling, and the city of Dundee.
(3) Peripheral: the highland region plus Argyll, Grampian region, Perth and Angus – all to the north of the central belt, plus Dumfries and Galloway and the Borders regions to the south.

Secondly, areas can be categorized by social geography. I will use an urban–rural division and also a socio-economic class division:

Urban–rural:
(1) City: Glasgow, Edinburgh, Aberdeen, Dundee.
(2) Town and urban: everywhere not in categories (1) and (3).
(3) Rural: wherever more than a tenth worked in agriculture (according to the 1971 census).

Socio-economic class:
(1) Low managers: under 10 per cent employers and managers.

(2) Medium mangers: 10–15 per cent employers and managers.
(3) High managers: over 15 per cent employers and managers (according to the 1971 census).

Since employers and managers tend to form a higher proportion of the work force in rural areas, the high managers' category has a rural bias, but in our sample three of the eleven high managers' seats were highly urban middle-class districts of Glasgow, Edinburgh, and Aberdeen.

Finally, areas can be divided according to political geography. A simple choice would be a division according to which party won the seat. However, since our sample included only half the Scottish constituencies, the number of SNP seats was too small to provide a reliable sample of SNP areas. So I have put all seats where the SNP vote exceeded 35 per cent into the SNP category. The party did win one seat, Dunbarton East, with less than 35 per cent of the vote, but that seat was not in our sample. So the division is:

(1) Lab: Labour-held in October 1974 and SNP vote less than 35 per cent.
(2) SNP: SNP vote over 35 per cent in October 1974.
(3) Con: Conservative-held in October 1974 and SNP vote less than 35 per cent.

Liberal-held seats, plus Aberdeen West where the Liberals were a close second, were excluded.

Let us consider British issues first. We might expect that respondents in different areas would have different issue priorities, and so they did. Views on the importance of strikes, the social services, or the need for a coalition hardly varied throughout Scotland and there were only modest variations in the priority given to housing and pensions. State ownership of industry was considered notably unimportant in urban working-class seats. But on the principal economic issues – prices, wages, and unemployment – there were large differences in emphasis between urban and central Scotland on the one hand compared with rural, peripheral areas on the other. Economic affairs were distinctly less important to those on the periphery, at least as a factor in deciding their vote (Table 7.6). However, issue

Table 7.6. Principal economic issues

	West	East	% saying issue important Periphery	City	Town	Country
Prices	88	84	73	86	85	75
Wages	76	81	65	76	76	68
Unemployment	73	74	60	74	71	63
Average	79	80	66	79	77	69

priorities did not vary much with the socio-economic class or political partisanship of the area.

Perhaps surprisingly, attitudes on crime varied little. Urban and working-class areas were marginally more in favour of tougher action on crime but the differences were slight. Respondents in SNP areas, on the other hand, were 13 per cent more in favour of tougher action than those in Labour areas.

Religious affiliation varied greatly but attitudes to Catholic schools did not (Table 7.7). Respondents in all types of constituency came down by about four to one against the continuation of separate schools for Catholics. But in the cities and the working-class areas Catholics were far more numerous, as were those of no religion.

Table 7.7. Religious variations

	City	Town	Country	Low	Medium level of managers	High
% Catholic	19	16	4	21	13	5
% No church	35	29	16	37	24	18
% Keep RC schools	22	23	21	25	24	18

Table 7.8 Support for redistribution of wealth

	City	Town	Country	Low	Medium managers	High	Lab	SNP areas	Con
% supporting redistribution	67	79	57	76	60	58	71	58	61

Attitudes towards the redistribution of wealth were the most variable of all, and this time the variation extended to constituency partisanship (Table 7.8). Urban, working-class, and Labour areas strongly supported the notion of redistribution.

Trust in Labour and Conservative governments also varied though it was linked much more closely to class, urbanization, and geographic centrality than to constituency partisanship. Indeed the level of distrust in Conservative governments was virtually as high in Conservative seats as in Labour. The Conservatives were most distrusted in the cities and working-class seats. Labour was most distrusted on the periphery, in the rural areas, and the places with the highest level of managers. Only Labour enjoyed a high level of trust anywhere, and that was in Strathclyde, the urban areas outside the cities, and in seats with low or intermediate levels of managers (Table 7.9).

I have identified oil, decentralization, Scottish government, and possibly EEC membership as special Scottish issues. The priorities given to these issues were remarkably uniform throughout Scotland. Since these were such important issues perhaps it is as well to document that uniformity (Table 7.10).

The EEC was not considered a more important issue in rural or peripheral areas or SNP seats, despite SNP campaigns on that topic. Oil was scarcely more important in SNP seats than Labour ones. Scottish government was rated important by 68 per cent in SNP seats compared to 62 per cent in Labour and 60 per cent in Conservative but these differences were remarkable for their small size rather than their existence. After all, the whole basis for the SNP was its demand for self-government.

Positions on these Scottish issues also displayed a notable uniformity (Table 7.11). On oil and the EEC there was only a 4 per cent gap between attitudes in Labour and Conservative areas, and SNP areas were intermediate. On greater decentralization or devolution, SNP areas were only 2 per cent more favourable than Labour areas and 5 per cent more than Conservative. Strathclyde and working-class areas were more favourable than others but again by less than 6 per cent. Again these issues were so important that I want to document this uniformity.

Here is another paradox. The SNP did best among those individuals most favourable to independence yet it did best in

Table 7.9: Distrust

	West	East	Periphery	City	Town	Country	Low	(Managers) Medium	High	Lab	Area SNP	Con
Distrust												
% rarely trust Conservatives	28	27	25	34	25	23	35	22	24	29	23	27
% rarely trust Labour	15	20	28	22	14	28	15	17	29	15	23	24

Table 7.10. Importance of Scottish issues: % saying important

	West	East	Periphery	City	Town	Country	Low	(Managers) Medium	High	Lab	Area SNP	Con
Oil	58	65	52	60	58	56	60	59	55	59	61	53
Scottish government	64	67	57	61	64	62	65	64	59	62	68	60
EEC	57	62	55	60	57	55	57	60	54	57	57	58

Table 7.11: Positions on Scottish issues

	West	East	Periphery	City	Town	Country	Low	Managers Medium	High	Lab	Area SNP	Con
Scotland to get more oil	72	66	71	73	69	70	73	68	70	72	71	68
Get out of EEC	51	48	52	59	45	53	58	47	49	53	53	49
Very important to decentralize	44	33	33	38	42	33	44	37	34	43	39	32
Want devolution or self-government	65	73	64	66	66	66	67	68	65	64	72	69
Average for two government questions	55	53	49	52	54	50	56	53	50	54	56	51

constituencies which were not at all distinguished by a high level of support for independence. The answer to this paradox lies in the effects which environments had on relationships between individual characteristics and voting rather than on the levels of those characteristics.

The effect of environment on the class alignment is fairly well known and is replicated in many other countries besides Scotland. In middle-class areas both middle- and working-class individuals are much more Conservative than in working-class areas. Indeed the Labour lead over the Conservatives in Table 7.12 owes as much to the class mix in the environment as to individuals' own class. Both middle- and working-class individuals gave Labour a 40 per cent higher lead in areas with low rather than high levels of managers; while in both working- and middle-class environments the working-class individuals gave Labour 45 per cent higher lead than did middle-class individuals (Table 7.12).

Over all we know that SNP support was not aligned by class

Table 7.12. Class, the class environment, and Lab/ Con voting

| | Labour lead over Conservatives among | | |
	Middle-class individuals	Working-class individuals	Difference
When area has			
Low managers	+15	+59	44
High managers	−25	+20	45
Difference	40	39	

Table 7.13. Class, the partisan environment, and SNP voting

| | % SNP among | |
	Middle-class individuals	Working-class individuals
In Lab seats	28	22
In Con seats	21	33

but within certain areas it was. The working class was more SNP than the middle class on the periphery but less SNP in Strathclyde. However, the strongest class pattern was a pro-SNP vote by workers in Conservative areas balanced by a pro-SNP vote by the middle class in Labour areas. This could be interpreted as tactical voting but it is more plausible that this was yet another example of the effect of balanced cross-pressures towards Labour and Conservative which we have seen generally led to higher levels of SNP voting.

Catholics in all parts of the country showed an extreme reluctance to vote SNP. Even when, as in the highly middle-class seats outside the central belt, they did give substantial votes to parties other than Labour they tended more to the Conservatives than to the SNP. Since Church of Scotland and the irreligious did vary their votes that meant the Catholic – non-Catholic voting split automatically widened wherever the non-Catholics gave a higher than average vote to the SNP.

Issue alignments also varied from one area to another. Oil showed least variation. Those who wanted a Scottish bias in the oil revenues were around 20 per cent more likely to vote SNP in most parts of the country. Those who opposed EEC membership tended towards Labour and the SNP by a roughly similar aggregate percentage in most areas but with a clear trade-off between Labour and the SNP. Labour got the bulk of the anti-EEC vote in Strathclyde, but the SNP got more of it on the periphery. EEC attitudes were aligned more closely with Labour in working-class areas and with the SNP in the most middle-class areas. But all these patterns were relatively slight compared with the spatial variation in the devolution alignment.

Table 7.14 compares the variation in EEC, oil, and devolution alignments in each party's seats. What characterized the SNP seats most was a far better penetration of the devolution vote than in other areas. The SNP did badly among anti-devolutionists in all areas but had a very variable level of support among pro-devolutionists; lowest in Strathclyde, the urban areas, and Labour seats; highest on the periphery, in country areas, and in the SNP's own areas.

This finding, that the SNP vote varied because of varying success in penetrating the pro-devolution vote, has important implications. First, it allowed the party to win seats by getting

Table 7.14. SNP vote penetration by individual attitude and area partisanship

	pro-EEC	anti-EEC	difference between cols. 1 & 2	anti-Scottish bias in oil revenues	pro-Scottish bias in oil revenues	difference between cols. 4 & 5	anti-devo	pro-devo	difference between cols. 7 & 8
In Lab seats	23	26	3	9	29	20	11	29	18
In SNP seats	36	51	15	27	51	24	12	59	47
In Con seats	21	31	10	12	31	19	2	35	33

SNP share of vote among individuals who were:

much higher than average votes in some areas despite the uniformity of attitudes towards devolution. Second, the party won seats only by penetrating the pro-devolution vote, not by fielding generally attractive candidates who could gain personal support from all types of constituents; nor by using local issues unconnected with devolution. Even in its own areas it took only 12 per cent of anti-devolution votes, and zero per cent of those who supported a complete status quo on Scottish government. Third, there was a natural plateau for SNP votes. If SNP support increased it could not increase uniformly since much of the devolution vote had already been won in its own seats, and the devolution vote was no bigger there than elsewhere. Fourth, if SNP support increased it was likely to increase most in non-SNP areas but only among pro-devolutionists in those non-SNP areas.

Other surveys can be used to check these hypotheses in more detail (Table 7.15). Breaking down the ORC/*Scotsman* surveys from April 1974 to December 1975 according to the same classification of constituencies into Labour, SNP, and Conservative areas shows, first of all, that SNP support was well on the way to its October concentration as early as April 1974. When SNP support fell in the spring of 1975 it fell most in the SNP's own areas. Following publication of the 1975 White Paper on devolution, *Our Changing Democracy*, SNP support reached its peak for the seventies. But though SNP support was 7 per cent up on the 1974 general election it was actually down in the SNP seats but enormously up elsewhere: so that by the end of 1975 the level of SNP support was fairly uniform throughout the land. In passing, we should note that this uniformity in December 1975 was not the chance result of a bad ORC sample. Labour and Conservative preferences in that ORC sample remained sharply linked to the type of area.

The various surveys put rather different questions on devolution, all of them multi-option. But all offered independence as the single most extreme option, and all showed that support for independence varied very little by area. Taking, from each survey, the percentage favouring independence plus the percentage favouring the next most extreme constitutional option shows that the demand for a strong measure of devolution hardly varied at all between Labour, SNP, and Conservative

Table 7.15. Time trends in SNP penetration of different areas

	SNP share of votes or preferences			
	ORC Apr. 74	SES Oct. 74	ORC Apr. 75	ORC Dec. 75
In Lab areas	21	21	28	38
In SNP areas	34	46	32	40
In Con areas	19	24	25	36

	Demand for devolution or independence				
	Average all surveys	ORC Apr. 74	SES Oct. 74	ORC Apr. 75	ORC Dec.75
In Lab areas	51	40	64	52	49
In SNP areas	50	41	71	47	42
In Con areas	49	42	69	39	44

	SNP support across the constitutional spectrum				
		status quo			independence
Survey	Type of seat	A	B	C	D	E
ORC Apr. 74	Lab or Con	2	5	5	27	65
	SNP	0	13	17	41	81
	difference	2	8	12	14	16
SES Oct. 74	Lab or Con	0		9	19	52
	SNP	0		20	46	80
	difference	0		11	27	28
ORC Apr. 75	Lab or Con	1	17	12	26	74
	SNP	6	13	12	35	86
	difference	5	−4	0	9	12
ORC Dec. 75	Lab or Con	4	15	19	34	84
	SNP	10	23	21	47	80
	difference	6	8	2	13	−4

seats. Because the questions changed from survey to survey the percentages vary by survey but not, on average, by area.

Each of the ORC polls offered five constitutional options,

while the SES offered only four, and the options themselves changed. But in all the surveys we can arrange the constitutional options into a spectrum from status quo to independence and look at the rising levels of SNP support across this constitutional spectrum.

As hypothesized the pattern of great SNP penetration of the devolution and independence vote in SNP seats was evident in 1974, especially strongly in the October voting patterns, but it was weaker in April 1975 and virtually eliminated by the end of 1975. Let us compare the peak time of SNP support, December 1975, with the October 1974 election: at the election the SNP won 80 per cent of the independence vote in the SNP seats but only 52 per cent elsewhere; by December 1975 it still had 80 per cent of the independence vote in its own seats but now had 84 per cent of the independence vote in Labour and Conservative seats. At the same time the SNP had begun to gather a little support at the status quo end of the spectrum in the seats it had won in 1974, possibly as a modest response to the hard work of its newly elected MPs. Consequently, by 1975 the relationship between devolution attitudes and party support was similar in different types of seat, and since devolution attitudes themselves were uniform, the SNP support in 1975, unlike 1974, spread evenly throughout Scotland.

THE SPATIAL PATTERN OF SNP VOTING

The fact that devolution and self-government attitudes were uniform throughout Scotland had two spatial implications. First, high SNP votes could be expected nowhere, everywhere, anywhere – the party might do best in the towns one year and best outside them in the next; it all depended upon the presence of constraint-breaking influences that would allow it to take up the full measure of its natural support. Second, there was a natural plateau of SNP support – just as the independence vote was a natural target for SNP appeals those at the other end of the devolution spectrum would not vote SNP no matter how good the local candidate or how vigorous the local campaign.

So when seeking explanations for the spatial patterns to SNP voting we are not looking for local conditions that might dispose the voters towards self-government, but conditions that might free those who wanted self-government from the ties of habit and loyalty to the old parties: perhaps a social or political milieu which prevented the old parties establishing strong roots; perhaps nothing more than a good SNP candidate and a well-run campaign.

Jaensch has tried correlating constituency votes in 1974 with a range of social variables taken from the 1971 census: occupation, industry, age distribution, birth-place (percentage Scottish born), education levels, house tenure, and car ownership. While Labour and Conservative votes correlated highly with these census variables, SNP votes did not. It would be easy, but incorrect, to conclude that there was no pattern to SNP constituency votes, that pure accident determined where the party did well. The error lies in treating social conditions as the direct and principal cause of SNP voting. As a result Jaensch seriously underestimated the degree of social pattern that did exist because social conditions provided only one of several constraint-breaking influences.

Constituency boundaries, in Scotland and England, were revised between 1970 and 1974 but just over half the Scottish constituencies remained intact. These included ten of the eleven seats won by the SNP in 1974 and most of the areas of SNP voting strength. So it is possible to trace the political history of almost all the SNP seats. The single exception is Dunbarton East, won by a 31 per cent vote against exceptionally evenly split opposition. Paradoxically, Dunbarton East was not an area of SNP voting strength even though it returned on SNP member to parliament.

The first possibility is that the local peaks of SNP support in 1974 reflected a lengthy local political tradition of SNP campaigning. Table 7.16 shows that the very few seats which the SNP had contested since the fifties and early sixties did return

Table 7.16. SNP vote in February 1974 by length of tradition

	Since	1955	1959	1964	1966	1970	First contested 1970
No. of constituencies		2	3	7	7	17	10
SNP vote Feb. 1974		31	28	30	30	37	40

Note: To qualify seats had only to be contested in 1955 and 1959, but get over 10 per cent SNP in 1964 and over 15 per cent in 1966 and 1970.

votes which were significantly higher than the average in 1974; but the very best SNP results in 1974 were achieved in seats the party had not contested before 1970 yet where it had done fairly well on its first attempt. Of the eleven seats won by October 1974, only one had been contested at all elections since 1955 and two since 1964, while eight were first contested in 1970. A lengthy tradition, therefore, did lead to higher than average SNP votes but it applied to very few seats and could only account for SNP victories in Perth East, and perhaps Stirling East.

On the other hand, the connection between SNP support in 1970 and subsequent years was very strong. The correlation with February 1974 was 0.82 and the regression equation was

$$\text{Feb SNP } \% = 1.22 \times 1970 \text{ SNP } \% + 7\%$$

showing that the SNP's greatest gains in 1974 were where it was already strongest in 1970. The coefficient 1.22 means that February 1974 votes were roughly one and a quarter times 1970 votes plus an additional 7 per cent everywhere. So the most powerful of all SNP traditions began, overnight, as late as 1970.

In so far as the SNP had enjoyed success in local government elections this success created on balance an anti-tradition. Where the party had consistently done well – in Cumbernauld (part of Dunbarton East) and Stirling Burghs – its parliamentary votes were at or above the average in 1974. But its massive local government gains in 1968, when it took a third of the vote in the cities, were generally followed by a below average parliamentary vote. As if to confirm the inverse relation between local and parliamentary successes, the SNP's only victory in the cities was at Dundee East where the party had withdrawn from local government contests.

By-elections played a significant part in the growth of the SNP and their after-effects account for at least half the best SNP votes in former Labour areas. By coincidence all the outstanding SNP by-election results had been in Labour seats: West Lothian in 1962, Hamilton 1967, Dundee East and Govan in 1973. All of these produced a large SNP vote without precedent in the locality, the consequence of outstanding candidates, a legendary campaigning machine concentrated in a single place, and fortunate timing. So in February 1974 the SNP vote was declining locally, but still above the national average in Hamilton and Govan where the party had won by-elections. In West Lothian the February vote was less than in 1966, but still greatly above the national average. Only Dundee East showed an SNP gain in 1974. In addition, Stirling Burghs returned the same SNP vote in February 1974 as at the 1971 by-election though Stirling also enjoyed a long SNP tradition in both local and parliamentary contests.

So, of the eight best SNP performances against Labour in February 1974, five reflected the after-effects of by-elections, the three Stirling seats had an unusually long SNP tradition, and the Western isles was clearly a unique case. With some double counting that covers all eight. SNP candidates in these seats included the president and the Chairman of the party, plus Margo Macdonald who captured the heart of the media during her Govan campaign, STV's chief political presenter George Reid, and the inimitable Donald Stewart, former provost of Stornoway. It all adds up to a set of historical and personal accidents strengthening the SNP as a party in these areas.

But on the other side, in the former Conservative seats where the SNP did well in 1974, the pattern was one of opposition weakness rather than SNP strength. Here, there were no spectacular by-elections, no lengthy history of SNP candidates in parliamentary elections and, since local government councils were mainly 'non-political', there was no history of involvement in local contests either. Table 7.17 shows the average SNP vote in the seven seats the SNP took from the Conservatives in 1974 contrasted with the average in the seven ex-Labour seats where the SNP did best. The time scale runs from 1955 to 1975. In the Tory or ex-Tory areas SNP voting was trivially small throughout the sixties, then suddenly increased to 24 per cent in 1970, higher even than in the best Labour areas. In 1974 both types of seat gave similar average SNP votes but in 1979 the SNP vote held up significantly better in the Conservative areas.

Table 7.17. SNP trends in Labour and Conservative areas

	1955	1959	1964	1966	1970	1974	1974	1979
Ex Con seats	3	3	3	4	24	41	44	38
Ex Lab seats	1	1	8	16	21	40	44	30

Note: Entries are SNP percent votes (average).

According to the 1971 census there were nineteen Scottish seats where over a tenth of the work force were engaged in agriculture. In 1955 sixteen of the nineteen were held by the Conservatives, one by the Liberals, and only two by Labour – Ayr South where there was a mining tradition and the Western Isles. Moreover, the rural seats were apparently the safest Conservative seats in the land yet these seats were not natural Conservative territory. It is one of the ironies of politics that the Conservatives were accused of having an excessively rural image. But rural areas have persistently deviated towards the Liberals, not the Conservatives ever since the rural working classes received the vote a hundred years ago. That was as true for Scotland as for England. Indeed, the lands swept by the Crofters' Party in late Victorian times could hardly be an appropriate base for the Scottish Conservatives. So during the fifties the Conservatives held these seats not on the basis of genuine strength but because the traditional vanguard of the anti-Conservatives in rural areas, the Liberal Party, was on the point of collapse and failed even to contest most of the rural seats. Indeed the Liberals had only five candidates in the whole of Scotland.

At the end of the fifties the Liberal Party began to fight back and by the mid-sixties they had won five of the rural seats plus the service town of Inverness. In addition they held second place in another six and substantial votes in a further three, making the Liberals a major force throughout rural Scotland. But the basic strategy of the Liberal Party in the sixties was to move into suburban areas chasing the will-o'-the-wisp of major party status in parliament. When that failed their organization and enthusiasm failed even in the rural areas which were the party's natural base. And in Scotland their leaders, especially Jo Grimond, got caught up in home rule campaigns which the SNP could fight equally well. In 1970 they abandoned even seats like Moray where they had scored 18 per cent in 1966, Argyll where they won 27 per cent, and the Western Isles where they had won 19 per cent. Even where they did stand again they fought a weak campaign and lost votes.

In the years after 1955 Labour added Berwick, Caithness, and Lanark to the two rural seats it already held but two of these gains had mining connections and in the third the Conservative MP had resigned the whip and sponsored a breakaway candidate against his successor. Elsewhere Labour lacked the organization, the pro-rural policies, and the credibility to form the nucleus of an anti-Conservative front. It was Labour's weakness rather than a genuine Conservative strength which had made these seats safe for the Conservatives.

So, for a variety of reasons all three parties were weak in the rural areas by the end of the sixties and this gave the SNP an opening.

Table 7.18 shows the deviation from national trends in the seven Conservative seats won by the SNP. They were all in our rural category, including three of the four most rural. (Most rural of all was the Liberal's Orkney and Shetland.) From 1959 to 1966 these seats trended towards the Liberals by 10–14 per cent more than Scotland generally. But from 1970 onwards this bias almost disappeared, replaced by a trend towards the SNP that was 10–18 per cent greater than in Scotland generally. Inevitably other parties had to suffer. In the sixties Labour suffered more than the Conservatives but only by 2–3 per cent and by 1970 the two major parties were about equally down compared to 1955. Then in February 1974 and still more in October and in 1979 Labour was hit far worse than the Conservatives. Allowing for Scotland-wide trends between 1955 and 1979, that is allowing for the large swing to Labour that occurred nationally, the trends on this rural Conservative–SNP battle-ground were 18 per cent more favourable to the SNP than elsewhere, 5 per cent less favourable to the Conservatives, and 14 per cent less favourable to Labour.

Table 7.18. Deviation of trends in seven ex-Conservative seats from nation-wide Scottish trends

	Con	Lab	Lib	SNP
1959	−4	−6	10	0
1964	−5	−8	14	−2
1966	−2	−5	10	−4
1970	−7	−7	3	10
1974 Feb	−7	−10	1	17
1974 Oct	−2	−10	1	11
1979	−5	−14	1	18

It would be unnecessarily narrow-minded to interpret this as tactical voting by people who were 'really' Labour. Much more reasonable is the view that in seats which had only been Conservative strongholds by default, the SNP took over much of the Liberal part of the anti-Tory vote in 1970 and added much of the Labour part in 1974. The SNP succeeded in forming the nucleus of an anti-Tory coalition.

Though the Liberals had played a path-breaking role in the seven seats won by the SNP from the Conservatives their average vote climbed only to a maximum of 20 per cent and the Liberals failed to win any of the seats. In the six seats which the Liberals did win – five rurals plus Inverness – the SNP remained at a disadvantage even as late as 1979. The Liberal vote averaged 45 per cent in 1966 and although the party was down to three seats and 36 per cent of the vote by 1970 it still remained a major force and the SNP received less than average votes in every election from 1955 to 1979.

At the other extreme, in the Labour seats where the SNP did best in 1974 the Liberals seldom fielded candidates and obtained derisory votes when they did.

Thus Liberal votes only led to SNP votes in rural areas where the Liberals achieved sizeable votes but failed to win seats, where they had exposed the weakness of the two-party system without establishing a strength of their own. Where they did succeed in establishing their own strength, Liberal votes in the sixties led to below average rather than above average SNP votes in the seventies.

One way or another, however, the majority of the rural areas turned out their Conservative MPs. In 1955 sixteen of the nineteen seats had been Conservative, many held by very large majorities. By 1974 the Conservatives held only five of the nineteen and only two by even moderately large majorities. The Liberals held three, Labour four, and the SNP seven.

One measure of the vigour of a local campaign is the amount spent on the candidate's expenses. In most constituencies the vast majority of election expenses go on printing and stationery. So, in general, large expenses mean many leaflets and many leaflets mean many workers to address the envelopes or deliver the leaflets by hand. Few Scots candidates spent anywhere near the legal maximum and most spent far less. So there is no reason to believe that expenses statistics have been unduly manipulated to keep within the law. What is clear, however, is that in some areas none of the candidates spent very much while in others they all did. So the best measure of the vigour of an SNP constituency campaign relative to the vigour of its opponents' is the ratio of SNP expenses to the maximum spent by any candidate in the same constituency rather than the legal maximum.

This statistic identifies the places where the SNP fought a purely nominal campaign in February 1974 doing little more than file a candidate's nomination papers. There were nine seats where the SNP spent only a fifth as much as one of its opponents, and altogether nineteen seats where it spent less than a third. Ten of the nineteen were in Glasgow, and all but one were near Glasgow. At the other extreme, fourteen of the twenty seats with the largest SNP expenditures were in our set of nineteen rural seats. So, whatever the natural political responses of the electorate, or the pattern of 1970 voting, the SNP itself mounted a 1974 campaign that was clearly directed at rural Scotland and away from Glasgow and its environs (Table 7.19).

Table 7.19 SNP twenty top spenders in February 1974 (Relative to highest spender in constituency)

			% SNP vote		
% Exp.	% Agric.		1970	Feb.	Oct.
100	12	Western Isles	43	67	62
100	26	Aberdeen East	30	51	49
100	–	Stirling East	16	44	51
100	13	Angus South	23	37	44
100	–	Govan	10	41	41
100	–	West Lothian	28	35	41
99	10	Perth East	17	27	41
96	11	Moray	28	49	41
95	24	Banff	23	46	46
95	14	Dumfries	13	19	26
90	25	Galloway	21	31	40
90	–	Stirling Burghs	15	35	40
90	10	Fife East	12	20	32
85	17	Caithness	16	16	24
84	–	Dundee East	9	40	48
83	17	Argyll	30	49	50
83	–	Edinburgh South	7	13	22
82	21	Angus North	17	23	34
78	21	Aberdeen West	5	15	22
74	20	Kinross	19	23	41

The six exceptions, where the SNP spent heavily in non-rural areas, included Govan, West Lothian, and Stirling Burghs – all places where a party leader was candidate and a by-election had raised SNP hopes – plus Stirling East and Dundee East.

The weight of SNP campaigning went into the places, urban and rural, where the party had achieved high votes in 1970 or at a by-election. It was a strategy designed to reinforce success and make the party's vote as non-uniform as possible. High spending was no automatic guarantee of victory for the SNP or for other parties. Labour spent more than the Conservatives in an unsuccessful bid to take the highly marginal Cathcart from the Conservatives, and the Conservatives spent more than the SNP trying to hang on to Moray. But there were few places where the SNP spent heavily without getting a larger than average vote in return – only four seats in the list of twenty.

SNP candidates in 1970 averaged 12.5 per cent of the vote in the seats they contested. Let us look at the subsequent history of the seats where they did better than average in 1970. There were nine seats with votes of 15–21 per cent (average 18 per cent), and six with votes of 23–30 per cent (average 27 per cent). In February 1974 the SNP expenses ratio averaged 80 per cent in the first set and 96 per cent in the second; and the SNP vote went up by 11 per cent in the first set and 18 per cent in the second. The party put in most effort and made the greatest gain where it already had most votes.

But between February and October the SNP made no further gains in its best seats: it had hit a plateau, perhaps fully taken up its natural support. Meanwhile, in the moderately strong SNP areas it again made an above average gain, halving the gap between SNP votes in the strong and moderate SNP seats. Finally, when SNP support dropped in 1979, the drop was least in its strongest seats (Table 7.20, Fig. 7.3).

To summarize: the SNP did particularly well in Labour areas where a by-election campaign, a party leader as candidate, or a long tradition of SNP contests had locally strengthened the party. It also did well in the rural ex-Conservative areas where the Liberals had won votes but not seats in the sixties. The SNP directed its 1974 campaign expenditure at these constituencies and turned them into political 'growth points' giving the SNP its

Table 7.20 Average SNP votes 1970–9 by size of vote in 1970

	1970	Feb. 1974	Oct. 1974	1979
Seats with 23–30 per cent in 1970	27	45	45	37
Seats with 15–21 per cent in 1970	18	28	38	29
All Scottish seats	13*	22*	30	17

* adjusted for number of seats contested in 1970 and February 1974.

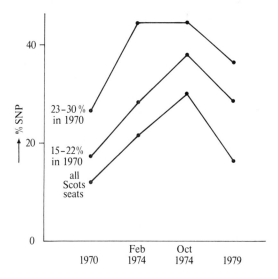

Fig. 7.3. Average SNP votes 1970–9 by size of vote in 1970

greatest gains where it already had most votes – a highly desirable pattern for a new party under a first-past-the-post voting system. At around 45 per cent the SNP vote hit a plateau and did no more than hold its own as the party made further gains in less favourable seats in October 1974 but when SNP votes declined in 1979 they held up best in the party's best seats. So at the end of the seventies the seats which had been 14 per cent more SNP than average in 1970 had become 20 per cent more SNP than average.

So whereas SNP support became more uniform throughout Scotland at its peak in December 1975, it became increasingly non-uniform as the tide of party popularity ebbed, reflecting perhaps the tendency of the party's MPs in 1979 to retreat to their own constituencies and fight personal, local campaigns rather than a national issue-based campaign.

CLASS ALIGNMENTS AND CLASS ENVIRONMENTS

Constituency class alignments like class alignments among individuals survived the growth of SNP voting remarkably unchanged. Right through from the mid-fifties to the late seventies the class alignment of constituency voting remained roughly equal and constant in Scotland and England.

As we saw in Table 7.12 the relationship between class and constituency voting was much more than a mere reflection of the link between individuals' occupations and their party choices. Everyone in middle-class areas – manual workers as well as professional people – was much more Conservative, and less Labour than in working-class areas. This can be illustrated diagramatically in the Z model. The highly simplified Z model shown in Fig. 7.4 applies strictly to a pure two-party system but it conveys the idea of individual and environmental class influences rather well.

The top line of the Z shows the hypothetical per cent Conservative among middle-class individuals. Since that percentage is not a constant but depends upon the local class mix the top line of the Z slopes upwards to the right instead of being horizontal. Similarly, the bottom line of the Z, which represents

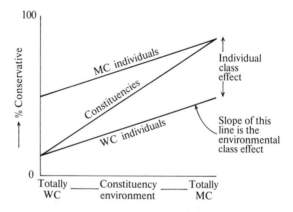

Fig. 7.4. Z model of class alignments

working-class support for the Conservatives, also slopes upwards towards the right since they too become more Conservative when they live in more middle-class areas.

If individuals in both classes are equally sensitive and responsive to the local class mix then the top and bottom lines of the Z will be parallel. There is evidence that this is so. The vertical gap between these two parallel lines represents the individual component of class polarization, the difference between the Conservative vote of middle- and working-class individuals living in the same social environment.

But the relationship between constituency voting and the constituency class mix has both an individual and an environmental component. It is given by the cross member of the Z. The Conservative vote in middle-class areas is high for two reasons: first, the people are middle class; second, they live in a middle-class environment and therefore support the Conservatives more strongly than other middle-class people who live elsewhere. Generally, in Britain the environmental component has been growing as the individual component has been declining and the environmental component of class polarization is now larger than the individual component. To put it another way: our choice between Conservative and Labour now depends more on the mix of occupations in our surroundings than on our own occupation. Class, in its political aspects, has become a social rather than individual attribute.

That does not apply to everyone. There are some positions or activities which merit the title 'core' classes and these are the ones responsible for the class polarization of Labour–Conservative voting. But few individuals are so closely linked to these pure class roles that they can be described as truly belonging to a core class. For most, their class position is defined by the relative strength and quantity of their links to each of the core classes. These links depend upon (among other things) contact with other people and contacts are structured by (among other things) the local spatial environment. Manual workers with managerial family connections tend to be much more Conservative than other manual workers but, provided they are evenly distributed, this has no effect on the environmental component of class polarization. On the other hand manual workers who have managers for neighbours also tend to be much more Conservative than other manual workers and this does affect the environmental component of class polarization.

Analysis suggests that one core class consists of employers and managers though the opposite core is less easy to define and almost impossible to measure. Thus the local density of employers and managers is the critical variable for defining the partisanship of an area. It is not just that they themselves vote solidly against Labour but their presence seems to make all others less likely to vote Labour also. It was for this reason that I used the level of employers and managers to define spatial environments with different class characteristics.

The implication for constituency voting is that although the managerial class themselves scarcely ever exceed a quarter of a constituency electorate their presence is the best predictor of Conservative versus Labour voting and so I shall use it to measure the strength of the constituency class alignment.

When more than the two class parties contest an election, especially when the other parties gain as many votes as in Scotland in the mid-seventies the statistic chosen to measure the Labour–Conservative balance of votes is critical. One obvious measure is the Conservative share of the Conservative plus Labour vote but this turns out to be highly misleading because the SNP and Liberals tend to take votes from the other parties more evenly than proportionately. Let me illustrate the effect this has. Suppose that in one election constituency A votes 60 per cent Labour and 40 per cent Conservative, while B votes 40 per cent Labour and 60 per cent Conservative. Then, at a second election third parties put up candidates and take 20 per cent from Labour and Conservative everywhere. Then according the Conservative share of the two-party vote these two seats have polarized:

			Seat A	Seat B
First election:	Con		40	60
	Lab		60	40
Con share of two-party vote		=	40	60
Second election:	Con		20	40
	Lab		40	20
	Oth		40	40
Con share of two-party vote		=	33	66

the difference between their levels of Conservative versus Labour voting has gone up from 20 per cent to 33 per cent.

If the new third parties had taken more votes from the party that was locally stronger – more from Labour in seat A and more from the Conservatives in seat B – then the Conservative share of the two-party vote would not have indicated an increased polarization. But this is not the normal pattern in Britain. Third parties do not take more votes from a party where it has more votes 'at risk' because the greater level of support for the party in its safer seats tends to reinforce the loyalty of its supporters there: there are more of them who could defect but each individual supporter is less likely to do so because his party choice is reinforced by contact with other people who also support his party.

So if we took the Conservative share of the two-party vote as a measure of Conservative/Labour partisanship we should automatically record increased class polarization between constituencies at any election when third parties gained unusually large numbers of votes. But it would not be a genuine class polarization; indeed, fewer people would be voting for class parties.

Hence, I will take the Conservative lead over Labour as the measure of Conservative/Labour partisanship. This measure is totally unaffected by third-party incursions which take votes evenly from an old party, as many in its worst areas as in its best. A reference back will show, for example, that it would record the difference between seats A and B as 40 per cent in both the hypothetical elections.

The strength of the class alignment between constituencies is measured by a regression of the form

% Con lead over Lab = $a + b \times$ (% employers and managers)

The coefficient b shows how much the Conservative lead goes up for every increase of 1 per cent in the level of the managerial classes. If constituency B has 10 per cent more managers than A, we should expect the Conservative lead to be 10b per cent more in B than A.

Table 7.21 shows the values for the b coefficient at each election from 1955 to 1979 in Scotland and England. Constituency class polarization was very similar on both sides of the

Table 7.21. Class polarization of constituencie.

	1955	1959	1964	1966	1970	Feb. 74	Oct. 74	1979
England	4.4	4.3	4.1	4.4	4.4	4.0	4.2	4.3
Scotland	4.6	4.6	5.0	5.2	5.0	4.2	4.5	4.9

Note: entries are unstandardized regression coefficients in equation predicting Conservative per cent lead over Labour from per cent employers and managers.

border and remarkably constant through time. Despite survey evidence that individuals in different social classes have come closer together politically, constituency class polarization has been maintained. Class polarization was always a little stronger in Scotland, particularly in the mid-sixties and to a lesser extent in 1970 and 1979 but the Nationalist breakthrough in 1974 left class polarization in Scotland where it had been in the late fifties, at the height of two-party politics.

The managerial classes in Scotland were somewhat smaller than in England and this explained part of Labour's greater electoral success north of the border. But does it explain it all? Table 7.22 shows the level of Conservative lead over Labour predicted by the Scottish and English class regressions for a typical constituency with 12.5 per cent employers and managers – rather more middle class than the Scottish average but less than the English average. The difference between the Scottish and English class-based predictions is a measure of the pro-Labour effect of non-class factors in Scotland, including any nation-wide attachment to Labour.

So allowing for class effects, Scotland as a whole deviated slightly towards the Conservatives in 1959, 1966, and February 1974, slightly towards Labour in 1964, 1970, and October 1974.

Table 7.22. Class-based predictions of Conservative lead in a typical constituency with 12.5 per cent employers and managers (10.5 per cent for 1955–70)

	1955	1959	1964	1966	1970	1974	1974	1979
England	1.5	4.0	−2.9	−9.5	0.1	−2.4	−6.8	4.6
Scotland	7.9	5.7	−3.8	−8.2	−2.5	0.0	−7.2	−6.7
(Scot.−Eng.)	+6.4	+1.7	−1.1	+1.3	−2.6	+2.4	−0.4	−11.3

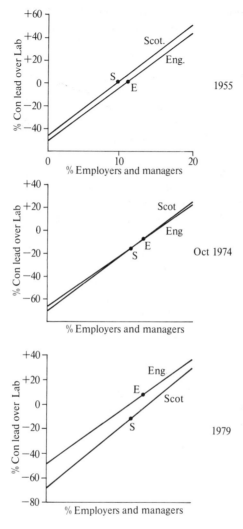

Fig. 7.5. Class regressions for Scotland and England 1955, 1974, and 1979

But the big Scottish national deviations were in 1955 and 1979: strongly towards the Conservatives in 1955 but very strongly towards Labour in 1979.

Over the four elections from 1964 to February 1974 there was no net pro- or anti-Conservative bias in Scotland once the effect of class is discounted. Now over those four elections the over-all difference between the Conservative lead in Scotland and England averaged 8 per cent. So that should be regarded as the normal Scots–English difference which is due entirely to class. Coincidentally the average gross national difference at all elections between 1923 and 1979 was also 8 per cent which confirms that figure as the norm.

Figure 7.5 shows the relationship between constituency class and constituency voting in Scotland and England for 1955, October 1974, and 1979. The points marked on the regression lines correspond to the average levels of employers and managers in Scotland and England. The point for Scottish constituencies is to the left of that for England and since the regression lines slope down to the left that implies a smaller Conservative lead in Scotland – other things being equal. But though other things were fairly equal in 1974 and the gross national difference of 10 per cent was attributable mainly to class differences, in 1955 and 1979 other things were far from equal.

At any given level of class, Scottish constituencies were *more* Conservative than English in 1955 but *less* Conservative in 1979. So in 1955 the Scots national tendency towards the Conservatives exactly cancelled the Scots class tendency towards Labour. Conversely, in 1979 the Scots national tendency towards Labour cumulated with a Scots class tendency towards Labour. The purely national effect was stronger than the class effect. So in 1979 the nations differed by 21 per cent instead of a normal class-based 8 per cent.

Chapter 8

Voting – 4: A Causal Model

In this chapter I want to summarize and co-ordinate many of the findings of earlier chapters by constructing what is technically known as a recursive causal model applied to cross-sectional data. This is not meant to be anything like an engineering blueprint, still less a working model. What this model does is to:

(1) list the major influences on voting but only the major influences, so that the reader is not overwhelmed with relatively unimportant detail;

(2) show how these influences combined and interacted to produce their effects on voting; and

(3) assess the relative power of different influences.

In short, the model seeks to give a highly simplified but powerfully predictive overview of voting patterns in the mid-seventies.

Let me take two examples of questions the model attempts to answer. First, we know that manual workers and council tenants tended to support Labour, but we also know that council tenants tended to be manual workers; so did council tenants only tend towards Labour for reasons of occupational class? And if not, which was the more significant determinant of Labour voting – occupation or housing? Second, we know that young people and pro-devolutionists tended to vote SNP but young people were also relatively pro-devolution: so did young people only support the SNP because they favoured devolution? or because youth in general were attracted towards a new rising party? or because they had not yet developed restraints of habit and loyalty to other parties sufficient to stop them indulging their devolution preferences and voting SNP?

Answers to questions such as these have considerable implications for our understanding of what happened in 1974 and what might happen in the future.

However, it is as well to emphasize right at the beginning that this model is a cross-sectional model and not a 'working' model. By that I mean that it displays the patterns of voting at one time. A high coefficient on the link between devolution attitudes and SNP voting means that the SNP did relatively well among those at the independence end of the devolution spectrum and relatively badly among those who favoured the status quo. But the whole model refers to patterns as they existed at one point in time. All the coefficients could change over time. The SNP could either gain or lose by breaking the link between devolution attitudes and SNP voting: it could gain if it won over the anti-devolution voters and it could lose by losing the support of pro-devolution and pro-independence voters. Either way the model would then show less of a connection between attitudes and votes. So by describing the model as 'cross-sectional' I mean that when the model outputs – party votes – change over time this change may be just as much the product of structural changes in the model as changing inputs. Even though the model shows that SNP voting was highly dependent upon devolution attitudes in 1974, SNP support could change as much because the attitude–vote relationship changed, as because devolution attitudes themselves changed. Thus the model is a valuable tool for describing 1974 voting patterns but it makes no pretence to permanence. It may help us speculate about future changes, but does not forecast them in any mechanical way.

My rationale for including variables in this model was to include only the minimum necessary to sketch the broad outlines of party choice. Social background, urban or rural residence, class, religion, house tenure, age, and perhaps sex, all appeared to affect either the choice between Labour and Conservative or between SNP and the rest. A minimum set of attitude measures would have to include devolution and oil attitudes because of their link with SNP support, and also some measure of voters' attraction to either, both, or neither of the old governing parties. I ran the model calculations twice, first using trust in Labour and Conservative governments, then attitudes towards the redistribution of wealth as the bases for measures of attraction towards the old parties. In broad terms the results were similar and I will only show those which used trust patterns.

The essence of a 'recursive' model is that there are no loops or circuits of causation in it: that we can assign all the variables to groups and assume that variables in one group may be influenced by those in earlier groups but not by those in the same or later groups. My postulated recursive structure was as follows:

Group 1: Rural residence
Group 2: Age
Group 3: Occupational class
Group 4: Religion
Group 5: House tenure
Group 6: Class identification
Group 7: Trust in governments; attitudes on oil and devolution
Group 8: Vote

The implications of this set of assumptions are, for example, that class identification depends on class, but not vice versa: that those with middle-class occupations were more likely as a result to feel middle class but that no one could get a senior manager's job just by feeling he was that sort of person.

Now any analytical assumptions are likely to be only approximately true. Some people may feel such a sense of identification with the working class that they go straight from university to an unskilled manual occupation and a council house. But if we admit such reciprocal influences then it becomes very much more difficult in theory, and perhaps impossible in practice, to quantify the degree of influence in each direction along such reciprocal causal links. The weight of influence is, I think, from the earlier groups to the later groups in the model and the assumption of a recursive structure is a reasonable analytical assumption.

Quantitative results depend critically upon the precise interpretation put on such variables as class. So it is important to list the definitions explicitly:

Group 1:   *Rural residence*: respondents who lived in constituencies where 10 per cent or more were employed in agriculture according to the 1971 census versus the rest.

Group 2:   *Age*: aged under 35 versus 35 to 55 versus over 55, with a requirement that the effects of youth and old age must be equal and opposite.

Group 3:   *Occupational class*: respondents whose head of household had a non-manual occupation versus a manual occupation.

Group 4:   *Religion*: was modelled by three variables: CATH which distinguished Catholics from the combination of Protestants and irreligious; PROT which distinguished Protestants from the combination of Catholics and irreligious; NONE which distinguished the irreligious from the rest. Any two of these variables used in harness could model a three-way religious split while one or other of them by itself could model any of the three possible religious dichotomies.

Group 5: *House tenure*: Council tenants versus the rest.

Group 6: *Class identification*: respondents who chose the term 'middle class' as a self-description versus those who chose 'working class'.

Group 7: *Trust*: initially trust or rather distrust in Labour (DT LAB) and Conservative (DT CON) government was coded as −1 for 'usually trust', zero for 'sometimes trust', +1 for 'rarely trust'. Then from these raw measures I constructed three indicators of trust in Labour and Conservative governments viewed as a pair. These indicators were: DT GAP, the difference between trust in Labour and Conservative, defined as (DT LAB − DT CON). That could range from −2 up to +2 with positive values indicating a pro-Conservative attitude. DT UB, the balance between trust in Labour and Conservative irrespective of which party was more trusted, defined as the absolute value of DT GAP. Thus it could range from zero for completely balanced trust up to 2 for extremely unbalanced trust. DT TOT, the total level of distrust in Labour and Conservative governments, defined as DT LAB + DT CON.

The values of DT GAP, DT UB, DT TOT corresponding to each of the nine trust combinations are:

Trust Con	Trust Lab			Trust Lab			Trust Lab		
	U	S	R	U	S	R	U	S	R
Usually	0	+1	+2	0	1	2	−2	−1	0
Sometimes	−1	0	+1	1	0	1	−1	0	1
Rarely	−2	−1	0	2	1	0	0	1	2
	DT GAP			DT UB			DT TOT		

The purpose of these three indicators was to model the notions of old-party identification (DT GAP), balance (DT UB), and protest (DT TOT).

Group 7:   *Oil*: respondents who favoured a purely British share-out of oil revenues were coded zero, those who wanted 'more' for Scotland coded 2, 'most' coded 3, 'all' coded 4. The significance of the unequal steps on this scale is that I took the distinction between wanting and not wanting a Scottish bias in the oil revenues as larger than between wanting 'more' and 'most'.

Devolution: respondents who wanted the status quo were coded zero, 'more understanding' coded 1, 'more decisions' coded 2, and 'completely run own affairs' coded 4. This time the unequal steps meant that the distinction between wanting independence or not was regarded as being greater than the distinction between other adjacent categories on the devolution scale.

Group 8:   *Vote*: I used two measures of voting: GAP which was coded 1 for Conservatives, zero for SNP, − 1 for Labour; and SNP which was coded 1 for the SNP, zero for Labour or Conservative. The results of model calculations for these two measures can be combined using the triangular, three-way partisan analysis techniques. This combination would be most obviously useful for influences that affected both GAP and SNP. On the other hand some influences affected mainly Labour versus Conservative choice or the SNP versus the rest choice and for them there was little point in using three-way partisan measures.

All respondents whose social characteristics or attitudes were unknown, or who failed to vote or voted Liberal were excluded from the model calculations.

In addition to the variables listed so far I also used a set of fifteen 'interactive' variables. Each of these was simply formed by multiplying the devolution attitudes variable by one of the other social or attitudinal variables. Together they allowed for 'interaction affects' between devolution attitudes and all other predictive variables in the model. They were included in Group 7. They allowed for the possibility that other variables amplified or damped the relationship between devolution and voting rather than acting on voting independently from devolution attitudes.

Figure 8.1 shows the results of model calculations as applied to Scotland. Each line drawn in the figure is a line of direct influence. Where a line is present it means there was a statistically

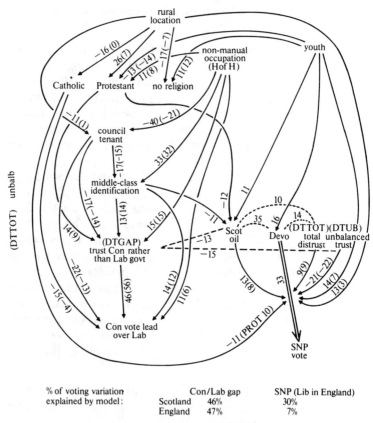

% of voting variation		Con/Lab gap	SNP (Lib in England)
explained by model:	Scotland	46%	30%
	England	47%	7%

Note. The path coefficients for Liberal votes are for non-interactive versions of the variables

Fig. 8.1. A causal model of Scots and English voting

significant and reasonably large influence by one variable on another even allowing for the concurrent effect of all the other variables in the model. The numbers printed beside the lines indicate the strength of influence. These numbers are called 'path coefficients' or 'standardized regression coefficients'. While it is technically possible for them to exceed 100 in very unusual circumstances it is fair to think of a value of 100 as indicating that one variable completely determines the patterns in another. Positive signs indicate that two variables go up and down together, negative signs indicate an inverse relationship. (Path coefficients were calculated using the stepwise multiple regression routine included in the SPSS statistical package.)

Path coefficients in brackets show the corresponding coefficients for voting patterns in England with English Liberal votes taking the place of SNP votes in Scotland. Dotted lines stand for 'unanalysed correlations', i.e. correlations where no causal direction is assumed or even implied.

Many pairs of variables which could have lines of influence drawn between them do not. This is because the estimated path coefficient was less than 10. All the coefficients shown are statistically significant according to standard tests but some other links which were statistically significant were also so weak (i.e. had coefficients less than 10) that they have been suppressed in the interests of clarity and simplicity.

The most outstanding feature of the model is the way it breaks into two parts – one predicting the Labour lead over the Conservatives, and the other predicting SNP voting. Class, house tenure, and religion influenced Labour/Conservative voting, age and rurality influenced SNP voting. Rurality had only a very indirect and weak effect on Labour/Conservative voting via religion and house tenure. The only social variable which strongly affected both Labour/Conservative and SNP voting was religion – Catholics were pro-Labour, but both anti-Conservative and anti-SNP.

Relative distrust in Labour and Conservative governments, DT GAP, was highly dependent upon class, house tenure, and religion, and highly predictive of Labour/Conservative voting, but almost unrelated to SNP voting. Conversely, oil and devolution attitudes, the degree of unbalanced trust (DT UB), or the total level of distrust (DT TOT) were unrelated to Labour/

Conservative voting but highly predictive of SNP voting. Moreover, while oil and devolution attitudes were somewhat dependent on class identification, religion, and age, levels of DT BAL and DT TOT were fairly constant across all social categories.

So, both the social and attitudinal variables, except for religion, divided into those which influenced Labour versus Conservative voting and those which influenced SNP voting. In part this sharp division occurs because I have suppressed relatively weak lines of influence (path coefficients less than 10) but that does not alter the reality of the conclusion: major effects were either on the Labour/Conservative or SNP/rest vote but not both.

The model divided still more on structural properties. Though I allowed the possibility that oil attitudes, age, religion, rurality, balanced trust, and total distrust might add to the chances of voting SNP, the calculations showed that this was not the case. The interactive versions of these variables proved far more influential. That is why, in the part of Fig. 8.1 that relates to SNP voting, all these variables are shown as influencing not SNP voting itself, but the link between devolution attitudes and SNP voting. The function of all other variables was to amplify or damp the devolution–SNP relationship, not to increase or decrease the SNP vote across the whole spectrum of devolution attitudes.

Let us follow through the chain of influence from rurality to Labour/Conservative voting (GAP) and at the same time compare findings for Scotland and England.

In rural areas, Scots were far more likely to be Protestants, and less likely to be either Catholics or irreligious than in urban areas. They were also less likely to live in council houses. In England the rural variable had very little effect at all, partly because so few English constituencies had over a tenth employed in agriculture. Young people were less likely to be Protestants and more likely to be irreligious both in Scotland and England. People in the non-manual classes were also a little more likely to be Protestants on both sides of the border.

But while manual working-class people tended to live in council houses in both countries, the influence of class on tenure was twice as high in Scotland as in England. Perhaps the easiest way to calibrate the path coefficients is to notice that in Scotland the link between class and tenure (path coeff = 40) was almost as strong as between differential trust (DT GAP) and Labour/Conservative voting choices (GAP) (path coeff = 46). Indeed the Scottish occupation–tenure link was the second highest coefficient in the model.

Class identification – respondents' self-description as 'middle' or 'working class' – depended on occupation and tenure but in both Scotland and England occupation was twice as powerful as house tenure in determining people's class image of themselves.

Relative distrust (DT GAP) – respondents' tendency to distrust Labour and trust the Conservatives – was influenced by house tenure, occupational class, class identification, and by religion, all of which had separate, independent and approximately equal effects in Scotland. The pattern was very similar in England, though religion and tenure were rather more important in Scotland. Council tenants, manual workers, those who felt themselves to be working class, Catholics, and the irreligious tended to trust Labour more than the Conservatives.

Finally, the voter's decision to vote Labour rather than Conservative was directly influenced by relative trust, house tenure, class identification, and religion. Relative trust was between two and three times as powerful as any one of the other influences. That is hardly surprising. What is less expected is the extent to which these other variables, which themselves influenced trust, also had a direct and independent effect on voting. This means that even when the relative degree of trust in Labour and Conservative governments was fixed there were still large, socially related variations in voting within categories of trust.

Scots choice between Labour and Conservative was noticeably less dependent on trust in their governments (path coeff = 46 in Scotland, 58 in England), less dependent on occupation (path coeff = 6 in Scotland, 11 in England), more dependent upon religion (path coeff = 15 in Scotland, 4 in England), and more dependent upon house tenure (path coeff = 22 in Scotland, 13 in England).

Over all, in this section of the model the picture is one of very considerable cross-national similarities except for a much tighter relationship between class and tenure in Scotland, and larger housing and religious impacts on voting in Scotland.

The dominant influence in the other half of the model was clearly devolution attitudes. By itself devolution had a strong effect on SNP voting and every other variable that influenced SNP support did so only in an interactive combination with devolution.

Young people were more inclined towards devolution. Catholics and the irreligious, the manual working classes and the young were more inclined to want a Scottish bias in the oil revenues, but apart from that none of the four attitudinal variables affecting SNP votes was socially dependent. However, there was a degree of interrelation between the various attitudes themselves.

Devolution attitudes correlated with total distrust and to a greater extent with oil attitudes. We can leave those as 'unanalyzed' correlations without altering the rest of our model calculations. It is peculiarly difficult to determine the direction of influence between these attitudes. Distrust in both London governments or a desire for all the oil revenues might be expected to influence respondents towards devolution or independence but since we know that support for independence did not increase when North Sea oil broke into the news, it seems more probable that attitudes on the constitutional question determined whether Scots felt they had a right to oil and perhaps also influenced their trust in London governments. However, it must be emphasized that whether or not this is true, it in no way affects calculations of any of the other coefficients in the model, in particular the relative power of different influences on SNP support.

Six variables met my criterion for an important influence on SNP voting and a seventh (DT TOT) is included for its theoretical significance even though it just failed to meet the arithmetical requirement. The chief influence on SNP voting was devolution attitudes. If only devolution were used as a predictor of SNP voting its path coefficient would be 42 instead of 33. Even when supplemented by six interactive variables which to some extent substituted for it, the devolution coefficient remained at 33. All the other variables represented amplification or damping influences on that basic devolution alignment. The most important of these was a balance of trust in the parties of government (path coeff = 21); then youth, rurality, and oil attitudes (path coeff = 14, 13, 13); finally, Catholicism (coeff = 11) and total distrust (coeff = 9).

Oil was clearly a much less important influence than constitutional attitudes. It acted as an amplifier rather than as a fully separate influence. Even then it was not the most powerful amplifying variable.

The coefficients of DT TOT and DT UB show that balanced trust in the two governing parties was well over twice as powerful an amplifier as total distrust: that balance was over twice as important as protest.

For an English comparison I took English Liberal voting in place of SNP. The oil and trust questions were asked in England as well as Scotland. But there was no exact equivalent of the central issue of Scottish devolution. So there were inevitably great differences between English and Scots voting patterns in this part of the model. Yet there were similarities also. Balanced trust was the most powerful influence on English Liberal voting, over twice as effective as total distrust. The only other variable with any power was religion. It had much the same size of effect as in Scotland, though in England both the irreligious and the Catholics tended not to vote Liberal.

Over all, the model explained almost half the variation in Conservative/Labour voting in both nations – 46 per cent in Scotland, 47 per cent in England. But the lack of a devolution equivalent in England was sorely missed in the other part of the model. The model explained 30 per cent of the variation in SNP support, but only 7 per cent of the variation in English Liberal voting. No doubt other, purely English-oriented models might do better south of the border but *this* model was four times as effective for predicting SNP votes as English Liberals.

While the model compares the effect of different influences on Labour/Conservative voting and separately on SNP voting, in its present form it does not compare the one with the other. To do that we have to combine predictions of GAP and SNP into a general prediction of three-way voting. Since that would also involve combining additive and interactive effects the result would be highly complex. So I will work with two extremely primitive versions of the model to answer the questions: which had the greater effect on Scottish voting in October 1974: (1)

occupational class or devolution attitudes? (2) relative trust (DT GAP) or devolution attitudes? The first question uses class which was clearly at the base of Labour/Conservative voting; the second uses relative trust which was the most powerful proximate cause of a Labour or Conservative choice.

To answer each question I have used the two predictors – class and devolution or trust and devolution – in regression equations predicting GAP and SNP, then applied the methods outlined in the Appendix to convert these regressions into predictions of the *size* and *direction* of the predictor variables' political effects. Instead of path coefficients it is necessary to use semi-standardized regression coefficients to measure political effects. These show the partisan effect in voting percentages, of a single standard deviation of shift on the predictor variable. The results are shown in Table 8.1.

These calculations suggest that the class and relative trust effects were oriented close to a pure Labour/Conservative direction and the devolution effect close to a pure SNP gain.

As for size or power, devolution attitudes had more influence on Scottish voting than class but less effect than relative trust in Labour and Conservative governments: more influence than the underlying social alignment but less than the proximate cause of Labour/Conservative choice.

Table 8.1: Three-way voting regressions (Scotland only)

Political effect = 17.2 DEVO + 13.8 CLASS		$(R^2{}_T = 15)$
(at 176°) (at 96°)		
Political effect = 17.4 DEVO + 24.3 DT GAP		$(R^2{}_T = 27)$
(at 173°) (at 95°)		

Notes: (1) DEVO: devolution attitude coded as in the full model. (2) CLASS: non-manual head of household versus manual, as in the full model. (3) An orientation of 180° is a straight pro-SNP direction, disadvantaging both other parties equally. (4) An orientation of 90° is a bipolar Conservative gain from Labour with no change in SNP voting. (5) The $R^2{}_T$ are 'trichotomous' R^2s, i.e., they measure the proportion of *three-party* voting variations which are explained by the equations. Since these equations contain only two predictors the $R^2{}_T$ are necessarily smaller than the R^2 values for the full model. (6) Coding the predictors differently would inevitably alter the regression coefficients. Coding class from 1 to 6 for the six social grades (unskilled manual, up to higher managerial) instead of using a class dichotomy hardly alters the results. Substituting class identification instead of objective class increases the class coefficient but only very slightly. Dichotomizing devolution attitudes into SG + MD versus MU + SQ reduced devolution coefficients by a third.

Chapter 9

The Consequences of October 1974

'The next Labour Government will create elected
Assemblies in Scotland and Wales' (UK Labour
manifesto, October 1974).
'In Scotland we will set up a Scottish Assembly' (UK
Conservative manifesto, October 1974).

Scottish politics had a British dimension. With some variation in
attitude and emphasis Scots worried about the same issues and
personalities as other Britons. But the election in October 1974
increased, for a time at least, the significance of the Scottish
dimension not just for Scots voters but for London politicians as
well. Both Scots and British politics in the years between 1974
and 1979 were greatly affected by the struggle over the Scotland
Act: Labour's plan for devolution.

What did the Scotland Act represent? Certainly not
independence, for while it proposed a substantial measure of self-
government it offered no independence at all: all the Scottish
Assembly's actions would be subject to scrutiny, veto, and
parliamentary tolerance. Was it devolution? At first, supporters
in all parties claimed it was the 'only devolution on offer': support
devolution and you must support the Act, oppose the Act and
you opposed devolution. Prior to 1974 the debate on the Scottish
constitution was about the status quo versus devolution and
except for the SNP it took place within rather than between the
parties. By 1 March 1979, however, the issue was not devolution
but the Labour Government's Scotland Act, firmly established
by then as binding Labour policy and bitterly opposed by the
Conservative Party: support Labour and you must support the
Act, oppose the Act and you opposed Labour. Even so committed a devolutionist as Lord Home could bring himself to do that.

According to the ORC poll in April 1974 one-third of all Scots,
including a clear majority of SNP supporters, would still want
more decisions transferred to Scotland even if that meant

Scotland being worse off than other parts of Britain. Perhaps they thought the hypothetical scenario was unrealistic, given the recent discovery of North Sea oil. But how did the economy progress under the constitutional status quo?

The years 1974 to 1979 were not boom years on either side of the border but at first several indicators suggested a narrowing of the gap between Scots and English prosperity. Though unemployment doubled, the rate of employment remained virtually unchanged and the ratio of Scots to UK unemployment rates which had been as high as 2.1 in 1964 and 1.7 in 1974 dropped right down to 1.2 in 1976 before rising again. Car registrations per capita, traditionally lower in Scotland, almost reached the GB rate in 1976 before dropping back again in 1977. Scottish GDP per capita rose from 90 per cent of the UK figure in 1968 to 97 per cent in 1976 and relative PDI followed a similar trend. The Scottish level of male manual earnings went 2 per cent ahead of the GB figure in 1975 before dropping back towards the GB level again. So in the middle of the Parliament the gap between Scottish and English prosperity almost closed, before it began to widen again.

What credit could the Labour Government take for these trends? Its special employment protection measures (SEM) supported up to twice as many jobs per capita in Scotland as in England, but growth in the oil industry provided twice as many as the whole of Labour's battery of employment measures and the Government could take little credit for oil jobs. Labour set up the promised Scottish Development Agency but its effect on jobs was minute compared to the British NEB's. During the October 1974 campaign Labour claimed that the Conservatives had planned to abolish REP (Regional Employment Premium) whereas the new Labour Government had just doubled it. Labour also promised to transfer 7,000 civil service jobs from London to Glasgow. In the event Labour postponed the civil service transfer into the eighties and announced the abolition of REP three days after the guillotine defeat on the Scotland and Wales Bill. The negative effect of these two decisions probably cancelled out the total positive effect of SEM. It is difficult to be certain because REP had a pervasive effect throughout the economy; no one could point to the particular jobs which were saved by REP. There lay the political advantage (there may be economic ones also) in switching resources from REP to SEM.

Of course, REP was abolished in England at the same time as in Scotland but SEM which replaced it was far less biased towards Scotland than REP had been. In December 1978, for example, only 12 per cent of SEM-covered GB jobs were in Scotland. Scotland's share of REP had been over three times that figure. In terms of closing the unemployment gap oil should get more credit than government while government, by withdrawing REP, contributed to the subsequent reopening of the gap.

As for the economic consequences of independence, in 1975 the *Scotsman* published a budget for the year 1973–4, the last year before oil disturbed such calculations, which suggested that Scottish government was overspending at two and a half times the rate of UK government generally. So an independent Scotland would either have to raise taxes and cut services compared to England, or subsist by consuming rather than investing the oil revenues. However, the Fraser Institute later used input–output techniques to estimate the Scottish trade balance for 1973 and showed that while Scotland had a trading deficit it was no more per capita than the UK's. Indeed, after allowing for large deficits incurred by importing North Sea oil equipment, it was not far out of balance.

Since there is a British dimension to Scottish politics part of the raw trends in Scottish party popularity must be explained by British factors. Conversely, comparative measures of popularity in Scotland and England are required to gauge the significance of the Scottish dimension. Using the same indicators as in Chapter 5, SNP voting and the difference between the Conservative lead over Labour in Scotland and England, Fig. 9.1 shows the trends in both after 1974.

The October 1974 election and the opinion polls during the 1975–9 parliament convinced many doubters that there was something very special about Scottish politics. Even the SNP's 22 per cent share of the vote in February could be discounted as equivalent to English third-party (i.e. Liberal) voting at that time. But while the English Liberal vote had declined by October, the SNP vote went up to 30 per cent. By this measure Scotland moved back towards mainstream British politics in 1979 when the SNP vote fell to 17 per cent.

Monthly polls show SNP support falling throughout 1975 but leaping to a peak of 37 per cent in December in response to the Government's so-called 'colonial' White Paper on devolution.

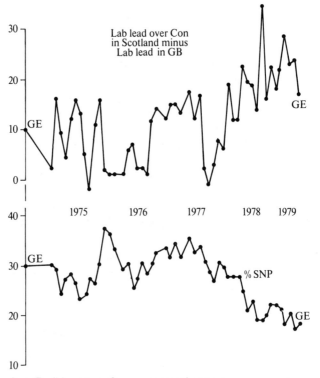

Fig. 9.1. Scots/English party preferences compared, 1974–9

Then the SNP declined until the summer. Support began to flow back to the SNP when Tam Dalyell and seventy Labour MPs published their letter threatening to vote against a guillotine on the devolution bill. The second peak of SNP popularity came just after that guillotine motion was defeated but it did not quite reach 37 per cent. From the summer of 1977 the SNP suffered a long decline, particularly sharp in the four months leading up to the Royal Assent for the Scotland Act. All of which fits the theory that SNP support ebbed as Labour fulfilled its election promises on devolution and flowed when Labour appeared to renege.

The difference between the Conservative lead over Labour in Scotland and England doubled between 1974 and 1979. So by this measure, Scotland moved away from mainstream British politics in 1979. Scotland was not alone in deviating towards

Labour in 1979: there was a clear North–South division within England. But Scottish trends were far more deviant than those in the North of England. Between 1951 and 1979 Labour's lead over the Conservatives increased by 2 per cent in North West England, and decreased by 3 per cent in North and North East England, but it went up by 16 per cent in the comparable Strathclyde region of Scotland.

The monthly trend in comparative Conservative leads is subject to a high degree of sampling fluctuation: Scottish–British differences must be computed from four percentages taken from two different polls. None the less a pattern emerges. Throughout 1975 the gap averaged 8 per cent, the long-term historical norm. For most of 1976 it was much less than that. Then at the end of the year, when the Conservatives decided to oppose Labour's devolution plans, the gap increased to 12 per cent and gradually widened thereafter. For three months at the end of 1977 it disappeared, and in September 1978 it rose to 35 per cent but both these departures from trend may be due to sampling problems or imperfect synchronization of two fast-moving national poll series. The trend was towards a 25 per cent gap in April 1979, significantly but temporarily reduced in the last fortnight of the general election campaign.

Sometimes, election results can be explained by the events of the campaign, the few weeks or even days before the vote. The Scottish referendum is one example. But Fig. 9.1 shows that the result of the 1979 general election in Scotland represented the culmination of trends established in the years after 1974. Indeed the 1979 election campaign itself only prevented the electoral patterns from being even more extreme.

Reactions to government can be expressed in less peaceful forms than opinion poll results but though Scotland had a high level of criminal violence it had a very low level of political violence. There was nothing comparable to the IRA bombings, Angry Brigade attacks on ministers, the Grunwick seige, inter-racial muggings and riotings, or the NF versus marxist violence which seemed so typical of England in the seventies. Leading politicians, usually non-Scots like Short, Foot, Thorpe, or Jenkins, warned of another Ireland if Westminster reneged on its promise of a Scottish Assembly. In the longer term they may now be right but not in the short term. Reaction to the guillotine defeat in 1977 came in opinion polls and local elections, not violence. Terrorism in Scotland was mainly concerned with UVF and UDA attempts to obtain supplies for use in Ireland.

When nationalist violence did occur it was promptly and vehemently denounced by spokesmen for the SNP. When party members were convicted by the courts they were expelled by the party. Two major terrorist trials involved the APG (Army of the Provisional Government) and the Tartan Army. They were accused of robbing the Royal Bank of Scotland and bombing electricity lines, oil pipelines, a railway line, and the Glasgow office of the Bank of England. They were heavily infiltrated by the special branch. At the Tartan Army trial in 1976 there were as many Crown witnesses who admitted their crimes but had immunity, as there were convicted terrorists. Altogether, nationalist violence appeared incompetent, possibly provoked, not very threatening, and completely overshadowed by the parliamentary battle for devolution.

Under cover of the general battle over devolution another group of nationalist guerrillas was more successful. Labour's plan for devolution would transfer powers from the Secretary of State to the new, directly elected Assembly. So to justify his status in Cabinet and in Scotland he must get new powers in compensation. Informally, he had long been regarded as responsible for all government in Scotland but he had lacked the power to match his responsibility. In particular he lacked industrial patronage. So in December 1975 Wilson announced that 'section 7' powers would be transferred to the Secretary of State from the Department of Industry, then ruled by the troublesome Mr Benn. 'Section 7' was the part of the 1972 Industry Act which provided for selective, discretionary aid to industry. Although the sums of money involved were never large, section 7's discretionary nature gave the Scottish Office political power rather than an administrative chore. In the event, the Scottish Office got the whole of the Department of Industry's Office for Scotland, powers, personnel, and all.

THE PARTIES AND THE SCOTLAND ACT

Labour

Without Scotland Labour would have been defeated by the Conservatives in 1964 and February 1974. The question of increasing its majority in 1966 or October 1974 would never have arisen. So Labour had reason to thank the Scots, but it also had reason to fear them: its forty Scottish seats after February 1974, forty-one after October, were hostages for good behaviour in a way that the thirty-nine Yorkshire Labour seats were not, especially after October when the challenger in all but one of the Labour marginals was the SNP, not the Conservatives. All the evidence suggested voters were far less reluctant to switch to (and from) the SNP than between Labour and Conservative. The risk was real.

Much of the progress towards the Scotland Act can thus be seen as a dialogue between Labour and the Scots in which Labour displayed a genuine sympathy for Scottish aspirations coupled with an equally genuine fear of losing a significant part of its Westminster majority. Labour had adopted devolution to appease its friends, the Scots, not its enemies, the SNP. But while Dalintober, coupled with the subsequent election campaign, committed Scottish Labour to an Assembly more firmly than the English wing of the party was committed to any policy at all, an English Labour MP was not so committed: the NEC had spoken but conference had not, the British manifesto contained a twelve-line Assembly promise but no one could claim it was a central part of an English MP's compact with his electorate.

As the SNP campaigned for a 'No' vote in the EEC referendum their support in opinion polls slipped from 30 per cent to 22 per cent while Labour's increased and also switched from being anti-EEC to pro-EEC. Consequently the 'Yes' side won 58 per cent of the Scots vote in the EEC referendum – significantly less than in England but still a clear majority. Shortly afterwards the Cabinet held a full day meeting at Chequers to discuss devolution. Jenkins, Crosland, Williams, Prentice, and Healey were reported as opposing devolution but being overruled.

After the EEC referendum, SNP support in the polls made a modest recovery but this was eclipsed by a sequence of spectacular victories in local government by-elections. In normal times local government by-elections do not make headlines in Scotland any more than in England, but nation-wide council elections were not due until 1977 and, as it turned out, no parliamentary by-elections came up before 1978. Only one organization produced frequent Scottish opinion polls and it had only started in 1974. So at a time when public opinion was being quoted as the basis for constitutional change every indicator of popular attitudes became front-page news. Stephen Maxwell began the series of SNP victories by taking Slateford/Hailes, on the outskirts of Edinburgh, with a swing of 22 per cent against Labour. A week later Labour's home policy committee which included pro-devolutionists Judith Hart and Alex Kitson declared they were 'worried sick' about Scotland. Twice in the next two months the Scottish Labour executive reminded Labour MPs that the Assembly was a manifesto commitment and a meeting of the Scottish Labour group at Westminster unanimously reaffirmed their commitment.

Our Changing Democracy was published at the end of November. Containing detailed Assembly proposals, it should have reaped Labour a rich reward for honouring the manifesto but had just the opposite effect. Even Secretary Ross, once the arch opponent of devolution, used a meeting of the Scottish executive to attack its constant references to the Secretary of State's veto powers – immediately dubbed 'Governor-General' powers.

Jim Sillars had publicly voiced the idea of a separate SLP (Scottish Labour Party) in November 1974, and again just after the EEC result. Now he resigned along with another member of Labour's Scottish executive, and the party's research officer. Together they helped to found the SLP. John Robertson, Labour MP for Paisley, gave the SLP a second voice in Parliament. At first, polls suggested the SLP might take a quarter of Labour's vote but support ebbed rapidly. Ross spoke of a 'special hell' for those who deserted to the SLP but Labour was careful not to make martyrs and the two SLP MPs were left to resign the Labour whip.

The White Paper got an almost uniformly bad press in Scotland and England and the Government was left fighting rather desperately on two fronts. English MPs were becoming increasingly aware that the Government had a Scottish devolution policy and a considerable number did not like the idea. Viewed from Scotland, the White Paper honoured the manifesto, but not the campaign broadcasts nor the post-election hints. Quite apart from the insulting veto powers, the Assembly was to get no oil revenues, no trade and industry powers, and no tax power other than the right to put a small surcharge on the local government rates. It would be financed by a block grant, voted annually by Westminster.

So in Scotland, Ross had to attack those like the STUC or the new SLP who demanded economic powers while in England he tóld MPs 'You can say good-by – if you do not agree with this White Paper – to the Labour Party in Scotland and possibly to Willie Ross as well'. The plan from now on was to make mainly cosmetic changes in the proposals to reduce the insult to Scots while threatening English Labour MPs with the wrath of Scotland should they obstruct the Government. In England the air was full of threats about the break up of the UK and, what was worse, the end of Labour governments for a generation or more. These melodramatic threats did their job at the time but they later formed a context within which a 52 per cent referendum vote for the Government's devolution proposals at a time of extreme government unpopularity could be interpreted as a rejection of the concept of devolution.

When Wilson resigned as party leader several former anti-devolutionists who were candidates for the leadership took the opportunity to speak up for an Assembly. Away from the leadership contest, the 1976 Labour conference at Troon resolved that the Secretary's veto powers be abolished, tax powers be investigated, the universities should come under the Assembly, and the block grant should take account of the environmental burden of North Sea oil.

Ross resigned along with Wilson. Callaghan appointed Ross's deputy Bruce Millan in his place. At the same time the Government's devolution team of Short and Hunt was replaced by the veteran Michael Foot backed up by John Smith, the young MP for North Lanark. Foot announced a package of concessions designed to placate Scottish feelings and a poll showed a swing from the SNP to Labour compared with the October election. It was the only poll between the 1975 White Paper and the passage of the guillotine on the Scotland Bill at the end of 1977 to show a pro-Labour swing. A fortnight after Foot's concessions Tam Dalyell sent him an open letter signed by seventy Labour MPs: 'We could not support a guillotine motion' on the devolution bill. Since the Conservatives were sliding towards opposition to Labour's plans a guillotine was essential. The polls began to swing back to the SNP.

Delegates to the British Labour conference met at Blackpool in September. 'If we were to renege on devolution now, I do not believe the Labour Party would be a credible political force at the next general election', Millan warned them. A retreat, said Foot, 'would invite the destruction of the whole of our movement'. As recently as May, Foot had rejected proposals for a referendum on devolution. Now he tried to win over reluctant English delegates by conceding that devolution plans would not be implemented unless approved in a referendum. The British Conference backed devolution by a majority of six to one.

Helped by the referendum concession, the Government had a majority of forty-five when the principle of the Scotland and Wales Bill was put to a Commons vote in mid-December. Ten Labour rebels voted with the Conservatives but only Dalyell represented a Scottish seat. Thirty, almost all of them English, abstained. Despite this clear majority for the principle, progress on the details was very slow. After much hesitation, arm-twisting, and head-counting, the Government finally risked a guillotine motion on 22 February 1977. It failed by twenty-nine votes and that was the end of the bill. Tam Dalyell and Willie Hamilton were the only Scots out of twenty-two Labour MPs to vote against the guillotine. Dick Buchanan and Bob Hughes were the only Scots among the twenty or so abstainers. Concessions and pressures had reduced guillotine opponents from the seventy who had signed Dalyell's letter, but not by enough. All the Scots and Welsh nationalists, the two SLP members, two Welsh Liberals, and two Ulster Unionists voted with the Government while the majority of the Liberals, including all three Scots, supported the Conservatives, despite the similarity of Labour's bill to their own earlier proposals for 'phased federalism'.

Still, it was clearly Labour votes which defeated the guillotine. A disciplined and loyal Labour Party would have had a majority around thirty. Between June 1976, just before Dalyell's letter, and March 1977, just after the guillotine defeat, polls showed a 10 per cent swing from Labour to the SNP but much of that swing had already occurred in expectation of a guillotine defeat and the relatively small shock reaction convinced reluctant devolutionist MPs that they would be safe to oppose an Assembly. Ross told a demoralized Labour conference in Perth that he was 'outraged to see how people went back on a manifesto commitment'. But not all of the fault lay with disloyal back-benchers: the Government lacked the nerve to make devolution an issue of confidence.

Three weeks later the Government tried to duck a vote on its public expenditure White Paper and when the Conservatives responded to this second act of parliamentary cowardice with a straightforward motion of no confidence, the SNP voted with the Conservatives and only the hurriedly constructed Lib-Lab pact saved the day.

Given the breathing space provided by the Lib-Lab pact, Callaghan and Foot both stated their determination to have another crack at devolution.

Meanwhile Labour adopted a new set of rules at its 1977 Scottish conference which changed the nature of the party in Scotland. The new rules were riddled with references to the Assembly, Assemblymen, and the ALP which was to be an Assembly version of the PLP. Throughout, Assemblymen generally had the same rights and duties as MPs. The Scottish executive and the ALP were given the right to draw up the Assembly manifesto and validate candidates and the Scottish conference would decide the party programme. The British NEC retained no more than the formal right to be consulted. Like the proposals for the nation itself these changes conceded devolution within the party – not federalism or independence – on devolved subjects.

The verdict of the opinion polls received some confirmation when Labour had a net loss of 129 seats at the Scottish district elections in May and the SNP a net gain of 107. The Nationalists tied with Labour in West Lothian and won control of Clackmannan, Falkirk, Clydebank, Strathkelvin, Cumbernauld, East Kilbride, and Cunninghame districts. Labour even lost control of Glasgow. Callaghan edged slowly towards making devolution an issue of confidence, 'Either this government governs or it goes', he said to the Commons in June; 'back us or sack us' to conference in the autumn; and in October he told the NEC that a defeat on devolution, 'would deprive the Labour government of choosing its own time for a general election'. Prophetic words!

Bribes accompanied the threats. North of England MPs had been particularly jealous of the Scots and particularly well organized in opposition to Scottish devolution. At the end of the day they could point to symbolic achievements like the headquarters of British Shipbuilders and the visit of President Carter, to the offer of regional devolution, regional offshoots of the NEB, the Tyneside Metro, the Drax B Order for Parsons, or the government partnership plan to renew inner-city areas on Tyneside. In the quarter year after defeat of the guillotine, Department of Industry figures showed that the North received the highest public expenditure per capita of any UK region, thanks to a huge bias in the allocation of Regional Development Grants; and while the Scottish rate of male manual earnings went ahead of the UK average at the end of 1975 it was overtaken by earnings in the 'North of England and the gap widened throughout 1977.

In November, a new Scotland Bill – excluding Wales this time – got a majority of forty-four in the vote on principle. Only eleven Labour members voted against: Dalyell was the lone Scot. Two days later there was a majority of twenty-six for the guillotine. Only nine Labour members voted against and Dalyell was again the lone Scot. Exactly a year after the first guillotine defeat, on 22 February 1978, the Commons approved the detailed provisions and sent the bill to the Lords.

Success came only just in time because the Scottish Labour MPs for Garscadden, Hamilton, and Berwick died in 1978. By-elections held in the political climate of 1977 would certainly have cut Labour's Westminster representation by three, but they might also have produced a surge in SNP support like the ones which followed the Hamilton and Govan by-elections in 1967 and 1973. Every ward of Garscadden had elected an SNP councillor in 1977 but less than a year later Donald Dewar held the seat for Labour though on a reduced majority compared to 1974. At Hamilton Labour went on to double its 1974 majority even though the SNP fielded Margo MacDonald, victor of the Govan by-election. And at Berwick in the autumn Labour again increased its majority and the SNP lost its deposit.

The Act had received the Royal Assent on 31 July 1978 and from then onwards until the end of the year monthly polls averaged Labour 50 per cent, Conservatives 26 per cent, SNP 19 per cent, and Liberals 4 per cent with very little month to month variation. When the new session of Parliament opened John Smith who had piloted the Scotland Act through the Commons was appointed Trade Secretary and became the youngest member of the Cabinet. Perseverance had been rewarded. Or so it appeared.

The Conservatives

A few days after the Conservatives' dismal showing in the October 1974 general election, Alick Buchanan-Smith, Shadow Secretary of State, issued a public statement committing the party to an elected Assembly. He talked of supporting Labour's proposals, even of pressing Labour to deliver devolution fast. Lord Home, too, felt that stronger proposals than his 1970 plan were now required. When Thatcher replaced Heath she told a rally in Glasgow City Hall that an 'Assembly must be a top priority to ensure that more decisions affecting Scotland are taken in Scotland by Scotsmen'.

But after the SNP's defeat and the Conservative success in the 1975 EEC referendum, Iain Sproat began a public campaign against devolution. By November the sixteen Scots Conservative MPs were split three ways: five firmly opposed to devolution – traditional unionists Hutchison, Anderson, and Galbraith plus populists Sproat and Taylor; five clear devolutionists – Buchanan-Smith, Younger, Fairgrieve, Gray, and Rifkind; with the others less firmly committed.

The Tories needed a Dalintober Street conference. It was held in the Music Hall, Edinburgh on 10 January 1976. By 103 to 60 it voted for Malcolm Rifkind's resolution accepting an elected Assembly but rejecting the Government's proposals as 'unworkable'. In short, it decided against the only devolution on offer with the only dissent being from those who opposed devolution even in principle. Rifkind later joined Buchanan-Smith in campaigning for a 'Yes' vote in the Scotland Act referendum. The normal annual conference met at Perth in May. In near riot conditions and amid allegations that anti-devolutionists had rigged the card ballot, the chairman declared that a show of hands confirmed the Music Hall policy.

So British Conservative leaders failed to give the Scottish party a strong lead on devolution and the Scottish party failed to articulate a well-defined demand. The instincts of Unionism and the habits of parliamentary opposition produced a drift towards simple opposition to Labour's proposals: a policy defined only by what it was not. At the time, and possibly again in the future, it seemed a weakness, but it had its advantages in the 1979 referendum campaign.

Thatcher issued a three-line whip against the principle of the Scotland and Wales Bill in December 1976, but five Conservatives, including three Scots, voted with the Government and twenty-eight, including seven Scots, abstained. Out of sixteen Scottish MPs only six obeyed Thatcher's whip and two of them retired at the next election. Only Sproat, Taylor, Fairbairn, and Galbraith backed Thatcher in 1976 and stood for re-election in 1979.

Conservatives went further than disobeying the whip: six spokesmen, including the Shadow Secretary and the party chairman, resigned before the vote and another resigned after it. Thatcher persuaded most of them to withdraw their resignations almost at once, and later rewarded them with office in her first Government. She did, however, replace Buchanan-Smith as Shadow Scots Secretary though he became a junior Agriculture Minister in her 1979 government. Taylor took over as Shadow Secretary of State. By an irony of fate, Taylor lost his seat in 1979 and Younger, who resigned in protest against Conservative opposition to the Scotland and Wales Act, was the man who became Thatcher's first Secretary of State and repealed the Scotland Act.

In her speech to the 1977 conference in Perth, Thatcher avoided reference to devolution and Pym described the Assembly commitment as 'inoperative'. After their flurry of resignations in December 1976 Conservative devolutionists fell back into line. They grumbled to the press but they voted solidly against the Scotland and Wales guillotine in February 1977. Four Conservatives voted for the Scotland Act in November but not one supported the guillotine on it.

Three months after the passage of the Scotland Act, Conservatives were disappointed by the Berwick by-election result though it is difficult to see why. Labour put up a very inexperienced young farmer as successor to the late Professor Mackintosh; the Conservatives needed only a 3 per cent swing to win the seat and on the very day of the by-election they achieved over twice that swing at an English by-election. Yet Labour increased its majority over the Conservatives in Berwick. By any reasonable interpretation of the monthly opinion polls Labour should have done even better. Berwick could only be a disappointment to Conservatives who thought in terms of English politics.

The SNP

The Scotland Act was not SNP policy. The party stood for full independence as soon as possible. Yet it was not intransigent. It tried to win what it could for Scotland. In October 1974 it closed a television broadcast with a long list of concessions won since February and the final slogan 'It pays to vote SNP'. But did it pay?

The Scottish electorate's threat of voting SNP must appear as one of the greatest influences towards devolution. Actual SNP votes made the threat of still more SNP votes at once more realistic and more dangerous. But did SNP MPs achieve by their actions any more than the electorate achieved by electing them? In March 1974 SNP members began by rejecting all pacts and forcing a vote of confidence when Wilson's Government was only a fortnight old. Every year thereafter they voted against the Government in confidence motions. Their votes failed to carry the guillotine on the Scotland and Wales Bill; the guillotine on the Scotland Bill and the votes of principle on either bill would have been carried even if the SNP had switched sides and opposed them. Finally, in March 1979 they succeeded in defeating the Government but were unable to show how that advanced the interests of self-government or of Scotland.

Their problem was not a refusal to compromise on nationalist ideology but the inevitable weakness of a party of eleven facing a party of over three hundred. In April 1974 the SNP had listed their devolution demands: the Secretary of State to stay in the Cabinet, backed by seventy-one Scottish MPs, the Assembly to have trade and tax powers plus control of North Sea oil. Strong but not extravagant demands and the first two were only nationalist in the sense of giving Scotland a strong voice at Westminster; ideologically they were Unionist not nationalist. They contributed to a moderate, business-like image.

Following the White Paper *Our Changing Democracy* the SNP had to cope with a surge in popularity added to their own sense of disappointment at the lack of powers offered. Their policy was to start negotiating independence if they won thirty-six of the seventy-one Scottish seats. Polls now indicated they might now come close to the magic thirty-six seats if an election were held soon and Wolfe rushed to stress the word 'negotiate'. Conference at Motherwell re-affirmed the party's policy that full independence was their aim but the Assembly proposals were a welcome first step. There was no surprise in that. But a move to delete the welcome for an Assembly was defeated by the surprisingly narrow margin of 594 to 425.

The next conference met in Dundee shortly after the guillotine defeat. Even Margo MacDonald, a well-known gradualist, felt that the middle way had been destroyed 'the only choice [now] facing Scots is the helplessness of the status quo or the hope that independence will bring'. A natural reaction but one that left Labour an undisputed position as the party of devolution when the unexpected happened and the Government produced the Scotland Bill.

In 1978 they met in Edinburgh just before the Hamilton by-election. Devolution was ignored but conference passed a long resolution on the structure of government. Its appendix listed sixteen ministries with a note that the first eleven would be needed under devolution and the powers of the various ministries were to be transferred either immediately, i.e. under devolution, or 'in due course', i.e. on independence. A useful multi-purpose policy. But 1978 was a bad year for the SNP. The one bright spot was a legacy of £250,000 in August. Otherwise it was a tale of declining public support and disputes over strategy and personalities.

Keith Bovey fought an accident-prone by-election campaign in Garscadden beginning with a letter signed by six MPs criticizing his pacifist views. At Hamilton Margo MacDonald suffered an even worse swing than Bovey. She claimed to have fought an 'independence campaign' but her address read 'Make Sure of Your Assembly – now dangerously at risk, yet essential to force Scottish unemployment down and living standards up'. Hardly a straight independence appeal.

Bovey was sacked after his Garscadden failure. Paterson, the SNP candidate for Berwick, was sacked before his campaign began. The executive wanted a more experienced candidate for a by-election campaign. Unfortunately he objected and the con-stituency association backed him up with resolutions and resignations. Isobel Lindsay, SNP vice-chairman for policy, took over as candidate and lost her deposit.

It looked as though Labour had satisfied Scottish nationalism and Nationalists were redundant.

The Queen and Duke of Edinburgh occasionally reminded their
subjects 'of the benefits which union has conferred' but at the
highest political level Englishmen charged with the government
of the United Kingdom were among the strongest advocates of
Scottish devolution: Heath, Wilson, Callaghan, Foot, while the
mass electorate had no fixed views beyond the desire for a quiet
life.

Just before *Our Changing Democracy* was published at the end of
1975 Marplan found that 56 per cent of the English were opposed
to a Scottish Assembly and 64 per cent were against English
regional assemblies. But just after the guillotine defeat in 1977
ORC found half the English accepted Scotland as a nation: they
were equally divided on whether the Government should press
on with new devolution plans; but by two to one they accepted
'Scotland should have a greater say in running its own affairs'
and by three to one they accepted that the Scots themselves
wanted devolution. Later polls, like Gallup in autumn 1978
revealed the English did not 'like' Scottish devolution but clearly
their attitudes were lightly held and by no means deeply
antagonistic towards Scotland.

The English backlash was real, but it was strongest at the level
of back-bench MPs and local government councillors, groups
who had most personal prestige to lose if Britain introduced a new
tier of central government, and who also tended towards a
narrow local-interest view of politics. Instinctively they felt
anything that was 'good for Scotland' must be bad for their
locality and for their own personal status.

Tynesiders took the lead. They provided seven of the forty
rebels against the guillotine – not a high proportion of the total
rebels but a high proportion of Tynesiders were rebels. There
were several devolution conferences on the Tyne in 1976 and
1977, beginning with the one called by the Development Council
and chaired by Ted Short. Margo MacDonald told them that the
proposed Assembly would have no power 'to take bread out of
English mouths or jobs out of your factories'. Smith, Foot, and
Mackintosh also tried to soothe Tynesiders' fears. Tyne and
Wear Council held a conference with the unambiguous title
'Devolution – the Case Against'. It was a gathering of local

councillors to hear several speakers attack the SNP as 'fascist' and one Conservative MP declare he would vote for Scottish independence only when the Scots were 'really prepared to fight for it'. Labour's Scottish executive was so concerned that they sent a special delegation to Newcastle to try and work out a common strategy.

Later in 1977 and 1978 the Northern blacklash subsided. If British politics was·reduced to a question of the pigs with the strongest shoulders getting their snouts in the trough the North might do badly. They lacked the numbers of Midlands and Southern MPs and had no credible independence option to fall back on. They consoled themselves with the concessions I quoted earlier.

THE SHETLAND ISLANDS COUNCIL

Long before oil was discovered neither Shetland nor Orkney regarded themselves as completely Scottish. Edinburgh and Glasgow were a long way off. Oil threatened Shetland with an enormous but temporary influx of population for islands whose electorate ran to only 13,000 in 1974. It threatened pollution. It threatened the destruction of traditional industries which would soon be needed again when the oil ceased to flow. So the Council struck a unique financial deal with the British Government and the oil companies. Effectively it gained the right denied to other councils and the proposed Assembly: the right to tax North Sea oil. By the end of the century Shetland's multitude of oil levies was expected to reach a total of £121 million (at 1978 prices).

The Council feared a Scottish Assembly might reform the Council, rescind the Zetland County Council Act of 1974, adjust the rate-support grant, or nationalize the oil port at Sullom Voe. Some of these fears went beyond the powers detailed in the Scotland Act but the fears were real enough and Acts can always be changed, powers increased.

On Burns Night 1978 the Commons passed two amendments to the Scotland Bill: the 40 per cent rule and the Grimond amendment. Jo Grimond's plan gave Orkney and Shetland the right to secede from the area governed by the Scottish Assembly (not from Scotland). If they chose to secede a Royal Commission would investigate constitutional alternatives. The Council held a postal referendum and on a 72 per cent response a nine-to-one majority approved its actions in fighting for the right of secession. Under the Grimond amendment, however, the islands would get no Constitutional Commission *unless* they seceded. Eventually, on Grimond's advice the Council narrowly accepted Millan's compromise plan: no right of secession, but the guarantee of a Constitutional Commission if Scotland voted for an Assembly irrespective of whether the islands voted 'Yes' or 'No'.

THE SCOTTISH REFERENDUM

When the Government originally conceded a referendum as an inducement for unionist back-benchers to toe the party line it was a purely face-saving gesture. Any referendum, in Scotland though not Wales, would produce a large majority in favour of devolution, or so it was thought at the time. But George Cunningham, MP for Islington, persuaded the Commons to pass the 40 per cent rule. The Government opposed it, 72 per cent of Scots MPs and 81 per cent of Scots Labour MPs voted against it but they were overruled. If, in the opinion of the Secretary of State, less than 40 per cent of eligible Scots voted for the Act he was required to lay a repeal order before parliament. The requirement was without precedent in British electoral history. Less than 40 per cent of Scots had voted for EEC membership but the very people who now voted for the 40 per cent rule had hailed the EEC vote as decisive and unifying. If less than 40 per cent of the registered electorate voted for the Act the Secretary might still take the view that 40 per cent of those entitled to vote had voted for it, or he might persuade the Commons to vote down the repeal order. But the opposite of repeal was not implementation: before the Act could come into operation the Secretary had to get parliamentary approval for a commencement order.

A System Three poll in October 1978 confirmed there was a two-to-one majority in favour of the Act but under the 40 per cent rule a two-to-one majority might not be enough. Bruce Millan had two real options: he could discount a high percentage of the register as not being 'entitled to vote' or he could try to discredit the 40 per cent rule and rely on parliament to reject a repeal order. Evidence abounded that the number of names on the register was larger than the number eligible to vote: the gross electorate included the dead, it listed many electors several times over, especially students, nurses, and those with two homes. Some argued that those who had moved, were in hospital, ill at home, or seriously disabled should also be discounted. Cunningham replied that by setting the rule at 40 per cent rather than 50 per cent such people were already discounted. There had been a 79 per cent turn-out in February 1974 and 40 per cent of the unadjusted electorate therefore meant about half the numbers who had somehow managed to vote in 1974. If the Government discounted names unreasonably, parliament though deprived of the opportunity to vote for repeal, might vote against the commencement order.

Millan adopted the second strategy: minimal adjustments to the register, so small they formed part of his campaign to discredit the whole idea of the 40 per cent rule. With or without a repeal order parliament still had to vote on the Act after the referendum. But while parliament might be persuaded to overlook a short-fall of 2 or 3 per cent, they had already specifically rejected Robin Cook's amendment lowering the 40 per cent to 33 per cent. Hence it was vital to get a vote as close to 40 per cent as possible, better still above 40 per cent. That implied waiting until the new register came into effect in mid-February 1979. The first of March was named as the day. Since the Lib-Lab pact had now ended, delay had the further advantage that it put the SNP under pressure to replace the Liberals as a parliamentary prop for the Labour Government.

This decision split the SNP. The majority of MPs wanted to keep up the momentum towards devolution with an autumn referendum. If parliament rejected the decision of the Scottish people, so be it: the SNP would win both ways. So nine out of the eleven MPs voted against the Government in both the autumn confidence debates. George Reid and Hamish Watt did not. Like the party executive, but unlike his fellow MPs, Reid considered it vital to maintain Labour in office to 'manage' the referendum. The Government survived both confidence motions.

But SNP votes provided the margin needed to end the Government's pay sanctions policy. So the background to the referendum campaign was the road haulage strike, followed by the public service strikes. Labour had refused to 'soil its hands' (their words, not mine) with a joint Labour-SNP campaign for a 'Yes' vote and Labour's posters pictured Callaghan superimposed on the word 'Yes'. Throughout Britain, Gallup showed a Labour lead of 5 per cent in November 1978 but Conservative leads of 5½ per cent, 7½ per cent, and 20 per cent in the next three months. In November 54 per cent were satisfied with Callaghan and only 36 per cent dissatisfied but by February it was 58 per cent dissatisfied to only 33 per cent satisfied. For a critical few weeks Callaghan's prestige became a negative factor.

In Scotland, Dalyell added to Labour's troubles. He set up a 'Yes' versus 'No' travelling circus with Sillars. Though Sillars was an excellent debator he had quit the Labour Party. So by appearing against him Dalyell looked less of a rebel than he was. John Mackintosh, who could be as eloquent as Sillars in favour of devolution and had not quit the Labour Party, had unfortunately died in 1978. Dalyell also formed a 'Labour Vote No' campaign in an audacious and successful bid to associate the Labour name with an anti-Labour policy. Since three of the four main parties supported the Act it looked as if three of the four special party broadcasts on television would support the Act. Dalyell got a court order requiring two 'Yes' and two 'No' programmes instead. That would have given the 'Labour Vote No' group as much television time as the Labour Party. So in the end there were no special broadcasts at all. Dalyell had the advantage over Smith, Foot, and Callaghan that he was not in the Cabinet, not struggling for the Government's survival in the midst of a severe industrial crisis. He could be ruthlessly single minded.

While Dalyell and the economic crisis combined to encourage Labour supporters to desert the party line, Thatcher and Home tried to make their line acceptable even to those of their supporters who favoured devolution. In a well-publicized speech at Edinburgh University in mid-February, Home declared: 'I should hesitate to vote "No" if I did not think that the parties will keep the devolution issue at the top of their priorities', but he said he would vote 'No' because he wanted an Assembly with tax powers, proportional representation, and a well-defined formula for separating Scottish and English business at Westminster. Two days before the vote Lord Thorneycroft persuaded Michael Swan to force BBC Scotland into re-scheduling its programmes so as to screen an interview with Home in which he repeated these points. On the day before the vote the press printed a short message from Thatcher beginning: 'A "No" vote does not mean the devolution question will be buried.'

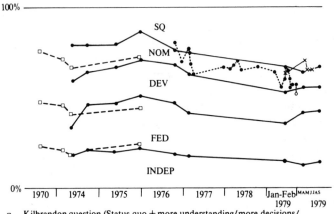

100% ──────────────────────────────

SQ

NOM

DEV

FED

INDEP

0%

1970	1974	1975	1976	1977	1978	Jan-Feb	MAMJJAS
						1979	1979

□ Kilbrandon question (Status quo + more understanding/more decisions/
   new system/independence)

● ORC question (Status quo/nominated ass/devolution/federalism/independence)

● Referendum question (% YES of YES plus NO)

× Post referendum question (% Scotland Act + new devolution plans/scrap devolution)

Fig. 9.2. Attitudes to devolution

How did the public react? Figure 9.2 charts their attitudes to devolution from 1970 to September 1979. To ensure comparability it only shows the results of polls which asked one of four recurrent questions. From 1970 to the end of 1975 four polls asked the 'Kilbrandon question'. Overlapping this period, nine polls between 1974 and 1979 asked the *Scotsman*/ORC question. Both of these offered the respondent a range of options. From 1976 to 1979, twenty polls asked whether respondents would vote 'Yes' or 'No' in the referendum on the Government's proposals, and four polls in 1979 asked whether devolution should be dropped, the Act implemented, or new plans devised.

Support for devolution appeared to decline slightly between 1970 and 1974 but with every party advocating it, support went up again between 1974 and 1975. Support dropped óver the winter of 1976–7 and suffered a further decline between then and the referendum, but rose slightly just after the referendum. A detailed comparison of the first and last *Scotsman* series questions is instructive. They were put in April 1974 and September 1979. The dividing line between those who wanted independence, a federal system, or a directly elected Assembly versus those who wanted none of these scarcely changed. But support for a federal system almost doubled while the numbers who wanted more and less extreme change decline. Similarly the total of those who opted for either the status quo or the 1974 Conservative suggestion of a nominated Assembly also remained almost constant but within the total, support for a nominated Assembly declined and that for the status quo increased.

As for referendum voting intentions there were three distinct phases. Over the short interval from October 1976 to March 1977 the 'Yes' side lost 12 per cent as the Conservatives moved to a position of outright rejection of the Labour plan. There followed a long period of stability until January 1979, then a swift collapse in the last weeks before the vote. On the day only 52 per cent of voters, 33 per cent of electors, voted 'Yes'.

Figure 9.3 shows how the Scotland Act became very much a party issue but devolution did not. It plots the level of support for the 'Yes' side (or for devolution) among Labour supporters minus the level among Conservatives. SNP supporters were almost unanimously in favour at all times. In October 1976

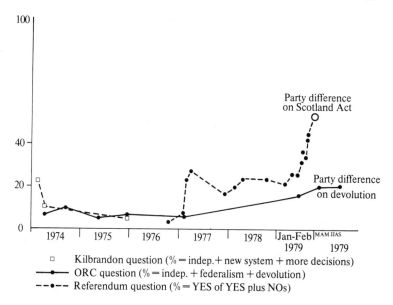

Fig. 9.3. How the Scotland Act became a party issue

Conservative and Labour supporters had much the same referendum intentions but by March 1977 the gap was 28 per cent and in 1979 it increased steadily from 22 per cent in mid-January to 53 per cent on referendum day. Yet even by September 1979 party differences on the principle of devolution or whether to press on with some form of devolution after the referendum reached only 21 per cent. The Thatcher–Home strategy worked. Pro-devolution Conservatives voted 'No' to the Scotland Act without giving up their expressed desire for devolution. Perhaps they believed the pledges given by Thatcher and Home; perhaps they only wanted some face-saving excuse to put party loyalty before devolution.

No doubt it was inevitable that the referendum campaign should make the Scotland Act more of a party issue though not to the extent that it became. But even the extreme party differences in 'Yes' support cannot completely explain why the 'Yes' side got only 52 per cent of the vote. The Conservatives were enjoying an unusual burst of popularity throughout Britain so there were an unusual number of them around. Secondly, Conservative leaders were much more successful than Labour in getting their supporters to back the party line – 81 per cent compared to 72 per cent according to the ITN poll – and this despite the underlying and continuing popularity of devolution. If Labour had been as popular as in the general election on 3 May and if Labour rather than the Conservatives had achieved the higher loyalty rate then even with a 53 per cent difference between the parties a simple arithmetical calculation shows the 'Yes' vote would have been 66 rather than 52 per cent and the 40 per cent requirement would have been met.

Certainly the Conservatives made the Act a party issue but they cut the 'Yes' vote to 52 per cent by being so much more successful than Labour in making it a party issue despite taking the basically unpopular position. Moss Evans and Tam Dalyell must, in their different ways, share some responsibility for the devolution result. In 1978 devolution carried Labour to a new height of popularity; in 1979 it sank under the weight of an unpopular and distracted Government.

After the referendum several polls showed that only a third of Scots wanted devolution dropped but relatively few expected the Government to proceed as if the referendum had never happened. Some change in the plans, if only cosmetic, was expected.

THE FRANKENSTEIN SOLUTION

Parliament had already rejected an amendment to the 40 per cent rule lowering the threshold to 33 per cent. So as soon as the result became known it was universally agreed that there was little chance of persuading the present parliament to implement the Act. On the very day of the result a government spokesman outlined the 'Frankenstein solution' – neither repeal nor implement the Act until after the general election. For a few weeks the Government tried exerting pressure on its anti-devolution back-benchers but it was plainly irritated by the Scots electorate and would take no more risks for devolution. In particular Callaghan would not make implementation a confidence issue which might have gained him the votes of Liberals and Nationalists on the issue and of his own rebels on the confidence and so saved both devolution and his Government.

A highly stage-managed Labour conference met in Perth on 10 March and approved the executive statement which declared devolution would 'remain at the forefront of our programme' and urged the Government to do 'all in its power' to implement the Act. Significantly, the final draft stopped short of demanding even a three-line whip. Aware that it would have to face an election within weeks the party closed ranks.

SNP support was so low in the polls that it looked as though they would lose all but one of their seats if they precipitated an election, but both the executive and the MPs agreed to end the Government if it would not at least put the Act to the vote. They disagreed only on the time limit before action, and when Callaghan proposed to continue discussions until the end of April the SNP responded with a motion of no confidence. In the final vote which ended the Labour Government every SNP member voted against it. If even one of them had refused to do so, as Reid and Watt had in the autumn, Callaghan would have survived through the spring and might well have won an election in the autumn. The SNP hoped that the Government would be blamed for the failure to implement devolution but Callaghan's careful behaviour made the SNP appear the most immediate cause of that failure.

The SNP view was that the Government had dished devolution by refusing a three-line whip and an early vote; that the people of Scotland could see it; but that Scots would gradually lose interest as the referendum faded into history. They had made the same claim after the guillotine defeat but the Government had gone on to produce the Scotland Act. Moreover, the voters were not in a rage over the Government's delaying tactics; they were well aware of the damage done by their own 52 per cent vote. An ORC poll found that only 28 per cent wanted the Assembly plans scrapped but still less, only 14 per cent expected the Government to go ahead as if nothing had happened; 16 per cent opted for the Frankenstein plan, and a massive 41 per cent for all-party talks as proposed by Callaghan. Several other polls, by Gallup and System Three, confirm that the largest body of electors wanted neither the status quo nor the Act as it stood but some revised devolution plan. Whether the revision was to be major or minor they did not say.

A BRITISH ELECTION

The essential feature of the 1979 general election campaign in Scotland was the temporary eclipse of the Scottish dimension. Neal Ascherson caught the mood in his *Scotsman* review:

If this is a dreich, colourless election in Scotland, the Scots made it so. The referendum and its aftermath abruptly withdrew the brightest theme . . . For five years, political argument and planning has been conducted in the Scottish dimension. Now, suddenly, the dimension is hardly there. The campaign in Scotland is part of the UK campaign, on smooth worn issues which the big UK parties present in Bathgate as they would present them in Blackpool. We had forgotten, perhaps, how dull British politics are.

The campaign marked a return to British politics. After the referendum the parties could find very little to say about devolution and the issue was not raised all that often on doorsteps. The media which had given devolution saturation coverage in January and February switched to UK news and personalities in April as much in the search for novelty as for its inherent importance. While Callaghan, Thatcher, and Steel provided travelling circuses to attract media attention, only the Scottish Conservatives planned their campaign to focus on a limited number of personalities – Teddy Taylor, George Younger, and Alex Fletcher – who took the daily press conferences in rotation and did the radio and television broadcasts. The SNP especially had a rooted objection to personality cults. It had no leader in the sense in which that term is applied to other parties and whereas its chairman, Billy Wolfe, had done a helicopter tour in 1974, he was too busy fighting West Lothian to do it again in 1979. SNP MPs stuck to their own constituencies in a desperate struggle to hang on to their seats against the tide. Since Margo MacDonald was not a candidate she could have provided a touring circus but her popularity with the media aroused resentment in the party and she was instructed to stay off television till after the election.

The seats most likely to change hands on national (Scottish) swings were SNP seats at risk to the Conservatives. Neither party was popular in Scotland at the time; so both fought sub-national campaigns appealing to the special interests of the electors in the atypical SNP/Tory marginals. SNP MPs emphasized their role as good local MPs. The Conservatives routed Thatcher's Scottish tour through the critical Grampian region – Aberdeenshire, Banff, Moray and Nairn – and the Grampian Tory candidates made a public attempt to force Thatcher into a very hard line against EEC fishing policy. In this they had a partial success.

The Scottish Conservatives opted out of three of the five UK Conservative election broadcasts. But all three opt-outs were filmed in a Glasgow hotel by Saatchi and Saatchi, their UK advertising agents, instead of relying on BBC Scotland as in the past. Two of the three were typical Saatchi and Saatchi programmes with only a Scottish-accented presenter.

Scottish manifestos must be judged on different criteria from the London manifestos of the UK parties. For a start, the SNP manifesto is a party manifesto rather than an election manifesto. Though updated from time to time it is not a plan for a five-year parliament written after the declaration of an election. *Return to Nationhood*, published in September 1978, was aptly described by its subtitle – 'a summary of the ideology of Scotland's right to independence, the guiding principle of the SNP and an outline of its programme for self-government'. It included proposals from the twenty-five policy committees that sat during the parliament, draft articles for a Scottish constitution, and excerpts from the

Declaration of Arbroath which had been sent to the Pope in 1320. On more immediate matters, under the slogan 'Good for Scotland' it listed the party's 'major achievements' since 1974 beginning with the Assembly: 'without the SNP presence in London, Devolution would not have happened.' It was perhaps just as well that, as an official said afterwards, 'we didn't fight the election on our manifesto'. Instead, SNP pamphlets and press advertisements carried the slogan 'Make sure Jim or Maggie don't sell Scotland short'.

Labour's approach to the manifesto was the very opposite of the SNP's. The Scottish manifesto was hurriedly written after the party obtained the text of the UK manifesto. In contrast to its preparations for a completely Scottish-generated Assembly manifesto, the parliamentary manifesto was mainly a word-for-word copy of the UK manifesto though the typography was far better. Even the critical devolution section ignored the resolution passed by the Scottish conference and used the UK manifesto's form of words which omitted the term 'legislative' and the phrase 'in the forefront of our programme'.

The Conservatives' manifesto included a whole battery of tougher measures on crime which the Scottish shadow team had pressed for and which were not included in the UK manifesto. But apart from that the manifesto was thin on specifically Scottish proposals.

Both Labour and the Conservatives' Scottish manifestos in 1979 made a threadbare comparsion with their efforts in 1974. They were far more remarkable for the Scottish elements they dropped than those they retained and not at all for new Scottish elements. Labour could quote an increase in the SDA budget to £800 million but otherwise the tone was muted though commitments, in some form, still stood. The Conservative manifesto dropped 1974 plans for an Assembly, for the abolition of toll charges, for uniform coal and gas prices, for the transfer of oil civil servants to Aberdeen, and instead of offering a Scottish Development Fund it talked darkly of restricting the activities of the SDA.

Despite the extreme concentration on British personalities and policies however, the 1979 election campaign was followed by a very un-British election result: Scots voting diverged from English at least as much in 1979 as in 1974, though in a different

direction. The effect of the British-oriented 1979 election campaign was indeed to drive Scots and English voting intentions
somewhat closer together but they had drifted so far apart in the
years between 1974 and 1979 that an enormous difference
remained. And once the campaign and election were over, they
drifted even further apart.

Chapter 10

The End of British Politics?

Widely expressed fears that 1974 marked the collapse of the old system of Labour/Conservative hegemony were clearly premature. In England the Liberal vote was already in decline by October 1974 and fell still more in 1979. Since Liberal votes represented no coherent policy preferences there was no reason to expect that high Liberal votes would occur outside the special circumstances of spring 1974.

But SNP votes were founded on a coherent policy choice. Sometimes the SNP is described as a 'one-issue' party because it is about self-government and nothing more. As a party it has tried to develop a range of detailed policies on the whole range of government activities; but some members have been reluctant to concentrate on such details, and the mass electorate has ignored them. To ordinary folk the SNP is a one-issue party but only in the sense that Labour is also a one-issue party, and the Conservatives a zero-issue party. Self-government is not another issue like a 2 per cent rise in VAT or a better pension plan: it is a grand issue like Labour's commitment to advance the interests of ordinary working people. At that level of generality the Conservatives are best defined as the party of resistance to the parties of change – resistance to Labour and resistance to the SNP.

Fully 61 per cent of Scots declared that the question of Scottish government was important in helping decide their party vote, and the parties themselves gave the issue priority in their election campaigns. For the next five years Scottish government was to be a major item on the British political agenda.

There was no more reason for pro-devolution Scots to automatically vote SNP than there is for working-class people to automatically vote Communist. But there clearly was a large body of opinion in Scotland which favoured a large measure of devolution and which was therefore a natural target for the SNP. Moreover, the purely party, as distinct from policy characteristics of the SNP were far from repulsive. While the party might never have been able to take up a large measure of its natural support without the help of conditions such as those in 1974 which predisposed people throughout Britain towards deserting the old governing parties, the SNP had the image, the organization, and the enthusiasm to take the opportunity in 1974 and to consolidate its gains thereafter.

Labour fought the SNP on its own ground by presenting a devolution policy that was even closer to Scots popular demand than the SNP's. And as Labour displayed its commitment to that devolution policy despite the parliamentary obstacles, Scots voting preferences continued to diverge from the English but increasingly to Labour's benefit rather than the SNP's. Labour has done well out of devolution, in Scotland at least.

The referendum result came as a shock even to those who had compaigned strongly against devolution. It has forced devolution off the British political agenda and even in Scotland the devolution debate went underground for a year. As a leading Scots journalist commented in the summer of 1979: 'devolution is now a topic for discussion only among consenting adults in private.'

So, in 1979 Labour had more to show for the devolution episode than did Scotland. For decades now, the city of Edinburgh has considered building an opera house and has commissioned and paid for several different designs but never decided to build; and now Glasgow has a highly successful opera house and company – so there is little need for one in Edinburgh. In Edinburgh only the architects have gained from the opera plans. So it is with Labour and devolution. Scotland has little to show for it all except bruises. Devolution, promised by every party in 1974, has failed to materialize; the civil service dispersal was postponed by Labour and postponed again by the new 1979 Conservative Government; REP was abolished and not replaced by anything so favourable to Scotland or so permanent; the oil revenues exceeded all expectations but flowed straight into the UK Treasury. English MPs were sensitized to the traditionally higher levels of public expenditure in Scotland which in future would need to be justified as never before. The economic gap between Scotland and England, which had almost closed, began to widen again. Apart from the Labour Party, the only winner was the Scottish Office, which lost nothing to an Assembly, but retained the new industrial powers it had been given in compensation.

Yet, in a sense, the repeal of the Scotland Act was its greatest justification. On 20 June 1979 George Younger who had resigned from the Conservative front bench when Thatcher decided to oppose the Scotland and Wales Bill, rose to move the repeal of the Scotland Act. Scottish MPs voted forty-three to nineteen against repeal but the Conservative Government had a majority of ninenty-five. An English Conservative majority overruled the overwhelming majority of Scots MPs, overruled the small majority of Scots voters in the referendum, and overruled the very much larger majority which surveys have always revealed and continue to reveal exists among Scots people in favour of the general concept of a Scots Assembly.

Ultimately it is the British government and parliament that keeps Scots devolution on the agenda by refusing to integrate Scotland with England and Wales. It is manifestly absurd to maintain and develop a separate system of laws, legislation, and administration for Scotland, run by Scots in Westminster and Scots in the Scottish Office and explicitly justified as an exercise in self-government, yet make the content of Scots laws depend upon English votes and give control of the Scottish Office to a politician whose twin qualifications are that he represents a Scots constituency and is acceptable to English MPs however unacceptable he is to the mass of his fellow Scots.

The whole of British government is riddled with logical absurdities but often they work well enough in practice. So it was with the Scottish Office for the first seventy years of this century. Despite the fact that the sheer size of England compared to Scotland always implied the probability that English votes would decide who ran the Scottish Office and devised Scots legislation, it only happened in one year out of the seventy. For the rest of the time the Scottish Secretary could claim the backing of a majority of Scots votes or a majority of Scots MPs, and usually a majority of both. True, Scots voted rather less than the English for the Conservatives but either the Conservatives had so much support that they still had a majority in Scotland – as happened between the wars; or when the Conservatives had only a narrow majority in Britain – as during the fifties – they had coincidentally reversed their usual disadvantage in Scotland. So Gordon

Campbell, between 1970 and 1974, was the first Secretary of State for Scotland this century who had to serve a full term without any trace of Scots electoral backing. George Younger from 1979 onwards is likely to be the second. He knows, and so does everyone else in Scotland and London, that he has the backing of only twenty-one other Scots Conservatives against forty-four Labour MPs, three Liberals, and two SNP. He knows his party won 10 per cent less votes than Labour in Scotland. Indeed, the 31 per cent Conservative vote in the May 1979 general election was a high point of Scots Conservative support. Over the ten months August 1979 to May 1980 they averaged under 25 per cent in the polls.

The gap between the Conservative lead over Labour in Scotland and England rose to a record 21 per cent at the 1979 election. If the Scots were to forget the Conservative Party's behaviour over devolution that gap might narrow again but there is no reason to expect it to fall beneath the 8 per cent implied by class differences alone. So for the foreseeable future Scotland can expect an externally imposed Secretary of State whenever the Conservatives are in office. And this is a new situation, not a traditional one, because although it was always statistically likely it just never actually happened until the seventies.

On what basis then can a Conservative Secretary govern without further alienating the Scots electorate and thereby exacerbating the problem? He has no mandate for the policies contained in the Scottish Conservatives' own manifesto. The Cabinet will not let him adopt the policies on devolution or, for example, nuclear dumping that he supported when he was only the MP for Ayr. He can pose as the protector of Scotland against the interests or inclinations of his Cabinet colleagues, but only if he can obtain blatant favours for Scotland or alternatively if he is willing to slander his own Cabinet by hinting at its originally anti-Scots intentions. The first is unlikely and the second would only help the Secretary at the expense of his party. He could justify his appointment and his actions by emphasizing the British nature of the election and pointing to the Conservatives' British manifesto: Scotland should just defer to the wider UK. But that justifies his appointment to the Secretaryship by attacking the basic justification for the Secretaryship itself.

Very modestly, he could claim no more than that he had been appointed by the PM to remind the Cabinet of Scottish interests – to speak for Scotland purely in the way that an advocate speaks for his client. Yet he does not represent his client in the way we expect of a lawyer in Britain. He is more like the defence counsel in some totalitarian dictatorship, chosen by the prosecutor from among his junior colleagues and imposed on the defendant against his protests.

There are other options of course. He could try to divert attention to policies on which his party has majority support even though the party itself is in the minority – principally the social rather than economic policies, crime and punishment instead of devolution, prices and employment policies.

But whenever a Conservative Secretary without the backing of either Scots votes or Scots MPs finds it necessary to impose unpopular policies he runs the risk of damaging not only his party but the Union itself. The SNP are bound to attack an imposed Secretary imposing unpopular policies, both because they dislike the policies and because they feel the policies have not been produced by 'due process'. Scots Labour who now control most local councils will have to decide whether to treat the Conservative Secretary gently and so risk abdicating the role of opposition to the SNP, or risk making the SNP's case by attacking strongly. The unionists in Labour's ranks may wish to attack Conservative policy decisions with vigour while avoiding any attack on the system that imposes such decisions in Scotland. But that may prove too fine a distinction and devolutionists in the Labour Party will find it difficult to forget that they came so close to winning control of Scots domestic government in 1979. The Act granting an Assembly and the rules granting NEC powers to the Scots party are still tucked away on the bookshelf at home and still remain official policy.

There is another future for Scots politics, Scots parties, and for devolution. The Conservatives might just try to regain their hold over Scots voters by conceding a substantial measure of political devolution. At worst that would rationalize the position of Conservative Secretaries of State by making them spokemen in Scotland for the Westminster government, relieving them of the role they cannot at present fulfil – of being spokesmen for Scotland at Westminster. At best it might give the Conservative

Party enough support in Scotland to win a Scottish majority at least in good years like 1955.

Teddy Taylor who, as Shadow Secretary of State after Alick Buchanan-Smith, led the Conservative opposition to Labour devolution proposals was asked during the 1979 campaign whether the Conservatives really would honour the promises they had made at all elections since 1970 and again during the referendum campaign: namely to set up a Scottish Assembly. He could hardly say 'No', but what he did say was rather more than 'Yes': 'Quite frankly yes. Most sensible reforms have been implemented by the Conservatives.'

However, if the Conservatives do set up an Assembly in Edinburgh which turns out to be nothing more than the old Scottish Grand Committee meeting outside London, they are likely to cause more problems then they solve. Under the lights of Scottish television it would be much harder for Scots Labour MPs to persist in their parliamentary deference to the English Conservative majority at Westminster.

There remains, however, the possibility, of a darker future. Devolution represented a logically defensible middle way between independence and integration. If it ceases to be a credible option only the extremes are left. And if British governments will not accept the majority votes of Scots voters and Scots MPs, then voting itself may become less of a credible option. There is, at present, a remarkably low level of popular support in Scotland for political violence over devolution or indeed over other special Scots interests. But while low it is not negligible and attitudes to violence are coherently linked to other political attitudes. The Government could increase the danger by conceding a large measure of home rule to Northern Ireland while reneging on its promises to Scotland. Already the letter writers in the national press have asked 'are we about to be given the message from our government, loudly and clearly, that the machine-gun succeeds where the ballot-box fails?' while the Kirk's Church and Nation Committee have considered 'why all attempts to obtain self-government have failed and reasoned arguments [been] brushed aside. Looking back to the past it sometimes seems as though British Governments will yield only to violence, or at least to non-violent disobedience to the law.'

There is at present a lull in political activity in Scotland but there is an urgent need for constructive constitutional change and/or for some break in the vicious circle or growing estrangement between Scotland and the Conservative Party before we have to face another storm. The record of British governments in squandering the precious resource of peaceful times gives no ground for optimism.

Appendix: Analysing Three-Way Voting

Trichotomous Partisanship

The outcome of a three-way contest can be described completely by a single point located within an equilateral triangle. There are at least three ways of deriving what turns out to be the same triangular representation, and each contributes to our understanding of the representation's properties. I will call them the 'box-corner', the 'homogeneous coordinate', and the 'rectangular' derivations. The first two underline the symmetry of a triangular representation while the third is more convenient for statistical calculations.

Figure A.1a illustrates the box-corner derivation. Imagine that D is the bottom, left-hand, rear corner of a box. We can represent the outcome of a three-party Con/Lab/SNP contest by a single point whose coordinates in three-dimensional space are per cent Con measured to the right of D, per cent Lab measured forwards from D, and per cent SNP measured upwards from D. Then we shall find that any election outcome whatsoever, in this three-party system, corresponds to some point lying on the triangular surface ABC, where A, B, and C are located 100 per cent to the right, in front, and above D. This happens because the three percentages, whatever they are, add up to 100 per cent. (Note that the triangle sides AB, BC, CA will be approximately 141 per cent long.)

Figure A.1b illustrates the homogeneous coordinate derivation. The Con, Lab, and SNP percentages are plotted perpendicularly inwards from the sides of the triangle. Any two votes define a point within the triangle and any pair define the same point as any other pair. The triangle must be drawn to scale, such that the height of any vertex above the opposite side is 100 per cent. (The sides of the triangle will then be approximately 115 per cent long.)

Figure A.1c illustrates the rectangular coordinate derivation. The Conservative lead over Labour (= GAP = Con %–Lab %) is plotted horizontally, and the SNP percentage vertically. To

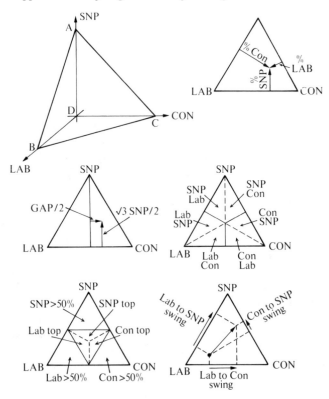

Fig. A.1. Triangular representation of trichotomous partisanship

make the triangle equilateral the SNP percentage has to be scaled by multiplying it by $\sqrt{3}$ before plotting. Then the representation will be symmetric and exactly equivalent to the first two representations in every way except scale: the side length of the triangle will be 200 per cent instead of 141 per cent or 115 per cent. There is some advantage in choosing a different scale, giving a side length of 100 per cent. This is done by plotting

$$\frac{GAP}{2} = \frac{Con\% - Lab\%}{2}$$ horizontally against $\frac{\sqrt{3}}{2}$ SNP per cent

vertically.

Amongst the properties of this representation are:

(P1) Despite the seemingly unsymmetric construction using rectangular coordinates, the representation is entirely symmetric, and identical with the representations derived from the other two approaches.

(P2) Each vertex represents an outcome in which one party gets all the votes.

(P3) The triangle can be divided into six areas according to which parties are first and second (see Fig. A.1d),

(P4) and into six areas according to whether any of the three parties has an absolute majority of votes, i.e. over 50 per cent, or only a plurality, i.e. the top vote but less than 50 per cent (see Fig. A.1e).

The Size and Orientation of Change

So much for symmetric representation, now for measures of change, difference, or effect. Let us start with two different election results in a three-party system. They correspond to two points within the equilateral triangle. Let us define the *size* of the difference between the two election outcomes as the length of the line joining the two election points; and the partisan *orientation* of that difference as the direction of the line.

The size of the difference, Z, is then equal to the root of the sum of the squares of the differences in the rectangular coordinates

$$\text{i.e.} \quad Z = \sqrt{\frac{\text{dGAP}^2}{4} + \frac{3\text{dSNP}^2}{4}}$$

where d stands for 'the difference in ...' e.g. dSNP = SNP per cent at second election minus SNP per cent at first. This can also be expressed in a form which emphasizes the symmetry of the measure:

$$Z = \sqrt{(\text{dCon}^2 + \text{dLab}^2 + \text{dSNP}^2)/2}$$

Z has a minimum of zero and a maximum of 100 per cent. The formula shows that in a two-party system, size, Z, equals the gain made by one party, which must necessarily be the same as the other's loss. When there is a bipolar change in a multi-party system, i.e. when one party gains X per cent, another loses X per cent and all others remain unchanged, then size $Z = X$.

Returning to the triangular representation of three-party election results, it can be shown that:

(P5) Movements parallel to the sides of the triangle represent bipolar changes.

(P6) Movements perpendicular to the sides of the triangle represent unipolar changes.

(P7) While, in general, movements are neither parallel nor perpendicular, the perpendicular projection (see Fig. A.1f) of a general movement on to any side exactly equals the 'Butler swing' which is traditionally used in Britain and elsewhere (see D. Butler and D. Kavanagh *The British General Election of October 1974*, Macmillan, London, 1975, p. 276) as a measure of the changing balance of support between two parties in a multi-party system. Butler swing can be defined as the average of one party's gain and the other's loss; or as half the change in one party's lead over the other. Thus the size measure Z is such that its perpendicular projection on to any triangle side equals the conventional measure of swing between a pair of parties.

Now for a quantitative measure of the partisan direction or orientation of change. We have to specify the direction of the line joining the two election result points, which we can do by quoting its angle θ relative to some reference direction. If we take the horizontal line from the Labour to the Conservative vertex as zero degrees and measure angles counter-clockwise (the usual geometric convention), then the tangent of θ equals the ratio of the vertical shift to the horizontal shift between the two election points. Thus

$$\theta = \arctan\left(\frac{d\left(\frac{\sqrt{3}}{2}SNP\right)}{d\left(\frac{CON-LAB}{2}\right)}\right) = \arctan\left(\sqrt{3}\,\frac{dSNP}{dGAP}\right)$$

where d means, as before, the change or difference between the percentages at one election and the other. Since anyone who has used a map and compass is familiar with the notion of measuring direction on a 360 degree compass this measure should be easily interpretable. In Chapters 5–8 I took the line vertically downwards as my zero degrees, reference direction, and consequently the angles quoted in the Tables of those chapters are θ +90 degrees.

Just as it helps interpretation with a geographic compass to define certain cardinal directions – north, south, east, and west – so with our political compass. Using properties P5 and P6 of the triangular representation (given above) we can list the angles corresponding to all bipolar and unipolar changes. These occur at 30 degree intervals round the political compass. They are shown in Fig. 5.3.

Trichotomous Regression

So far, I have described the size and political direction of the difference between two election outcomes, represented by two points in the symmetric diagram. If each point represented the over-all party percentages at each of two General Elections then we should be measuring a *change* in partisanship. If each point represented a constituency result at the same election, we should be measuring a *difference*. Again, if one point represented the party percentages in the middle-class part of a sample survey, and the other point represented partisanship amongst working-class respondents, then we should be measuring a class *effect*. We can generalize this sequence one step further: suppose that we are analysing the effect of the class mix in constituencies on their partisanship and we find, by regression or some other analysis procedure, that a unit shift on the class predictor appears to correspond to certain shifts in the levels of Con, Lab, and SNP voting. Then we know dCon, dLab and dSNP corresponding to a unit shift on the predictor. These three differences are all we need to calculate Z and θ. We can no longer locate the change at a particular point within the triangle. Indeed, it is usually an essential assumption of the analysis technique that the partisan response to a change in the predictor variable is independent of the prior level of partisanship. But we can still define a size and direction of change just as if we were comparing the partisanship of two subsets of survey respondents. (See Table 8.1 for examples of trichotomous regressions.)

For a more extended treatment of trichotomous methods of analysis (with extensions to multi-party systems, use of loglinear techniques, etc.) see also:

Miller, W. L. 'Symmetric Representation of Political Trends in Three-party Systems with some properties, extensions and examples', *Quality and Quantity*, 11 (1977) 27–41.

Miller, W. L. *Causal Modelling in Three-party Systems: Trichotomous Regression Studies of Scotland, England and America* (Glasgow, Strathclyde University, CSPP paper 10, 1977).

Miller, W. L. 'Beyond Two-party Analysis: some new methods for Linear and Loglinear Analyses in Three-party Systems', *Political Methodology* (1980) forthcoming.

Select Bibliography

This is in no way a comprehensive list of books and articles relevant to recent Scots and UK politics. For such a list see Laurence Pollock and Ian McAllister: *A Bibliography of United Kingdom Politics: Scotland, Wales and Northern Ireland* (Glasgow, Centre for the Study of Public Policy, Strathclyde University, 1980) which contains about 2,000 references.

Most of this book has been based on original analysis of the SSRC-funded Scottish Election Survey (1974) which formed part of the British Election Survey. I was myself the Scottish Director of that survey. The British Directors were Bö Sarlvik and Ivor Crewe, of the University of Essex. Their analyses of the data, from a British perspective, have appeared in I. Crewe, B. Sarlvik, and J. W. Alt, 'Partisan Dealignment in Britain 1964–74' *BJPS*, 7 (1977), 124–90; J. W. Alt, B. Sarlvik, and I. Crewe, 'Partisanship and Policy Choice: Issue Preferences in the British Electorate', *BJPS*, 6 (1976), 273–90; J. W. Alt, I. Crewe, and B. Sarlvik, 'Angels in Plastic: the Liberal Surge in 1974', *Pol. Stud.*, 25 (1977), 343–68; and B. Sarlvik, I. Crewe, and J. W. Alt, 'Britain's Membership of the EEC – a Profile of Electoral Opinions in the Spring of 1974 with a postscript on the referendum', *EJPR*, 4 (1976), 83–114. I must thank the SSRC for research funds and my colleagues at Essex for their very generous cooperation.

I have made very extensive use of the Scottish newspaper files held at the Mitchell Library, Glasgow. The newspapers consulted include the *Record*, the *Scottish Daily Express*, and especially the *Scotsman* and *Glasgow Herald*. The *Herald* published a particularly useful index–similar to the London *Times* index – until 1968, and the *Scotsman* made up for its lack of an index by giving very full coverage to Scots politics in general and devolution politics in particular. All my quotations of politicians are taken, unless otherwise stated, from *Glasgow Herald* or *Scotsman* reports. For the purpose of understanding popular political responses it is, of course, irrelevant whether the politicians were misreported or not.

This is the first full-length study based on a nation-wide Scottish political survey. So there are no exact equivalents for comparison. The nearest is *Scottish Political Behaviour* (London, Longmans, 1966) by Ian Budge and Derek Urwin which, despite its title, is based on a set of local surveys. Much has happened since 1966 in Scots politics, and for that reason alone readers might like to compare Budge and Urwin's findings with my own.

Particularly useful are several works which complement this book in

different ways and on which I myself have relied heavily. First, James
Kellas gives a thorough description of Scottish political institutions in
his *Modern Scotland* (London, Pall Mall, 1968) and especially in his
Scottish Political System (Cambridge, CUP, 1976). Michael Keating
analyses the consequences of separate Scottish institutions at Westminster in *A Test of Political Integration* (Glasgow, Strathclyde University,
CSPP Paper no. 6, 1977). Vernon Bogdanor presents an informed and
readable account of devolution throughout the last hundred years of
British politics in *Devolution* (London, OUP, 1979). More extended
analyses of the Scotland Act proposals appear in the volume edited by
Donald Mackay, *Scotland: the Framework for Change* (Edinburgh, Harris,
1979). Tam Dalyell's *Devolution: the End of Britain* (London, Cape, 1977)
conveys the flavour of the anti-devolutionists polemic, though it should
obviously not be read as a factual account.

Various aspects of Scots electoral behaviour are analysed in the
following:

Bochel, J. M. and Denver, D. T., 'Canvassing, Turnout and Party
  Support', *BJPS*, 1 (1971), 257–69.

Bochel, J. M. and Denver, D. T. 'The Decline of the Scottish National
  Party – an Alternative View', *Pol. Stud.*, 20 (1972), 311–16.

Bochel, J. M. and Denver, D. T. 'The Impact of the Campaign on the
  Results of Local Government Elections', *BJPS*, 2 (1972), 239–44.

Bochel, J. M. and Denver, D. T. 'Religion and Voting', *Pol. Stud.*, 18
  (1970), 205–19.

Bochel, J. M. and Denver, D. T. *The Scottish Local Government Elections
  1974: Results and Statistics* (Edinburgh, Scottish Academic Press, 1975).

Bochel, J. M. and Denver, D. T. *The Scottish District Elections 1977:
  Results and Statistics* (Pol. Sci. Dept., Dundee Univ., 1977).

Bochel, J. M., Denver, D. T., and B. J. McHardy, *The Scottish Regional
  Elections 1978: Results and Statistics* (Pol. Sci. Dept., Dundee Univ.,
  1978).

Brand, Jack. *The National Movement in Scotland* (London, Routledge &
  Kegan Paul, 1978).

Chrimes, S. B. (ed.) *The General Election in Glasgow, February, 1950: Essays
  by Members of the Staff of the University of Glasgow* (Glasgow, Jackson,
  1950).

Cornford, James, and Brand, Jack 'Scottish Voting Behaviour', in
  Government and Nationalism in Scotland, ed. J. N. Wolfe (Edinburgh
  Univ. Press, 1969).

Drucker, H. M. *Breakaway: The Scottish Labour Party* (Edinburgh,
  EUSPB, 1977).

Jaensch, Dean. 'The Scottish Vote 1974: A Realigning Party System',
  Pol. Stud., 24 (1976), 306–19.

McLean, Iain. 'The Rise and Fall of the Scottish National Party', *Pol. Stud.*, 18 (1970), 357–72.

Miller, W. L. 'The Scottish Voter', *Scotsman* 14th, 15th, 16th October 1975.

Miller, W. L. with Sarlvik, B., Crewe, I., and Alt, J. 'The Connection between SNP Voting and the Demand for Scottish Self-government', *EJPR*, 5 (1977) 88–102.

Miller, W. L. *Electoral Dynamics in Britain since 1918* (London, Macmillan 1977).

Miller, W. L. 'What was the Profit in following the Crowd?—Immigration and Devolution Strategy since 1970', *BJPS*, 10 (1979) 15–38.

Miller, W. L. 'Class, Region and Strata at the British General Election of 1979', *Parl Aff*, 32 (1979) 376–82.

Rose, R. *The Future of Scottish Politics* (Glasgow, Strathclyde University, Allander Institute Speculative Paper, no. 4, 1975).

Steed, M. 'The Results Analysed', in D. Butler and D. Kavanagh, *The British General Election of February 1974* and *The British General Election of October 1974* (London, Macmillan, 1974 and 1975).

Though not about Scottish voting, the papers by J. Alt *et al.* and by P. Lemieux (both in *Pol. Stud.*, 25 (1977), 323–42 and 343–68) on the bases of Liberal support in 1974 are obviously relevant for comparison purposes. So also is *Research Paper 7: Devolution and other Aspects of Government: An Attitudes Survey* published by HMSO in 1973 for the Commission on the Constitution (Kilbrandon Commission) despite its avoidance of party preference and voting.

The *Scottish Economic Bulletin* published by the Scottish Economic Planning Department of the Scottish Office gives information on national Scottish economic statistics and on Scotland's economic position in relation to GB or the UK. After the 1966 and 1971 censuses, the General Register Office for Scotland issued volumes of census information tabulated by parliamentary constituencies. I have used data from both these sources in the text.

For a technical report on the 1974 BES/SES surveys see James Spence, *The British Election Study of October 1974: Methodological Report* (London: Social and Community Planning Research, 1975) which gives the full questionnaires and describes the sampling methods. There were 2029 respondents interviewed in England, 1170 in Scotland, and 135 in Wales. I have excluded the few Welsh interviews from my analysis.

Index